The Geni

M000187847

The Genius of *Bob's Burgers*

Comedy, Culture and Onion-Tended Consequences

MARGARET FRANCE

McFarland & Company, Inc., Publishers
Jefferson, North Carolina

LIBRARY OF CONGRESS CATALOGUING-IN-PUBLICATION DATA

Names: France, Margaret, 1976– author.
Title: The genius of Bob's burgers : comedy, culture and
onion-tended consequences / Margaret France.
Description: Jefferson : McFarland & Company, Inc., Publishers, 2022. |
Includes bibliographical references and index.
Identifiers: LCCN 2021049790 | ISBN 9781476669373 (paperback : acid free paper) ∞
ISBN 9781476644578 (ebook)
Subjects: LCSH: Bob's Burgers (Television program) | BISAC: PERFORMING
ARTS / Television / Genres / Comedy | PERFORMING ARTS / Animation
(see also Film / Genres / Animated)
Classification: LCC PN1992.77.B58323 2022 | DDC 791.45/72—dc23/eng/20211014
LC record available at https://lccn.loc.gov/2021049790

BRITISH LIBRARY CATALOGUING DATA ARE AVAILABLE

ISBN (print) 978-1-4766-6937-3
ISBN (ebook) 978-1-4766-4457-8

© 2022 Margaret France. All rights reserved

*No part of this book may be reproduced or transmitted in any form
or by any means, electronic or mechanical, including photocopying
or recording, or by any information storage and retrieval system,
without permission in writing from the publisher.*

Front cover illustration © 2022 Shutterstock

Printed in the United States of America

*McFarland & Company, Inc., Publishers
Box 611, Jefferson, North Carolina 28640
www.mcfarlandpub.com*

To my teachers, who always believed I could write,
and my students, who always give me so much to write about.

Acknowledgments

This book would not have been possible without the unfailing enthusiasm, encouragement, and flexibility of my editor, Layla Milholen.

The project sprang directly from my desire to spend more time with the friends who also make up my writing group, "Out of Fucks": Melissa Bender, Maura Grady and Karma Waltonen. You are inspiring company: the only thing I value more than your writing is your friendship.

The support of my friends and family, particularly Shanti Rieber and Amelia Farrell, has been instrumental in the completion of this project. Early readers Emily Cranford, Olivia Hernández, and Charlie Hitchcock told me that what I was writing made sense when I wasn't so certain, and I am profoundly grateful to you all.

Table of Contents

Preface

At first glance, the animated series *Bob's Burgers* seems as undistinguished as its name. It either brings to mind a local burger place—my town has a pub called Bob's Burgers and Brews—or is easily confused with the formerly ubiquitous chain restaurant, Bob's Big Boy. Of course, if you're reading this, it's very likely that you are already quite capable of disambiguating the show from that diner that always smells like onion rings and despair. Still, to clarify, *Bob's Burgers* is an animated sitcom created by Loren Bouchard. It debuted on Fox in 2011 and is projected to run until at least 2023, with a film due in the spring of 2022. In the following pages, I make a series of arguments that *Bob's Burgers* deserves recognition as an ongoing meditation on what it means to be a member of a family, a class, and a country in 21st-century America.

This book collects nine of my own critical writings on *Bob's Burgers*. It was composed between 2015 and 2020, so it only refers to episodes from the first ten seasons. I approach this subject as someone trained in literary studies, thus rather than consulting the writers and performers or presenting the technical aspects of its creation, I use this show as a proxy for the culture that consumes it. Instead of exploring how *Bob's Burgers* came to be, these chapters ask what it means now that it exists. Of course, this book also collects a great deal of trivia about the show, its reception, and its fans, but for the most part each chapter presents a lens for understanding how the narratives in *Bob's Burgers* relate to larger cultural issues, particularly those of identity, whether that identity is defined by age, gender, sexuality, or family roles.

In exploring these questions, I rely on many concepts from gender studies, media studies, and critical theory. However, I explain these ideas within the chapters, so no background in these fields is necessary to follow the arguments I make herein. In fact, my hope is that if you come to this work with an earnest interest in *Bob's Burgers*, you will leave it with the assurance that your curiosity about the show makes you someone who is actually curious about many other things. In learning how to read *Bob's Burgers* as a series of critiques of Steven Spielberg's early blockbusters, or a rejection of Freudian psychology, you may decide that something else you love is making a similar contribution to our cultural consciousness. Perhaps you will read my assessments of Gene's masculinity, or Tina's desires, and decide that my understanding of the show is dead wrong. These chapters are arguments. In reading them, I hope to inspire you to make your own.

Introduction

Welcome to the Pundane Surreal

Thanks to *The Simpsons*, *South Park*, the Cartoon Network's Adult Swim lineup, and the expansion of platforms for consuming media in general, animation for adults in the United States has never been more mainstream. In a sense, animation has finally come full circle. It began as a cinematic technique in the early 20th century, first as a special effect for live action films and, eventually, as its own narrative medium, a kind of hybrid between a film and a comic strip (Stabile and Harrison 2–5). At that time, there was no question that animation was for adults. Early shorts replicated vaudeville gags, and early stars like burlesque beauty Betty Boop were meant to stir adult feelings. The rise of Disney shifted ideas about the audience for animation, to the extent that from the 1950s until the debut of *The Simpsons* in 1989, adult animation existed mostly on the margins (Dobson 32). Ralph Bakshi's *Fritz the Cat* (1972) and Gerald Potterton's *Heavy Metal* (1981), both feature films, typify adult animation from this period. Both were based on popular underground media properties: R. Crumb's comics for the former; *Heavy Metal* magazine spawned the latter. Though these films were commercially successful, it was the homely medium of television that would make adult consumption of animation widespread in the United States.[1]

I contend that *Bob's Burgers* could very well be the homeliest example of this homely medium. While I adore *Bob's Burgers*, I'm drawn to the program as a critic because so many invite the Belcher family into their homes. My focus on *Bob's Burgers* derives not from any qualitative aesthetic judgment; honestly, my current favorite animated sitcom is probably Netflix's *Big Mouth*. But *Bob's Burgers* is special. As a network program that is both widely syndicated and available on many streaming platforms, *Bob's Burgers* has a far greater reach than any program created exclusively for cable or streaming. The exigencies of network television require *Bob's Burgers* to appeal to people who might

3

not relate to the travails of a debauched and depressed horse (Netflix's *Bojack Horseman*) or the adventures of a narcissistic spy (F/X's *Archer*). Thus, *Bob's Burgers* makes broader, multivalent overtures in its attempts to appeal to an intergenerational audience. And *Bob's Burgers* succeeds. Squarely the product of folks in my own cohort, Generation X, *Bob's Burgers* breaks through generational barriers. My millennial students introduced me to *Bob's Burgers* during its second season, which gave me something in common with my peers' adolescent children. My Generation Z students treat *Bob's Burgers* almost like a utility; at this point they hardly remember a world without it. As screens have become less communal, *Bob's Burgers* has become a hearth around which a wide variety of adults and children can gather.

Bob's Burgers not only turns up in more homes than most contemporary animated sitcoms, it also feels more like home. *Bob's Burgers'* creator, Loren Bouchard, and executive producer, Jim Dautrieve, both previously worked on *King of the Hill* (1997–2010), an animated sitcom created by Mike Judge that also aired on Fox. While *King of the Hill's* premise—a glimpse into the life of a Texas propane salesman and his family—has more regional specificity, the shows are deeply intertwined in their engagement with the grittier aspects of daily life, particularly when it comes to money (Hugar). Like its spiritual predecessor, *Bob's Burgers* distinguishes itself by showing restraint in its settings and circumstances, and abandon in its development of the interior lives of its characters.

In the beginning, there was little indication that *Bob's Burgers* would rise to the level of *King of the Hill*, or really any of the animated sitcoms that came before it. *Bob's Burgers* debuted in 2011 as part of Fox's Animation Domination block of Sunday prime-time animated programs, a natural addition to family sitcoms like *The Simpsons, Family Guy, American Dad*, and *The Cleveland Show* (Hibberd). In the company of these brightly colored domestic comedies, *Bob's Burgers* hardly seemed like a departure. The cutting humor and rebellious nature of youngest daughter Louise could be uncharitably read as an homage to Bart Simpson, while middle child Gene's fartistry on the keyboard and Tina's itchy crotch suggested that the program would engage in the adolescent scatological humor of *Family Guy*. Hank Stuever of *The Washington Post* wrote as much in his review of the pilot, dismissing it as "pointlessly vulgar and derivatively dull." As the program engages in the kind of vast world-building that has typified the prime-time animated sitcom since *The Flintstones* debuted in 1960, *Bob's Burgers* diverges from its network brethren and predecessors by building its universe on a bedrock of verbal whimsy and celebrations of alterity as its cast diversifies and deepens.

The pleasure creators and consumers derive from animated sitcoms often springs from the medium's ability to incorporate a far broader range of sets, phenotypes, celebrity cameos, and a certain suspension of disbelief. What would be impractical or obscenely expensive in live action can be accomplished at a fraction of the cost in a cartoon. *The Simpsons* and *Family Guy, Bob's Burgers'* forerunners on Fox, use animation to, in *Family Guy's* case, insert an endless series of pop culture references and celebrity cameos. In *The Simpsons'* case, animation enables outlandish travel through time and space, including the reoccurring aliens of the annual Halloween-themed "Treehouse of Horror" episodes. In this company, *Bob's Burgers* feels gritty, as if the TV cop genre skipped directly from *Dragnet* to *The Wire*. *Bob's Burgers* keeps its plots close to home. An entire episode will focus on relatively mundane dilemmas like a disappointing open house at the children's school, finding a way to pay rent, or buying a couch. Though *Bob's Burgers* features wonderful guest voices (my favorite is Jon Hamm as a talking toilet), its projected 13 seasons do not lean heavily on celebrity cameos, intercontinental (or interstellar) travel, extreme weight gain, or talking pets (Andreeva). Instead, creator Loren Bouchard uses the medium for comparatively mundane ends, like to keep his characters from aging.

The way that animation introduced surrealist possibilities into the sitcom was established by the first animated sitcom. *The Flintstones* premiered on ABC in 1960 and ran in primetime until 1966, translating standard tropes from the sitcom to animation. In fact, "translating" might be too generous a term, while "sitcom" is unnecessarily vague. *The Flintstones* took the premise and structure of *The Honeymooners* and animated it, changing the setting to an utterly imaginary prehistoric age, where humans domesticate dinosaurs, employing them the way the 20th century employed the internal combustion engine. In the course of a single episode, a small dinosaur is strapped to a dolly allowing Fred to mow the lawn while Betty busies herself inside, dragging a mammoth around the house to suck up dirt like a vacuum cleaner ("Animal Tools").

The Flintstones was not only the first prime-time animated sitcom, it was influential enough to spawn so many failed imitators that the model was not attempted in primetime for three decades. *The Flintstones'* influence was great enough to buoy its futuristic sibling, *The*

Introduction

Jetsons, propelling even a knock-off into the popular imagination along with it, as it survived in remakes and syndication despite its swift cancellation during its run on network primetime. Even though *The Jetsons* lasted only a year in primetime, it built a much larger legacy than say, *Calvin and the Colonel* and *Matty's Funday Funnies* (Hilton-Morrow and McMahan 76). While the other stone-alikes floundered, the original episodes of *The Flintstones* were so widely syndicated that its popularity only grew in the 30-year period between the debut of first prime-time animated smash and the second (*The Simpsons*).

The Simpsons, vanguard of the next, more sustainable wave of prime-time television animation, pushed the medium to new heights of fantasy. Despite its contemporary setting, *The Simpsons* might have less fidelity to reality than its predecessor, because it plays at realism without adhering to its rules in the slightest. As I note above, though it dutifully resets at the end of every episode, *The Simpsons* imagines a universe of not just intelligent alien life, but outlandish extremes here on earth. No employer has tolerated more blatant incompetence than Homer's boss, Mr. Burns, while no employee has toiled for a purer architect of evil. But within these flights of fancy, *The Simpsons* also demonstrates ways that shows like *Bob's Burgers* might be able to more accurately render the human experience than live action programs. As critic Michael Tueth notes, in *The Simpsons* the abstraction of animation allows us to view at a jolly distance the very real consequences of Homer's binge eating and drinking, for example, issues that would be difficult to watch in a live action format ("Back to the Drawing Board" 142). Thus, the show introduced the notion that animation can in some instances bring more realistic situations to our screens because we could not tolerate them rendered with real people. A roadrunner struggling to escape a starving coyote is an entertaining scenario only when both are cartoons.

In grounding the show in recognizable settings and characters, *Bob's Burgers* deviates from the most foundational tropes of the genre established by shows like *The Flintstones* and *The Simpsons*. The animated sitcom began as a place where quotidian domestic or workplace conflict could be woven into bizarre new settings. In cartoons, dinosaurs frolic with humans, blue creatures with matching hats live in a socialist paradise, and Sonny and Cher show up to solve mysteries with a bunch of *avant le hashtag* #vanlife teens and their Great Dane. Just as an animated figure is a caricature of the human form, an animated personality becomes a caricature of the human psyche. While Lisa Simpson might inspire generations of young women surrounded by idiots, she almost never reveals the warmth or humor that might make her seem like a friend instead of an icon. Even actual humans lose their depth in two dimensions. Animation can reduce even Cher, a human with as many dimensions as contemporary celebrity allows, to just another scolding wife ("Secrets of Shark Island").

Defining realism requires critical context of the medium and genre under examination. For example, the standards for realism in fiction writing are complicated but still useful when applied to speculative fiction. While all speculative fiction builds a distinct imaginary universe, science fiction imagines a possible future, while hard science fiction does the same thing while limiting itself to advances based on current scientific knowledge and theories. Likewise, realism in *Bob's Burgers* must be measured by the standards established for animated sitcoms, standards distinct from live action sitcoms. These standards derive from the fundamentally abstract nature of animation. Thus, while no one actually lives in a community exclusively populated by people with receding chins, *Bob's Burgers* still strives for realism when compared with an animated sitcom like *The Flintstones*, which builds a lavish fantasy of prehistoric blue collar family life, or *Family Guy*, which has a similar setting—an imaginary town in Rhode Island, comparable to *Bob's Burgers'* imaginary town on the north Atlantic—but whose characters, particularly the talking family dog, sever the show from real life. Unlike these programs, *Bob's Burgers* often has plots that are not so dark that they couldn't happen in live action—many of the plots driven by economic strife could feasibly have occurred on *Roseanne*—nor so incredible that they would be beyond the budget of a live action network sitcom. Thus, the show mostly works within constraints that animation does not have.

This is not to say that *Bob's Burgers* might as well be a live action sitcom. Instead, it exploits the possibilities of its medium in subtler ways. Creator Loren Bouchard has repeatedly stated that the characters will not age, so the show will never completely embrace the limits of our world. The other area in which *Bob's Burgers* loses most contact with the real world is in its endless appetite for whimsy, particularly its earnest embrace of puns. The essence of the pun, be it cause for knee-slapping or face-palming, is the slipperiness of language. *Bob's Burgers'* equivalent of The Simpsons' "couch gag" is the double-barreled punning of its opening credits, in which we see a business open and close next door, and a pest control van arrive and leave. Failed businesses include "Magnum G.I. Colonoscopies," "Scroto-Rooter Vasectomy Clinic," and "Rude A-Bakening: Cakes for People You Hate," while exterminators from

Introduction

"Termite-mare on Elm Street" to "So You Think You Have Ants?" stop by.

Thus, the kind of realism *Bob's Burgers* achieves is what I'd like to call the "pundane surreal," in which the entire universe is swathed in a cheerful acknowledgment of the multivalent possibilities of language and identity. Part and parcel of this is the casting of two men in female roles, one clearly in drag, one doing something more akin to traditional animated cross-casting, in which women are regularly cast to play male roles. In building out its universe, *Bob's Burgers* reflects not the expansive possibilities of animation in general, but the small ways that we would all delight in a world that better reflected our personalities.

The chapters that follow will give you greater context for understanding the comingling of fantasy and reality in *Bob's Burgers*. They consider why these fantasies exist and how they look to different members of *Bob's Burgers'* diverse audience. None describe the technical aspects of the program, nor did I seek any input from its creators, though I tried to interact as much as possible with fans. This book explores *Bob's Burgers* as a cultural artifact, so I've focused on potential readings rather than the intentions of its creators. None of the chapters are meant to argue for the greatness of *Bob's Burgers*. Instead, each offers a framework for understanding how the show works—how it works for its time, how it works for different audiences, and how it reflects the culture that creates and consumes it. As I've established, *Bob's Burgers* is not the first animated sitcom, nor the longest running, nor the most popular, but it resonates with early 21st-century America in a very particular way.

The chapter on birth order, "From the Womb to the Tomb," allows even the casual viewer of *Bob's Burgers* to understand the significance of its relationship to popular psychology, and how that relationship allows the show to define itself against former upstart, now behemoth, *The Simpsons*.

Similarly, the "Spielberger of the Day" chapter examines the patterns in the way *Bob's Burgers* reinterprets a very specific part of the Spielberg oeuvre as a means of articulating the tensions between Baby Boomers and Generation X through their shared cultural landmarks. When I recommend *Bob's Burgers* to the uninitiated, my pitch often hinges on this Rorschach-like appeal across generations. These tensions surface in the way the Generation X–created show appropriates and interprets the work of that great exemplar of boomer hope and anxiety, Steven Spielberg.

The studied irony Generation X wears as a security blanket to hide their collective sadness that their small numbers and historical moment means that they will never have the affluence or influence of their baby boomer parents contrasts with the sincere passion millennials exhibit. Millennials care about what they love as if their feelings matter, and, unlike tiny, sad Generation X, they may be right! That participatory nature means that viewers born after 1980 are far more likely to express their fandom in writing their own stories or wearing their favorite moments from the show permanently on their bodies. Appropriately, the chapter on fan culture, "'We're not not-going to a toy-pony convention,'" focuses primarily on the artistic expression of the younger generations.

There might be no figure that inspires more intergenerational consensus than Bob, whose paternal excellence delights young and old. In "Our Father Who Art in Apron," I look at how fatherhood works within the show. In many ways, Bob parents in a vacuum. Like many of us, he finds his paternal role model on TV. Bob's oft-quoted "I love you but you're all terrible" evinces the kind of unconditional love sought by children of all ages (1.1).

The setting for Bob's utterance is, naturally, the eponymous restaurant in which so many of the show's plots unfold. In "Burger Boss" I examine the way the premise of *Bob's Burgers* allows it to combine the two classic settings of American situation comedy: the home and the workplace. *Bob's Burgers* is not only part of Fox's line-up of animated programming, it participates in an even older Fox ritual of scheduling family sitcoms on Sunday evenings, a tradition that began with the debut of *Married with Children* on April 5, 1987. I contend that *Bob's Burgers* might be best understood as something more than that. Considering *Bob's Burgers* alongside the American version of *The Office*, *The Mary Tyler Moore Show*, and other workplace comedies exposes the underlying sadness of finding family in the workplace.

Bob's Burgers also distinguishes itself from other animated programs in its unusual voice casting choices, particularly in having two of the core female characters voiced by men. In "'Boys are from Mars, girls are from Venus,'" I give a context for cross-casting in animation. Then, in exploring Dan Mintz's naturalistic performance as Tina and John Roberts' affectionate drag as Linda, I consider the way *Bob's Burgers* points out the artificiality of gendered behaviors by putting Tina's adolescent horndoggery and Linda's improvised wine-mom anthems in the mouths of men.

Introduction

ther way *Bob's Burgers* challenges gender norms is in its por-
__.., ... of the Belchers' lone son, Gene. In "Gene-der Trouble," I trace
Gene's habit of referring to himself in feminine roles, particularly as a
mother, and his passion for musicals and tablescaping, both interests
often coded as feminine in our culture. Gene dances to the beat of his
own Casio, and I look at what perceptions of Gene's gender and sexual
identity say about our cultural norms.

The diegetic cultural norms of the *Bob's Burgers* universe come
through in the treatment of Marshmallow, a Black trans woman who
has reoccurred on the show since the first season. In "The Marshmallow
Test," I read Marshmallow in the context of other trans characters in animation and consider how the characters' interactions with her over time
reflect changes in the way our culture understands the gender binary.

I developed these chapters organically. Some come from the way
my interest in the show intersects with my background and training as
a literary scholar. For example, as someone who teaches cultural history, I was intrigued to see the shift from using psychoanalysis to evolutionary psychology as a way of understanding family structures reflected
in *Bob's Burgers*. My students' responses to the show over the last five
years inflect every chapter, and specifically drove my excavation of Bob,
Marshmallow, and Gene as exemplars of the show dealing with issues of
gender and queerness. I conclude by imagining what my future students
might make of the show as an artifact of a more innocent but less just
time. The final chapter, "'You're so good at touching strangers,'" speculates on the future of *Bob's Burgers* in the face of one global threat and
one national one: the COVID-19 pandemic; and the overdue reckoning with America's deadly endemic racism, catalyzed by the murder of
George Floyd.

I have loosely grouped these chapters, but they are designed to be
modular: each will give you the context to understand the show in a new
way. If anything, I might recommend that you start with the final chapter. If you've made it this far into my introduction, then I don't need
to sell you on the transformative possibilities of art and culture, but in
considering the role *Bob's Burgers* played during a period of unparal-
leled turmoil and uncertainty, you may find some comfort in knowing
that you were not the only one who settled into an imaginary restaurant
while all our real ones were closed.

1

From the Womb to the Tomb

Bob's Burgers and Birth Order Theory

Despite employing bright primary colors, contemporary animated sitcoms illustrate dark theories of family strife. After all, the longest running and most acclaimed animated sitcom returns again and again to the Oedipal struggle of two jaundiced combatants seeking the approval of a giant blue phallus. As much as *The Simpsons* enacts psychoanalytic tropes, *Bob's Burgers* engages one of the most widely disseminated theories of evolutionary psychology, the birth-order hypothesis. In making the Belcher children inhabit the roles delineated by this hypothesis so consistently, the program demonstrates the way any trait taken to extremes can look like its opposite. The characters of Tina and Louise lie at either end of the spectrum set up by the birth order hypothesis. Eldest child Tina represents the conservatism of the approval-seeking niche taken to such an extreme that she appears to be coming out the other side, rebel guns blazing. Louise hews equally closely to this dynamic, becoming such a force for disorder within the show that she has been characterized as its most powerful antagonist. Gene, cooperative, attention-seeking, and sometimes overlooked, enthusiastically embodies the stereotypes of the middle child.

Birth order theory in popular culture can be summarized in three words: "Marcia, Marcia, Marcia." Jan Brady's lament, as the Brady girl without an adorable lisp or a perfectly brushed blonde mane, is emblematic of how intricately birth order theory has woven itself into television history. The basic precepts of birth order theory are so embedded in American popular culture that they might seem like second nature: the first-born child is a rule-governed authority figure; the middle born is a mediator, starved for attention; and the youngest child is the baby, allowed to break all the rules the firstborn so studiously follows. Just as a rudimentary knowledge of Sigmund Freud's Oedipus Complex complicates and enriches the conflicts between Bart and

Homer on *The Simpsons*, reading *Bob's Burgers* through the lens of birth order theory allows a far more nuanced understanding of the show's family dynamics.

Birth Order Theory in Psychology and Popular Culture

Birth order theory's popular appeal has always outstripped its academic standing. Francis Galton, an English polymath who made significant contributions to meteorology and statistics, surveyed his fellow scientists in 1874 and discovered that the majority of his peers were first-born sons. This observation was explored in the first half of the 20th century by Austrian psychiatrist Alfred Adler. Adler began from the observation that siblings often exhibit very different personality traits despite being raised in a similar environment by the same people. For Adler, these differences were evidence that each child must find a unique role in the family. In his studies, Adler claimed that children with the same ordinal position molded their personalities to suit that position. First-born children prefer order, structure, and identify with those in authority, often becoming them. Youngest children tend to be manipulative, because they have less direct access to power, and are sometimes spoiled. The middle child, in Adler's scheme, tends to receive less attention than either the eldest or the youngest, and thus struggles to capture the esteem of others (Stewart 78).

Over half a century after Adler's death, Frank Sulloway incorporated evolutionary theory with Adler's ideas about birth order and personality in his 1996 treatise, *Born to Rebel*. Sulloway imagines domestic life as an ecosystem with finite resources, requiring each participant to find a niche in order to survive. Birth order, according to Sulloway, underlies human personality traits, as children cultivate their characters to allow them to find and exploit available resources, namely the attention of their parents. Sulloway describes siblings as competing in an "an evolutionary arms race played out in the family" (Boynton 75). The defining household conflict shifts from seducing the mother to drawing the attention of both parents away from other siblings. First-borns identify closely with their parents and learn that they will be rewarded for pleasing them. In Sulloway's scheme, laterborns inevitably rebel because the niche of approval-seeker has already been filled by the firstborn. To support this hypothesis, Sulloway marshals the biographical data of scientific and political revolutionaries. Sulloway uses birth order to explain how siblings end up on opposing sides of the French Revolution, of evolution, even explaining the relative successes and failures among Henry VIII's marriages by looking at the birth order of his wives. Despite Martin Luther's status as a firstborn, Sulloway feasts on data from 718 other prominent figures from the Protestant Reformation, revealing that "only one other predictor—age—comes close to matching the explanatory power of birth order" (*Born to Rebel* 262).

Middleborns receive less attention from Sulloway than firstborns, and sometimes conclusions about them are undifferentiated from lastborns. To the extent that Sulloway considers middleborns' cases independently from laterborns in general, it is again with a prominent historical anecdote. Sulloway notes that middleborns tend to be mediators and appeasers. In terms of the big five personality traits Sulloway uses to differentiate his subjects, middleborns "score higher on Agreeableness than do firstborns or lastborns" ("Birth Order and Sibling Competition" 303). To illustrate his claim, Sulloway notes that Martin Luther King, Jr., began to practice coalition-building and non-violent resistance as a middle child (*Born to Rebel* 301). Sulloway speculates the middleborns become less aggressive because they are discouraged from lashing out at the younger, "baby," of the family, and would likely be dominated by the eldest (303). In his study of participants in the French Revolution, Sulloway classifies middleborns as "the most tender-minded," a classification that perhaps explains his lack of interest in middleborns as a category (321).

If this sounds both intuitive and possibly ridiculous, that pretty much sums up the scholarly response, first to Adler, then to Sulloway and *Born to Rebel*. In a cover story for *The New Republic*, Alan Wolfe lays out a series of critical flaws in both Sulloway's hypothesis and his methods. Most damning of any theory contrasting laterborns and firstborns is that when universalizing around human families, which until very recently tended to include more than one child, there will always be more variation among the laterborns, because only one child can be firstborn. In particular, Wolfe notes that Sulloway bases his study on functional birth order. Biological birth order, assuming the existence of accurate biographical data, is an objective category. Sulloway himself defines functional birth order, making it a subjective criterion. Thus, according to Wolfe, these results will not be replicable by other scientists. Wolfe's conclusions are born out by researchers Tor

Egil Førland, Trine Rogg Korsvik, and Knut-Andreas Christophersen, who attempted to find correlations similar to Sulloway's in their study of siblings' involvement in the radical movements of the 1960s. Førland, Korsvik, and Christophersen echo Wolfe's observation that laterborns, by definition, are born later, and so revolutions in science and politics will seem less revolutionary to them than to their older siblings. However, the notion has had remarkable traction in pop psychology, where Kevin Leman, Cliff Isaacson, Kris Radish, and others use it to refine approaches to parenting and mate selection, and life in general.

Leman may be the most successful adherent to birth order theory. His *Birth Order Book* has been revised and updated twice since its initial publication in 1985. Leman parlays his expertise into dozens of television appearances, noting that he correctly guessed television journalist Katie Couric's birth order just from watching her interact with her cohost (34). The following examples are typical of Leman's writing style, which presents a theory and then uses data drawn from anecdotal evidence, sometimes from Leman's clients, sometimes biographies, sometimes just lists of celebrities. For example, in defining lastborn tendencies Leman writes: "These social, outgoing creatures have never met a stranger. They are uncomplicated, spontaneous, humorous and high on people skills. To them, life's a party. They're most likely to get away with murder and least likely to be punished" (220). Leman follows up his definition with a long list of laterborn comedians (23). Setting aside the slippery use of terminology in his switch from lastborn to laterborn, Leman does something else here: he suggests that mastery of birth order theory allows the alert reader to comprehend not just themselves and their own family, but the broader world.

Where Leman distinguishes himself from scholarly researchers is in his push toward utility. He breaks down ordinal characteristics in a familiar way, but directs these characteristics very specifically toward family life. He addresses his initial assessment of each role toward the reader in the second person to emphasize that recognizing those traits in yourself will lead to a more fulfilling domestic life:

> If you're a firstborn or an only child, you'll learn why you're so driven to do everything.... If you're a middleborn, you'll find out why you always find yourself in the role of mediator, why you're on a different path than your firstborn sibling, and how you can keep yourself from being squeezed in the middle. If you're a last you'll find out why sometimes you need to walk a little more softly around the older ones in the family, cut them a little slack [16].

The traits assigned to each are familiar, but the purpose to which these descriptions are put allows Leman to fill chapters like "What's Parenting Got to Do with It?" and "Birth Order Marriages Aren't Made in Heaven" with strategies that address domestic strife using birth order as the neutral, inescapable cluster of traits. Leman also spends a chapter giving rationales for those whose personalities fail to fit his models. Though he doesn't use the term "functional birth order," Leman details nine variables that impact birth order including mixing the more objective traits, like sibling deaths, illness, or sex,[1] with subjective ones, like "the critical eye of the parent," and "emotional differences" (37). For Leman as for Sulloway, these exceptions prove the rule. The individuals whose personalities don't coincide with their ordinal birth status show that they are exceptional by expressing the traits of their true birth order. Again, my purpose here is not to focus on the circularity of this logic, but to note the extent to which each shores up the notion of birth order as an essential and constant indicator of character.

Another representative of popular birth order theory, *The Birth Order Effect: How to Better Understand Yourself and Others*, posits birth order as an immutable quality that, once understood, can be leveraged for self-actualization. Authors Cliff Isaacson and Kris Radish list eleven rules that account for exceptions to what they term, "Birth Order Personality." Many of them cover similar ground to Leman, including the notion that a five-year gap between births starts the cycle over again. Where they distinguish themselves from Leman is in their final rule, "In harmonious families the Birth Order of children can be quite mild," an optimistic exception for any reader who fails to recognize themselves in their descriptions (43). Isaacson and Radish maintain that birth order is established by age two. They provide tools for determining your Birth Order Personality, including a lengthy ranked inventory and multiple-choice assessment (18–24).

Scientific merit aside, acknowledging the influence of birth order theory on *Bob's Burgers* allows for a reading that reframes the children's behavior, making fan-favorite Tina less daring than she might first appear, Gene more conflicted, and Louise, well, probably still a sociopath. The Belchers embody their ordinal positions so consistently that episodes might be selected at random to illustrate this phenomenon. Still, each of the following three episodes allows one of the Belcher children particular glory in their position, while affirming the status of the other two. In the interest of fairness, I begin with the character most likely to be overlooked, middle child Gene Belcher.

Gene Belcher as Jan Brady

More than a dozen years after *The Brady Bunch* left ABC prime-time in 1974, the 1990s ushered in a Brady renaissance, beginning on stage with *The Real Live Brady Bunch*, moving to television on *Saturday Night Live*, and culminating in two films, *The Brady Bunch Movie* (1995) and *A Very Brady Sequel* (1996). The greatest beneficiary of the renewed interest in the Bradys was middle daughter Jan. Melanie Hutsell, a cast member from *The Real Live Brady Bunch*, gave commentary on current events as Jan Brady on *Saturday Night Live* in 1992 and 1993. Each appearance derived humor from the limits of the character's perspective as she attempts to give opinions about the 1992 presidential election or breast implants using only her family history as guidance. Jan's character is so defined by her frustration at her status within her family that she can never escape it. More than 20 years later, Jan Brady still reigns, source of the meme, "Sure, Jan," a GIF generated from the first film that became a popular vehicle for expressing skepticism on the internet in January 2015 (Weber).[2] The self-identified "All-devouring Pop-Culture Wiki," *TV Tropes*, calls this phenomenon "Middle Child Syndrome." *TV Tropes* references *The Brady Bunch* and Jan but describes the trope as an affliction that crosses gender lines, using Lisa Simpson and Gene Belcher as examples, along with many others from live action television and other media.

"Full Bars," the second episode from *Bob's Burgers'* third season, is an excellent site for analyzing the extent to which the show integrates all birth order roles, particularly for middle child Gene. On Halloween, Louise successfully argues that they should be allowed to trick or treat without their parents. Tina instantly reverts to the status quo when Bob asserts his right to accompany them, but Louise prevails, claiming, "We're born alone, we die alone, and in between, we trick-or-treat alone." All that freedom comes to little more than oyster crackers and packets of hot sauce in their neighborhood, so Louise convinces her siblings to take the ferry to a wealthy enclave, King's Head Island. There the Belchers find the titular full-sized candy bars, given so freely that they are even left in unattended bowls. The Belchers meet locals Milo and Ned, who caution them about Hell Hunt, a King's Head tradition where teens round up and torture kids on the street after dark. The kids stay out, despite Milo and Ned's warning, and narrowly escape the teens. Milo and Ned are less fortunate. Tina convinces Louise and Gene that they must rescue Milo and Ned, a development that allows Louise to steal, lie, and inflict suffering on strangers, but forces Gene to sacrifice his candy in their final race to the last ferry home. Thus, all the sacrifices entailed in following Louise's drive for mischief and Tina's allegiance to conventional morality fall to Gene. In his willingness to follow both his sisters, Gene finds himself living up to Dr. Kevin Leman's threat, a middle child feeling the squeeze of the more dominant personalities to either side.

Beyond the plot outline of "Full Bars," the costume each character selects reinforces their status within the family. Tina is not just a mummy, but mummy-mommy, taking on more responsibility than she needs to by wrapping up a doll as well as herself. When Bob cautions that she will need to bring back the toilet paper, Tina immediately agrees, though Louise overrules her, and she spends the course of the adventure trying to steer her siblings toward the most responsible path, including holding them accountable for looking after their new friends Milo and Ned. Louise garbs herself as Tim Burton's greatest anti-hero, Edward Scissorhands, the sensitive young man with deadly sharp scissors instead of hands. The only other costume that could rival its tidy encapsulation of her potential for creativity and destruction would be the Hindu goddess Shiva.[3]

Still, it is Gene's costume that demonstrates the greatest debt to birth order theory. Gene's interpretation of "rapper/actress Queen Latifah from her U.N.I.T.Y. phase" parodies the idea of the approval seeking, mediating middle child, often acting as the substitute parent in conflicts between the firstborn and lastborn children. Queen Latifah, née Dana Owens, leverages her size and confidence into a regal, maternal bearing, despite her youth (Keyes).[4] Gene's comfort with his size (not only does he know that he's a little tubby, he traces it to a single ice cream sandwich) and willingness to draw power from it is a tribute to Queen Latifah. In "Family Fracas," Gene declares before an appearance on a *Family Feud*–like game show, "Camera, take the day off. I added ten pounds to myself!" (3.19).

Like Queen Latifah, Gene presents himself as a mother, unlikely as that might seem given both his sex and age. In the third season episode, "The Kids Run the Restaurant," Louise, bored while waiting for her parents to return from the hospital, complains, "Oh! This is gonna be the longest hour of my life," eliciting Gene's response, "Wait till childbirth, girlfriend" (3.20). While this might seem like simply a non sequitur, Gene's comment fits a pattern. In an earlier Season 3 episode, "OT: The Outside Toilet," Gene proclaims that he was "born to be a mother!"

In the third episode of the second season, Gene cries after some strenuous synchronized swimming, "Next time we do this I'm getting an epidural!" Season four's "Frond Files" depicts Gene with a rubber ball under his shirt. He waves at Louise and says, "I'm dodging for two!" Many critics and fans note the ambiguity of Gene's gender identity and sexuality. Jenny Jaffe, writing for *Bustle*, speculates that Gene is trans, while *Bob's Burgers* star H. Jon Benjamin claims that Gene is gay (Gebreyes). While Gene's potential as an animated queer icon is open for interpretation, his maternal tendencies live on the surface, however unlikely their realization.[5]

Though Gene cultivates his maternal resemblance, as a young artist, Queen Latifah expressed ambivalence about being treated like a mother. Cheryl Keyes attributes this ambivalence to a broader cultural tendency to shoehorn revolutionary female figures into traditional women's roles. Categorizing Queen Latifah as a mother allows a sexist, racist culture to read her ferocity and anger not as ways of chafing against the limitations of Black womanhood in 20th-century America, but as the protective, socially acceptable snarling of a mother protecting her young. The way that being a mother neutralizes aggression works very differently for Gene, who as the only son might be expected to dominate his sisters. Instead, Gene actively seeks opportunities to enlist himself in his sisters' schemes, bemoaning missed opportunities to get his legs waxed in "Mother Daughter Laser Razor," and attempting to insinuate himself into Louise and Tina's infiltration of a Thundergirls troop in "Tina, Tailor, Soldier, Spy" (3.10; 5.7).

The era of Queen Latifah that Gene depicts also deserves close consideration. In noting that it comes from her "U.N.I.T.Y. phase," Gene cites Queen Latifah's greatest mainstream triumph as a rapper.[6] Gene wears a paper or cardboard version of the crown-like kufi Queen Latifah wore on stage at the 1994 Grammy awards, along with a dark tunic and bright Africa pendant. At that ceremony, Queen Latifah's single "U.N.I.T.Y." won for "Best Solo Rap Performance," with lyrics that trumpeted the power of Black women without alienating other listeners.

The title alone fits Gene's costume tidily into stereotypes about middle children as mediators, both among their siblings and between children and parents. The song affirms that women must be treated with respect, but it falls short of claiming respect for all women, all the time. Queen Latifah declares her desire to take a stand against the prevalence use of the terms "bitch" and "ho" as virtual synonyms for women or girls in the hip hop idiom. However, in the next verse, she allows that some women should be called bitches and hos. Queen Latifah never explicitly details which women fall into the category of bitches and hos, but instead assumes that she and the listener have similar standards, as a way of building community with the listener who uses these terms. She specifies moments when she has been mistaken for the kind of women who should be called a bitch or a ho, citing moments of harassment, in order to clarify the behavior she protests in "U.N.I.T.Y." Still, there's a whiff of conciliation about the track, despite Queen Latifah declaring again and again that she is neither a bitch nor a ho, because she introduces the idea that some women, sometimes even herself, are or can be called bitches and hoes. She stakes out a middle space and claims it as a position of respect, despite seemingly weakening her argument (if not, truth be told, her song, which is amazing). Queen Latifah refuses to alienate either side of the spectrum, allowing for the possibility that individual women can be "bitches" (women who will not be courted) or "hos" (women who will be courted, but require compensation).

As a cultural figure, Queen Latifah personifies the impossible middle ground Gene inhabits as he attempts to mediate between Tina and Louise. In the late eighties and early nineties hip hop was a bifurcated genre, with artists like the Fresh Prince and DJ Jazzy Jeff, MC Hammer and Young MC finding mainstream success with danceable tracks. The music recycled familiar samples from funk, R&B, and rock, while the lyrics were breezy tours of young love punctuated by fast cars and slow hands. The other sound coming to the fore was "Gangsta Rap": tales of underground markets in women and drugs, where the fast car was not a way to attract girls but to outrun the authorities. Into this, Queen Latifah attempts to highlight the problems throughout the genre—namely the treatment of women as goods to be cherished or trafficked. Feminist scholar Joan Morgan returns to this contradiction throughout her study of women of the hip hop generation, *When the Chickenheads Come Home to Roost*. She attempts to claim a space she calls "the grays," staying in dialog with hip hop while confronting its misogyny (54).

In the conclusion to "Full Bars," Gene finds himself in a position less complicated than Queen Latifah's, but similarly compromised. He supports both Louise's plan for mischief and Tina's moral imperative to set things right, a volatile combination that leaves him racing to the last ferry to the mainland from King's Head Island. Risking his candy and urine-filled water balloons, he invokes his idol and analog, crying "Queen Latifah, give me strength!" Though Gene's enthusiasm for his sisters never flags, "Full Bars" demonstrates the sacrifices he makes to follow them. Though Gene can seem like the most self-aware of the three, particularly in his acceptance of his size, this episode shows that, unlike Jan Brady, he may not entirely realize the consequences of his ordinal role, just as Queen Latifah can't completely dedicate herself to lifting all her sisters from the labels "bitch" and "ho." As the only son, Gene might be expected to have a more dominant role in his family, but his accession to his ordinal role is greater than his dedication to his gender role.

Louise: The Revolution Will Wear Pink Bunny Ears

Like "Full Bars," "The Frond Files" reveals how closely the characters identify with the classic role according to their birth order, but is particularly revealing for Louise (4.12). The plot acts as a frame for each child's interpretation of the creative writing assignment, "Why I Love Wagstaff." Bob and Linda read each essay in Mr. Frond's office, as Frond tries to explain to them why, as the school's guidance counselor, he felt that he couldn't put the Belcher children's essays on display. Not only do the children put themselves into their classic birth order roles within the essays, they also recognize their siblings' niches.

"The Frond Files" allows each child to take over the point of view of the episode, presenting his or her own role as he or she imagines it. Thus, each vignette is as direct a representation of the Belcher children's perspective as the audience will ever see. Louise imagines herself as a hybrid of John and Sarah Connor from the Terminator series, saving her siblings almost as an afterthought. Gene's fantasy subtly concurs by giving her a punk piercing. Gene, true to his nature as a mediator, brings Tina and Louise together in his essay, and both of them assist him in singing about farts and making the school a better place to sing about farts by imprisoning Mr. Frond. Tina's so traditional that her vignette unspools in black and white. Just as Louise embodies rebellion, Tina grasps for symbols of conventional power. In her fantasy, Tina is dressed like the sheriff from the popular television program *The Walking Dead* (2010–present). Made over as an authority on zombie control, Tina must rescue not just her siblings, but the entire school and possibly the world. As the eldest, she takes it all upon her shoulders, and if that means she has 16 zombie buttfriends, er, boyfriends, then so be it. Though these vignettes provide plenty of evidence for each Belcher's investment in their ordinal position, Louise's fantasy, more than any other, clarifies the depth of her identification as a laterborn. As Frank Sulloway might put it, in her own mind Louise is "born to rebel."

Louise's essay riffs on James Cameron's *The Terminator* (1984) and his sequel, *Terminator 2: Judgment Day* (1991). Louise conflates the films in her essay, following the plot of the first while inserting set pieces and imagery from the second. The elements of both films that don't hold her interest, namely romance and motherhood, are completely excised from her account. As a combination of Sarah Connor and her son John Connor, Louise is the target of a Mr. Frond–like robot from the future, sent by Future Mr. Frond to execute her before she can put a brownie on his chair and humiliate him at her eighth-grade graduation ceremony by making him look like he's soiled himself. Louise learns this from Darryl, a classmate who has come from the future to warn her. Future Darryl is a version of the Kyle Reese character from the first film, portrayed by rugged, stubble-faced Michael Biehn. Within the series, Reese is Sarah Connor's lover, John Connor's father, and the first to say: "come with me if you want to live," a catch phrase that would reoccur in two other films, including *Terminator 2*. Future Darryl sports a patchy attempt at a mustache, but if that nod to the Reese character is too subtle, Future Darryl implores Louise to "come with me if you want to continue to be alive."[7] The visual and aural debt to Cameron's films is clear from the start. Robot Mr. Frond beams in naked, analyzing nearby people for clothes to steal, eyes glowing red, as the soundtrack fills with beeps and eerie, metallic synthesizers prominently featured in both films. Louise barely saves herself and her siblings from Robot Frond, escaping by tricking it into falling into a hot vat of creamed corn in the Wagstaff kitchen. This scene recalls the finale of *Terminator 2*, in which the T-1000 meets its end by being shot into a vat of molten steel. Just as in the first film, the Belchers must stay on the run, as an army of Robot Fronds appears to resume the mission. Louise and her siblings go into hiding in Mexico (or Belize, there's some confusion about that. To be fair, Louise is only nine years old). As the segment closes, Louise sports the same sunglasses worn by Sarah Connor in the second film, writing in her journal just as Sarah Connor narrates her story into a tape recorder at the end of *The Terminator*.

The Terminator and *Terminator 2* have all the blood, bullets, and collateral damage that viewers expect from R-rated action thrillers. However, both films stand out for having deep emotional cores. While many people are shot and crushed by Arnold Schwarzenegger in *The*

Terminator and *Terminator 2*, the first film is lauded as a love story, while the second, like James Cameron's *Aliens*, is read as a tribute to maternal affection.[8] Louise's retelling abandons both themes.

In *The Terminator*, Reese comes from the future to protect Sarah under orders from Sarah's son, John. Reese arrives already in love with Sarah after learning about her from her son, ready to train and protect her. Future Darryl does not perform to the same standards. After he explains the catalyst and provenance of Robot Frond, Louise snaps, "you came back through time to tell me this, just to be a narrator, and you didn't bring any special weapons or anything, just a bucketload of exposition and a stupid mustache?" Louise herself is the rebel leader in the future, so she must be protected for her own sake, not for her breeding potential. But she is not protected—instead Future Darryl becomes another hapless civilian for Louise to defend, making what was once a love story (Reese sacrifices himself to protect Sarah after impregnating her with John) into pure, possibly endless carnage. By becoming both Connors, Louise allows herself to take center stage in the bloody plot of both films without the romantic and maternal implications.

Louise's recall of the films, at least as they play out in her fantasy, emphasizes violent conflict—she literally gives the viewer the greatest hits. She draws on the second film primarily to insert another action set piece—the T-1000 melting in molten steel—into her story. Louise's other explicit integration of material from the second film involves the final shot of the vignette, when Louise wears aviator-style sunglasses as an homage to the Sarah Connor of *Terminator 2*. Some critics, particularly Margaret Goscilo, read Sarah Connor as utterly hapless in the first film (39). At the close, Louise aligns herself, as a character, with that later Sarah, while conveniently skipping over all the elements of Sarah that Louise would find inconvenient, like her initial dependence on and attraction to Kyle Reese in the first film, and the fact that her ferocity as a warrior derives from her maternal instincts in the second.

Perhaps the most radical part of Louise's homage to the *Terminator* series is that she is so taken with her own version that she freely interpolates scenes from other films. When Robot Frond follows Gene into the kitchen, Robot Frond is distracted by Gene's reflection on the stainless-steel surfaces. The kitchen looks very much like the one used in 1993's *Jurassic Park* in a scene where two children attempt to hide from a raptor. Louise, ever the rebel, doesn't recognize the conventions that might limit her to drawing on only one action film series in the course of her seven-minute vignette.[9]

Louise takes only what she wishes from the *Terminator* series, which summarizes her approach to pretty much everything in her life. She harvests the bits that serve her, which makes her vignette a pastiche that has very little thematic connection to the films that inspired it. Like the laterborn rebels described by Sulloway and Leman, Louise molds her source material to suit her. She takes pride in the scatological prank that sets Mr. Frond on his course of destruction, never expressing any guilt or regret about putting herself and her siblings in peril. Louise has an unwavering belief in herself that can't be challenged by authority figures, as well as a willingness to face the unknown. If Louise is, as Leman writes of lastborns, "rebellious, temperamental, manipulative, spoiled, impatient, and impetuous," she seems completely unbothered by her own anti-social tendencies (168). Because it is structured as a series of fantasies created by each Belcher child, the dystopian, hunted Louise is her idealized version of herself. In covering *Bob's Burgers* since 2013, *AV Club* writer Alasdair Wilkins notes that Louise can be "more of a chaotic force of nature than a character in her own right," while other critics and fans celebrate her even as they wonder if she might be a sociopath.[10]

Perhaps what might be more productive than weighing Louise's potential diagnoses is considering how treating her disruptive behavior as normal, as Bob and Linda do, impacts the program. While the show never directly references birth order theory, taking Leman's approach to Louise allows for far happier family dynamics than directly engaging in combat with a nine-year-old. Bob and Linda rarely seem shocked by her behavior. In fact, they both respond positively to the story, supporting her creativity and courage, while accepting her violent imagination without comment. Their acceptance of Louise on her own terms models an approach to parenting that anticipates that not every child will be eager to please, like Gene, or strictly rule-governed, like Tina.

Tina, Tina, Tina!

Of all the Belchers, 13-year-old Tina most preoccupies and delights critics and *Tumblr* denizens alike. Tina's bespectacled mug moans in memes, mugs, and all manner of merchandise. Critics like Sonia Saraiya attribute Tina's originality to show creator Loren Bouchard's willingness to ignore gender in creating a lusty yet oddly affectless adolescent. Tina started as a boy named Daniel, and when the character's gender changed, the lines and Dan Mintz's voice remained the same. The result, according to *Bitch* magazine, confers "the same awkward horniness we've always seen in television's teenaged boys on to a female character" (Moss). In fact, Tina's desire makes her more, not less, conformist, and this conformity is consistent with the larger popular psychological paradigm of birth order theory.

"Tina-Rannosaurus Wrecks" epitomizes Tina's firstborn tendencies to conform and follow rules. In the first scene, Bob, elated at purchasing "Six thousand low-fold dispenser napkins for fifty-eight dollars," decides that it's time to teach Tina to drive in the restaurant supply store's nearly empty parking lot. Tina notes that it is illegal for a 13-year-old to drive, but assents in the face of Bob's excitement. Paralyzed by the dissonance of disobeying either her father or the law, Tina very slowly crashes the car into the only other car in the lot, unable to stop or turn. Tina insists over Bob's objections that they leave a note on the barely scratched parked car. Because the damaged vehicle belongs to Bob's arch-nemesis Jimmy Pesto, the entire Belcher clan is eventually drawn into a scam, with Tina groaning audibly every step of the way. Bob insists to his insurance adjuster, Chase, voiced by reliably slippery Bob Odenkirk, that he was driving at the time of the accident. The adjuster is so taken with the Belchers that he hires them to cater a barbecue at his house. During the barbecue, Tina inadvertently sets Chase's house on fire. Tina breaks down, and Bob finally takes her to Chase's office. Chase explains that he never believed Bob's story of the accident but signed off on the claim in order to enlist the Belchers in a series of fraudulent insurance claims, starting with the fire. Louise, as a chaos-loving lastborn, is typically unsympathetic to Tina's plight. At the episode's denouement, when Tina has finally freed the family from Chase's schemes, Louise responds to Tina's characterization of the past week, saying "this was the worst week of your life? You got to crash a car and burn down a house!"

Tina's suffering throughout the episode punctuates how much dissembling and disobedience go against her firstborn nature. The only way Bob can enlist her in lying to Chase is by alluding to a greater authority: romantic desire. Bob finally finds a way to get Tina to go along with his lie in the following exchange:

> **Bob:** It's not even really a lie…. It's a secret. It's our shared secret.
> **Tina:** Huh. Maybe if I had a backstory?
> **Bob:** A backstory?
> **Tina:** Do I have a boyfriend in this scenario?

1. *From the Womb to the Tomb*

When Bob concedes, Tina must give the imaginary boyfriend a name and a tragic secret before they can move on. The scene takes place in the restaurant's basement with the napkins prominently depicted on a shelf behind Bob and Tina, almost centered in the frame when the shot features both characters, looming over Bob's right shoulder in his close-ups. Featuring the bulk napkins casts a melancholy pall over the scene, as the viewer can only escape the hulking manifestation of that joyful, prelapsarian moment when Bob had just claimed his bounty in the shots of Tina, who is confused and devastated.

The subtle melodramatic touches extend to the use of non-diegetic music. Like many scenes on *Bob's Burgers*, this scene begins without a score. Then, as Tina's secret boyfriend begins to come into focus, music comes in. Violins begin with "he plays lacrosse," accompanied by a plaintive piano when Tina reveals that lacrosse is dearer to his heart than she is. When Bob reveals that he has greasy hair, triumphant percussion emerges, adding impact and enthusiasm to Tina's "yes" as the scene ends and the music cuts out. The bale of napkins and soap opera–like score highlight both Tina's misery and the potential for its resolution. Tina, true to her firstborn nature, identifies with authority (Sulloway *BTR* 53). Most birth order experts link this to a tendency for firstborns to see the world in black and white, which explains Tina's turmoil, as she's confronted in the first minutes of the episode with two authorities (paternal and legal) in conflict with one another. When Bob fails in convincing her that there are shades of gray in deception, he wins her over by introducing, at Tina's urging, an imperative that outranks all others: romantic longing.

The notion of Tina as conservative firstborn seems incompatible with the "strong, smart, sensual woman," so widely celebrated on *Tumblr*, but Tina not only embodies the conformity that Frank Sulloway claims is innate to firstborns, her obedience to romantic imperatives above all others is symptom of the extent to which she strives to live up to the cultural expectations for contemporary adolescent girls. *Bob's Burgers'* critique of heterosexual romance's creep into childhood is revealed through the rules Tina finds to follow. She sexualizes every interaction with the opposite sex, from her dentist to her neighbor. Even the objects of her affections that seem more eccentric, like her fascination with zombies in her dreams and her erotic fiction, supports the reading of Tina as a typically conservative firstborn.

Tina's sexual attraction to zombies can be viewed as the pinnacle of her conformity to "dead" standards. While the format of sitcoms allows characters to become increasingly eccentric as the writers explore and expand their personalities over dozens of episodes, Tina reveals her peculiar relationship to the living dead right away. Within the first few minutes of *Bob's Burgers* second episode, "Crawl Space," Tina invites Gene, displaced by visiting grandparents, to share her room. As a caveat, she mentions, to Bob's surprise, that she still suffers night terrors from seeing *Night of the Living Dead* when she was eight years old. Tina explains to her wide-eyed siblings and parents, "I think my subconscious fears and my budding sexuality are getting all mixed up so I think I'm being attacked by zombies and I start screaming, do you want to make out? And then I make out with it." Tina's family pauses at this disclosure, then returns to planning for the grandparents' visit. However, Tina's desires are not merely a gag. Later in the same episode, Tina incorporates the sounds of her grandparents' lovemaking into her recurring dream, rendering it a nightmare again.

In "Bad Tina," Tina creates a zombie named Chad, a fellow student at Wagstaff who joins Tina and Jimmy Jr. for a three-way butt-touch. In a piece championing Tina as the harbinger of new possibilities for female adolescents on television, Katie Schenkel notes, "Tina's sexual desires aren't there to titillate the audience. They're there because they're a part of her." I agree that with Schenkel about the centrality of Tina's sexual desires to her character, but I posit that some of the humor of Tina's zombie encounter derives from the reification of another zombie theory: young women's lust is beyond their control. Tina's imagination can invest anything, even an empty shoebox named Jeff, with sufficient personality to commence a loving, romantic relationship. In this sense, Tina's love life is the ultimate illustration of the rule-governed conservative. For Tina, the idea of romance is enough to imbue that shoebox with a personality.

Tina imagines her first kiss with Jimmy Jr. at her 13th birthday party as "the moment she becomes a woman." To the strains of the Thompson Twins, "If You Were Here," Tina, in an homage to Molly Ringwald's bridesmaid dress in the deathless teen romance *Sixteen Candles* (1984), meets Jimmy Jr. at the center of the dance floor and kisses him. Tina's urge to conform makes her unable to imagine her first kiss without clothing it in the trappings of a 30-year-old romantic comedy. If Tina's dress seems dated, so too can the psychological theory used to explain her investment in tired notions.

The persistence of birth order theory in psychology despite a dearth of replicable studies makes it what psychologists Christopher J. Ferguson and Moritz Heene term an "undead theory" or "zombie theory." Essentially, the studies that disprove correlations are less likely to be published, while the ideas gain power through cultural exposure irrespective of their utility or accuracy. Tina's attraction to the zombies literalizes her conventional behavior. The program plays with Tina as a vessel who enacts old, bad ideas, again and again. These ideas end up being as unwieldy as the pink dress Tina wears to her party, which allows Tina to charm with her awkward sexuality while its source goes unexamined.

Tina's portrayal as roiling with sexual desire doesn't make her an iconoclast. She's part of a long line of young women unwilling or unable to control their sexual desires. Recall that one of the greatest threats to family stability in *Pride and Prejudice* is Lydia's inability to stymie her desire for any man in a red coat. The Victorians defined themselves against the notion that women swelled with barely concealable lust, but its resurgence of late is typified by the widespread popularity of the *Twilight* series. Nothing defines the heroine, Bella Swan, like her barely contained desire for cold, hard Edward Cullen. Gabrielle Moss calls Tina revolutionary because she does more than just respond to the sexual desires of adolescent boys, she has desires of her own. However, Tina understands the world as popular culture. She sees her own classmates as potential characters for her fan fiction because she doesn't draw any distinction between popular culture and her reality. Her exuberant sexual desires are simply another indicator of the extent to which she identifies as a typical adolescent girl. Only a culture that expects adolescent girls to be overcome with desire would make stars of the Duggar sisters, the good Christian reality television stars who will not give their suitors more than a side-hug until marriage.[11] Tina's insatiable lust is actually a parody of what it would look like to internalize cultural norms set for women since *The Simpsons* debuted in 1990: a vision of female/male desire that actually looks a lot like male/male desire. This current is subtly underscored by having Tina express her desires with the voice of an adult male.

While *The Simpsons*, at least in its first few seasons, enacts a perfectly Freudian model of internecine conflict with a father and son battling over an ever-nurturing blue phallus, *Bob's Burgers* escapes psychoanalytical tropes altogether, locating Belcher family conflicts in a Darwinist model in which near peers struggle to define and defend a niche. Understanding Tina as a conformist, Gene as a mediator, and Louise as a rebel deepens *Bob's Burgers* critique of popular culture by giving weight, even pathos, to the roles embodied by the Belchers.

2

Spielberger of the Day

Boomers Dream, Generation X Schemes

I can't hope to provide an exhaustive guide to the popular culture references in *Bob's Burgers*. Simply cataloging and sourcing the burgers of the day could take up several chapters in this book. It would take a writers' room like that for *Bob's Burgers* to excavate each homage. However, the writers' room in general and Loren Bouchard in particular share a fascination that makes them especially typical of Generation X. Defined as Americans born between 1965 and 1980, this generation is the first to grow up on Steven Spielberg films. The cinematic oeuvre of Spielberg might be the most pronounced cultural touchstone in the series, at times explicit. The allusion to *E.T. the Extra-Terrestrial* in "OT: The Outside Toilet," the recreation of the Spielberg-produced *The Goonies* in "The Belchies," and the *Jaws*-influenced, "The Deepening" are pretty tough to miss. A more subtle homage can be discovered in "Christmas in the Car," which enacts a chase reminiscent of Spielberg deep cut, *Duel*, but could read as another hilarious-yet-heartwarming holiday episode to the uninitiated.[1]

Few living filmmakers spur as much critical discussion as Steven Spielberg, but often that discussion focuses on his more explicitly "serious" films like *Schindler's List* (1993). *Bob's Burgers* concerns itself with the Spielberg films widely available to children in the 1970s and '80s. *Jaws* and *E.T.* were massive hits, rereleased to theaters and circulating widely on home video after their premiers in 1975 and 1982, respectively. The other two films with the greatest impact on *Bob's Burgers*, *The Goonies* and *Duel*, were swept along by the hunger for more Spielberg content in the 1980s, but not necessarily the films that anyone who was not a child in the '80s would deem essential. *The Goonies* wasn't even directed by Spielberg but was heavily marketed as a Spielberg film; he earned story credit and was an executive producer. As part of the same '80s zeal for Spiel, *Duel*, a 1971 made-for-television thriller, finally got

28

a United States theatrical release following *E.T.* and then a wide video release. The Spielberg films that *Bob's Burgers* devotes whole episodes to are not necessarily canonical choices, but movies that were in constant circulation in the '80s and '90s, whether as part of anniversary celebrations, career retrospectives, or, in the case of *The Goonies*, airing constantly on cable television. They each became objects of childhood fascination because of their omnipresence, regardless of whether they were meant for children. Analyzing *Bob's Burgers'* interpretations of these films allows us to see more than just how the show interprets contemporary popular culture, it's also a chance for *Bob's Burgers* to recuperate or reject Spielberg's moral preoccupations. Spielberg, born in 1946, is one of the most pervasive, influential voices of his generation, so his vision of family, masculinity, and childhood can in many ways act as synecdoche for a certain class and age that has had a historically long reign as the dominant culture in the United States. When *Bob's Burgers* brings in Spielberg's blockbusters of the '70s and '80s, it's an opportunity to see what a baby boomer fantasy looks like through the lens of Generation X. This vision becomes more acute as the series goes on, so I will consider the Spielberg parodies in the order in which they aired: "The Belchies," "The Deepening," "The OT" and finally, "Christmas in the Car."

The Goonies

The Goonies' place in Spielberg's career is somewhat contested. The opening of the film gives him a prominent place; "Steven Spielberg Presents" fills the screen before the title. However, Spielberg's actual relationship to the material becomes less clear as the credits roll on. He has story credit and is an executive producer, but according to actors on the film he also spent every day on set as a kind of shadow director (Astin 135). The plot of *The Goonies* certainly bears some of the hallmarks of a Spielberg film, though its direct address of class issues—something present in the novel *Jaws* but underplayed in the film—makes this new territory. Briefly, a group of kids who call themselves "Goonies" because of their proximity to the Goon Docks, are about to be forced from their homes to make way for a golf course. On the last weekend before their houses will be demolished, they find a treasure map. In joining forces in the hunt for the treasure—which they agree to apply toward rescuing their homes from the developers—they come into conflict with a crime family, the Fratellis. An unlikely friendship forms between one of the kids and the Fratellis' son, Sloth, who has developmental disabilities and facial deformities. Sloth ends up helping the Goonies escape from his mother and brothers, and they find enough loot to rescue their homes.

Of all the episodes I discuss in this chapter, the homage to a single Spielberg film is clearest in "The Belchies," from the title to the theme song to the plot elements that are repurposed in the show. Cindy Lauper sings "Taffy Butt" for "The Belchies," just as she sang "Goonies Are Good Enough," for the film. There are smaller moments as well, like the "Fratelli and Son" sign visible from the taffy factory, and Louise, listing off generic, randomly assigned nicknames as the kids—Tina and Gene, but also, against Louise's wishes, Jimmy Jr., Zeke, Andy, and Ollie—enter the condemned taffy factory.[2] However there are certain elements that become part of a critique of the film, calling attention to the rampant racism, sexism, and phallocentrism of the film.

The Goonies, like the other Spielberg films *Bob's Burgers* references, has its roots in horror. The bulk of the film is spent in caverns under local landmarks—the lighthouse, the wishing well—exposing, like *Jaws*, the potential danger that lies under the surface of what appears to be a family-friendly space. The streets of Astoria, as shown in the jailbreak chase that opens the film, are quaint, full of independent storefront shops, with just a single lane for each direction of traffic, and four-way stops signs instead of lights. However, like every soft smooth stretch of flesh, beneath the skin lies a damp, creepy skeleton—in this case a series of booby-trapped caverns, each one promising the possibility of treasures squirreled away in the 19th century by One-Eyed Willy.

Of course, this is a film about body horror and adolescent boys, so the fact that its major plot point is also a dick joke is truly no surprise. The terror of having a body or finding a body animates *The Goonies* from the start. The film opens with what seems like a corpse hanging in a jail cell (it turns out to be a member of the Fratelli family, alive and using the element of surprise to escape his captors), the camera circles and then shoots in to explore the silhouette and then fully realized form of the giant, pink, mostly hairless sloth, and throughout the adventure, skeletons that pop out at every turn. Bodies and bones are everywhere as this 13-year-old boy takes cryptic instructions from "One-Eyed Willy." That the girls are the first among the Goonies to express a desire to abandon the quest fails to surprise—they suffer enough at the whims of the one-eyed willies on the surface to subject themselves to the one calling the shots below ground. The film, focused as it is on the imaginations of adolescent boys, ends in twin fantasies—that pretty girls will identify the boys as objects of desire, and that they can redeem their fathers.

The racism of *The Goonies* is not subtle. One of the Goonies, called Data, has a lot of ingenious inventions. He has a belt that shoots a suction cup and automated reel so powerful that he sucks himself into a trash can. Data, given his propensity for developing technology and generic East Asian accent, is clearly supposed to be Japanese, as Japan in the 1980s was the United States' primary technological rival. However, Data is apparently Chinese—he comments when they are at the bottom of the wishing well that "If we keep going this far down we'll reach China!" Rather than just treating this as a joke, Data seems sincere, following it up with "Maybe I can visit my auntie or something. Yeah, my uncle!" His accent is a source of comedy, as the kids can't seem to understand his pronunciation of "booby trap." *Bob's Burgers* addresses this part of *The Goonies* early in the episode. Teddy explains that Mr. Caffrey set up taffy men throughout his secret tunnels to keep the feds away from his boot-legging operation, "like the terra cotta warriors of ancient China." Gene responds with "China! Stick to noodles, right? Is that racist?" Bob and Teddy agree that it is, and Teddy moves on with his story. Bringing up racism, specifically anti–Chinese racism, certainly alludes to the pain anyone who grew up watching the film feels as we see and hear Data portrayed as this barely comprehensible prodigy, an Asian stereotype through and through that can't even bother to reckon with the difference between Japan and China. *Bob's Burgers* brings the racism to the surface, incorporating into the story that makes it impossible to ignore—Gene, on some level, knows his joke is racist, or he wouldn't ask, and Bob, our guide to sane and civil behavior, confirms as much.

The way the dick joke comes into *Bob's Burgers* shows a similar level of exasperation with *The Goonies* as an appealing but problematic text. Mikey invokes One-Eyed Willy, the source of this treasure, again and again, directly addressing him and asking for guidance. Once you realize how puerile this joke is, it starts to become distressing to hear a child repeatedly invoke him as one might call on a god. Perhaps as adults we assume a child would simply accept that One-Eyed Willy is just the name of a pirate. *Bob's Burgers* makes its dick joke impossible to ignore. The kids sneak off to the taffy factory with ease, because it is Sunday, Bob and Linda's date night. Linda, plotting to make it special, spikes Bob's casserole with an erectile dysfunction pill. When Bob and Linda discover that the kids are gone, Bob worries that his erection won't go down and Linda admits that she secretly dosed him, because

"Sometimes you want to ride a roller coaster twice and you don't want to wait in line." Linda encourages Bob not to worry, and to make the best of things, saying, "that thing made the kids, maybe it can find them."

Bob tries his best to rely on other extremities in their search for the kids. For the remainder of the episode, Bob pulls down his shirt or keeps Linda in front of him until the finale. After the taffy man helps rescue Louise, he gets stuck on Bob. The look is so disturbing that Teddy says, "Your sex night took a weird turn, eh Bobby?" Bob's tumescence wanes, releasing Taffy, and Linda says, "I see you finally got the starch out of your shirt." This entire element of the plot proceeds without ever naming or showing Bob's erection. While Linda mentions "penis pills," the penis in question is referred to as "that thing," or gestured at. Just as in *The Goonies*, the dick joke might not be something that kids pick up on, but (forgive me) it just keeps coming up, no matter how unfortunate the setting. At least *Bob's Burgers* explicitly acknowledges how inappropriate it is for a grown man to join a children's adventure with his penis jutting out from his clothes.

My problem with One-Eyed Willy in *The Goonies* does not stem from a Puritanical wish that these children be unspoiled by the thought of genitalia. On the contrary, I think it's absurd that among this group, not a single one of them, not even the preternaturally gifted linguist, Mouth, would fail to recognize the name for what it is, or at least turn it into a dick joke. Given everyone's reaction to the map, One-Eyed Willy has been a part of the lore of Astoria for a long time. Kids between 12 and 17 enjoy little more than finding sexual innuendo in the world around them, but it never occurred to any of these kids that this figure of local folklore might share a name with a John Holmes character? That adults wrote this for a child actor, Sean Astin, to say over and over again, with no diegetic understanding of what it implies, is truly more disgusting than Bob running around the factory with an erection. Thus, what seems like a crass plot point of the B story in fact issues a major corrective for those familiar with the film. In this way, *Bob's Burgers* refuses to simply represent—it must also reckon with its problems, as it does in addressing the racism of Data's portrayal.

While mostly remembered for the camaraderie of the adolescent boys, *The Goonies* also had a romantic plot. Brand, Mikey's older brother, has a crush on designated prettiest girl in school, Andy. This sets up some of the class conflict that arises among the young people, as his rival for her affection, Troy, is a classic country club jock, driving a Mustang convertible while Brand makes do with a stolen little girl's bicycle. Andy and her best friend, Stef, end up joining the Goonies on their subterranean odyssey, allowing the film to touch on some classic romantic tropes. There's mistaken identity, as when Andy kisses Mikey, thinking that it's Brand, the sniping couple, Mouth and Stef, and, obviously, since he's played by an already absurdly handsome Josh Brolin, a working-class kid outshining his rich romantic rival in the eventual union of Brand and Andy.[3]

I object to the romantic elements of *The Goonies* on several fronts. First, Andy accidentally kissing Mikey can only be funny if one has never been a 16-year-old girl. From my year of experience, I can confidently state that nothing would be more mortifying than learning that I had made out with a 13-year-old boy.[4] Second, the coming together of Stef and Mouth, while not necessarily as gross as Andy's consensual molestation of Mikey, seems wildly unlikely, since Mouth is genuinely annoying. As part of the film's denouement, Andy reassures Mikey that even though she's going to date his brother now, he's a good kisser, and Mouth and Stef come to an acknowledgment that they hate each other so much that it must be love.

"The Belchies" parodies this obsession with romantic clichés through Tina's journey. At the beginning of the episode the kids return from the beach with treasures. Tina clutches a romance novel with the vaginally inspired title, *The Darkest Crevice*. Taking her cues from the novel's heroine, she puts herself in Jimmy Jr.'s path, feigning helplessness at every turn. When Louise and Taff, the man made of taffy, are trapped in a pit, Tina's willingness to play dumb dramatically expires. Tina says, "Stupid book. I'm sick of acting like a dumb, helpless girl just so a hot boy who dances his feelings will notice me. I'm a smart, strong, sensual woman." She then arranges her friends and family into a human chain, and they reach down to drag Louise up to the surface. This is a direct reference to the poster for *The Goonies'* theatrical run, which shows the Goonies forming a human chain with Brand at the head, gripping a stalactite—which, in the theme of *Bob's Burgers* correcting the original, is not actually a scene from the film. Thus, Tina's arc in the episode points out how stereotypically the girls in the film behave and also gives a reason for the theatrical poster that the original film lacks.

Finally, "The Belchies" takes its structure from the impending demolition of Caffrey's Taffy Factory. Like *The Goonies*, this creates a firm deadline for the action—the Goonies are about to be evicted from their homes, the Belcher kids only have one night before the building will be demolished. However, in a small seaside town, only one of these events will draw a crowd. While its possible that the Goonies parents might congregate somewhere, perhaps with the authorities, there's no reason for the entire town to gather on the same spot where the Goonies emerge from the cavern. In "The Belchies" we see the construction workers, everyone can hear the rumbles, it's clear time is limited, which not only makes the rescue of Louise dramatic, it also makes it completely logical that the entire town would be assembled outside the factory. In small towns, you only get to know your neighbors when you all start walking toward a local fire. A demolition, planned destruction, truly reaches more citizens than a municipal fireworks display. *Bob's Burgers* underlines its solution to this widely noted plot hole from the film in a bit of dialogue between notoriously negligent father, Jimmy Pesto, and his twin sons, Andy and Ollie.[5] They run up to him, excited, and assume that he came for them. Jimmy replies, "I'm just here to watch the demolition. You know.... I mean. Yes, I came here for you."

Within this episode Gene delivers practically Generation X's mantra during their youth: "ironic detachment is great! Nothing means anything!" That this idea would come up in an episode that explicitly references *The Goonies* and *Footloose* makes this episode an ideal site to explore the way *Bob's Burgers* uses Spielberg's oeuvre as a way to comment on broader generational differences. In general, "The Belchies" allows *Bob's Burgers* to reckon with a beloved text from childhood that becomes problematic a few decades on. While affectionate, "The Belchies" is very pointed. Bob's erection and Gene's China quip, while easily integrated into the broader storyline, is not required by the adventure, and Tina's romance novel (a pretty serious vagina joke) underlines how thoughtfully *Bob's Burgers* pursues these problems by bringing them to light.

Jaws

While *Jaws* might not seem like a family film, the menace of the shark can only become visceral if it is grounded in something both aspirational and familiar, like family life. In brief, the film, based on the 1974 best-selling novel by Peter Benchley, traces the response of a fictional Martha's Vineyard–like beach town, Amity, to a series of shark attacks. The police chief, Brody, wants to act on the first shark attack, but the mayor reclassifies it for fear of spooking tourists, which leads to more fatal attacks, and then a long, slow showdown at sea between the great white shark and three men: Brody, ichthyologist Matt Hooper, and veteran shark mauler, Quint.

Brody might be the best father to survive a Spielberg film. Early scenes between Brody and his wife establish that they are recent transplants from New York. They came to Amity seeking a more peaceful setting to raise their two children. Brody, despite being afraid of the water himself, even buys his older son, Michael, a boat for his birthday. While the interaction between Brody and his family is limited, Spielberg efficiently sketches a portrait of Brody as a man who sees the pleasure his wife and children derive from living on the island and decides that it supersedes his anxieties about boats and bodies of water. Brody sacrifices his own comfort for that of his family, but then must risk being severed from them forever to meet the demands of his profession, as Amity's chief of police.

After the second shark attack, which kills young Alex Kintner, Brody sits at the dinner table, feeling helpless. He has his head resting on his chin, then in his hands, while his youngest son Sean apes every gesture. Finally Brody notices, smiles, and asks Sean for a kiss. "I need it," Brody says. Sean, who looks about five years old, gives his father a kiss on the cheek and walks away, presumably heading to bed. This acutely tender moment represents a break between the two sections of the film. The first section depicts the attacks and Brody's resulting frustration with the people he terms the "city fathers." The mayor and prominent businessmen wish to keep the beaches open despite his conviction that the water is unsafe. In the second half of the film, Brody leaves his family and community behind to pursue the shark at sea. Rather than have Brody exposit his concerns and feelings of helplessness through dialogue, Spielberg shows us Brody thinking through his scenario. The audience sees Sean following Brody's gestures before Brody does, and the exaggerated way that he follows his father doubles the impact on two counts. First, seeing a child make the typical gestures of someone thinking through a difficult situation is both funny and painful. The contemplative gestures of an adult interpreted by a child have the comic power of caricature, but are also poignant because no one wants to think of children as tormented by anxious ruminations (though, as a former child, I can assure you that this happens all the time). The child seeks connection to a suffering father. Part of the father's suffering is due to the child. Brody's reference to the mayor and business owners not as the city's leaders, but as its fathers shows that he expects them to show paternal care for its residents. We have a quiet moment of mutual concern between father and son as a kind remediation for the moment we have just witnessed with the city leadership. While the vulnerable will often mimic the behavior of the powerful, as we see with Sean, it is up to those in power to set an example worth following. He wants the mayor and the business he represents to see the beachgoers with the same eyes that he has for his son.

Brody finally addresses the threat of the shark with a team representing three generations of masculinity. Quint, the swaggering, apricot brandy–fueled veteran, has the iconic weight and lived experience of a war hero. He decorates his boat and his home with the jaws of sharks he's killed. His boat, the *Orca*, connects him to the most famous of American mariners, Ahab from *Moby Dick*. By naming his boat after a whale, he frees himself to seek other targets which, in a comically over-determined version of masculinity, means that he has a home full of shark teeth without a single place to sit.[6] Molly Haskell describes him as a kind of swaggering jock, and the trophies support this (63).

Hooper, as played by Richard Dreyfus, is in many ways an avatar for Spielberg himself. He can't fit in on the island—he's always overdressed or underdressed. He shows up uninvited in a suit jacket at Brody's house with two bottles of wine, awkward and obviously confused about the protocol of winning over the police chief. In the scuba scene, Hooper dresses appropriately, but is still regarded with scorn, looking more like a sea creature than a man as he insists that he be put in his cage. Spielberg himself was treated with derision on set for wearing elaborate and expensive bell-bottoms during filming, and tried to avoid being thrown in the water by the crew by wearing an outfit made entirely from suede. As it turned out, this did not further endear him to the camera operators, grips, and teamsters. Thrown together, the binds forged beyond Brody and Hooper's common enemy are tenuous. They both feel like misunderstood outsiders on the island, but it's clear they have little else in common. Hooper's story of how he became interested in sharks when his first boat was sunk by a shark—a boat he received as a child, which, along with his education and soft hands—mark him as very different from Brody and Quint.

The way the archetypes are translated into *Bob's Burgers* makes Bob the Brody figure—he's the block captain and father, after all. Teddy, like Quint, has a history with sharks—at least the mechanical variety—as well as a disposition to over-indulge, though Teddy's feelings are appeased by burgers, not brandy. Mort takes on the expert nebbish role of Richard Dreyfus' Matt Hooper, and while Mort is certainly nerdy

and overdressed, he lacks any qualifications for the sho
mechanical shark aside from his interest in being with h\

Thus, putting Bob in Brody's situation is very natur\
seasons and change preceding this homage to *Jaws*, Bo
established himself as the kind of dad who will put his chi\
above his own. And the Brody character seems like someon\   .\o might
come into the restaurant. In an early scene, when Brody and his wife
have Hooper over for an impromptu dinner, Brody refills his beer glass
with wine, giving the other two dainty pours in stemmed wine glasses.
This almost feels like a lost scene from *Bob's Burgers*, albeit with Linda
in the Brody role.

As "The Deepening" opens, Bob realizes that the ice cream machine
is broken, as his attempt to make a small ice cream for Mort runs amok,
with ice cream streaming out of control and directly into the mouths
of Gene and Louise. The loss of control of a mechanical device both
foreshadows the horrors to come and their resolution. Mr. Fischoeder
comes in to use the kids as a focus group for new attractions at Wonder
Wharf. As they work through ideas, Bob suggests using the town's history as the shooting location for the horror movie *The Deepening 3*. Mr.
Fischoeder follows Bob's advice and buys the mechanical shark from the
film. The kids knock it over, and it goes on a slow but destructive rampage through the town, eventually making its way down Ocean Avenue
to the restaurant.

Bob's work as block captain, like Brody's as chief of police, at first
seems mundane. Early in the film, islanders accost Brody regarding various parking issues. Bob's role as block captain is revealed to us when
Hugo, the quadrant captain, tells Bob to take care of what Hugo believes
is an abandoned bicycle, thus casting a similar problem, already petty,
into the pettier scale of Bob's life on Ocean Avenue. Because this is
Bob's Burgers and not a Spielberg movie, we actually see Bob attempt
to address the problem, only to get mooned by the owner of the bike.
Unlike *Jaws*, *Bob's Burgers* explores rather than alludes to the daily
humiliations of being a person in a community.

Like *Jaws*, "The Deepening" has two antagonists: Mr. Fischoeder,
who stands in for Amity's craven mayor and the business interests he
represents; and the shark itself. The film forgets the initial antagonist
when the action shifts from land to water, but *Bob's Burgers* never allows
us to lose sight of Mr. Fischoeder. Once the men are on the boat, the
movie never references Mayor Vaughan, but of course he and everyone
he represents still have blood on their hands. However, the film closes

vith Hooper and Brody swimming back to shore after exterminating the shark, so it feels like they have come to the end of their struggle against nature. By ending there, the villainy of the mayor recedes, even though the kind of crisis precipitated by his greed could happen again, easily, in many other forms, particularly given the environmental challenges that would come to the Eastern seaboard in the decades following *Jaws'* release. The shark was an individual calamity, but the way that public officials, aside from Brody, approached that disaster all but guarantees that lives will be needlessly lost, as the mayor himself tries to cover up the existence of the shark rather than deal with it, putting profit over people. In the dramatic showdown between the men and the shark on the boat, it's easy to forget that if the city had just been willing to close the beach after the first attack, four lives would have been saved. By ending with the shark's death, there is no reckoning in the film with the other forces involved in creating Amity's crisis. *Bob's Burgers* brings those problems to the fore, by keeping the battle based in the community. The shark's rampage occurs on a crowded street full of onlookers. Bob, not the police, takes charge of the response, but the measures taken come from brainstorming during a meeting. Finally, because there's no distance between the public and the showdown, the man at fault, rabid capitalist Mr. Fischoeder, has to make a quick exit, but the audience, and Bob, sees and calls on him to take responsibility for his actions. Perhaps the most acute portrayal of Mr. Fischoeder's failure to protect the public occurs just after Gene knocks over the shark. Tina suggests that they might need to back up, but Louise, in a moment that reads as uncharacteristically naïve, says that they will be fine as long as they stay behind the safety barrier. Of course, that's not how that works. The way that Brody is played off against the mayor as a kind of good father vs. bad father comes through in *Bob's Burgers* as Mr. Fischoeder only takes an interest in the children to the extent that they can increase his profits. Mr. Fischoeder, like the mayor, deflects all responsibility for the mechanical shark to Bob, and then disappears at the end of the episode when Bob suggests that he take action to fix the damage the mechanical shark has done to the building that houses the Belchers and their restaurant.

By including elements from behind the scenes in the making of *Jaws* as well as plot elements from the film, *Bob's Burgers* calls in *Jaws'* historical context. Only Bob and Teddy seem to remember that the film was made in their town. When Bob screens *The Deepening* within the show, on the tiny television in the corner of the restaurant, he spends most of his time fast forwarding through gratuitous scenes of women's bodies— breasts coming out of a wetsuit, a topless carwash, a hot tub—to get to the shark parts. Bob tries to get to the shark parts, but as it turns out, those parts don't dominate the screen. Bob's confused that the film isn't what he thinks it is, and Teddy still bears the scars from his participation in it. The ironically titled film is presented by the show as a pure cash grab, an exploitation piece. *Jaws*, as critics love to note, established the pattern for the summer blockbuster as a film that would appeal particularly to young people and be released as widely as possible.

"The Deepening" portrays not just some of the most famous moments in Spielberg's *Jaws*, but also explores the variety of audience responses to the film, as it is both a pastiche of the film and a meditation on what it would be like to be part of the community that made *Jaws* (3.6). Thus, we not only have Teddy reenacting the scene where Robert Shaw as Quint gets the attention of everyone in the meeting by dragging his fingernails on the chalkboard (of course Teddy, not having any nails, just mimes it and makes the sound, which is even more annoying), we also have flashbacks of young Teddy, who was an extra in the film. In Teddy's life, the film, or at least the mechanical shark, is the equivalent of the shark in *Jaws*: the force beyond rationality or reckoning that can steal your youth in an instant by forcing you to accept your own mortality. Tina, by empathizing with the mechanical shark, reflects the ambivalence of the final scene of *Jaws*. There is no triumph, no glib one-liner, instead the music and the languor of the final shot suggests that these adversaries, the men in the boat and the beast in the water, respected each other, and were pitted against each other by circumstance, not malice.

Bob's Burgers plays in the realm of myth and reality at the same time. The show pays homage to *Jaws* and the making of *Jaws* within the same episode, The movie prop is a fake, yet it poses a real threat to the residents of their seaside town. The fake shark stalks a fake ocean— Ocean Avenue. The fact that all the sounds seem diegetic, at least in this episode, is another where the *Bob's Burgers* episode treads in a liminal space of fiction and reality. The musical cues in *Jaws* are comically aggressive, but of course, no one in the film reacts to them, because they are non-diegetic, they exist in the story as part of the narrative framing but not within the world that the characters inhabit. When the mechanical shark breaks free and starts undulating toward Ocean Avenue, Bob says, in perfect synchronicity with portentous drone, "This is my fault. I have to do something." Linda can't hear him, so he says it again, over the same ominous musical cue. Linda's "what?" reveals she hears the music, too, while the way the cue repeats itself prefigures the succession of failures to control the shark that will make up the rest of the episode. *Bob's Burgers* even literalizes Brody's struggle at the end of the movie, when he dispatches the shark with the only things left on the boat, the compressed air tanks and the harpoon gun. As Bob sees Teddy, saved from being crushed by the shark only by his Boydle (a girdle for men), he reaches for something to save them both and finds only a box of straws. "I'm grasping at straws!" Bob says.

The series of ways to cope with the mechanical shark follows the sequence that the men on the ship go through as they chase the great white. The puncture strip and hooking the shark with the crane both make the shark more destructive, just as the barrels attached to harpoons are eventually manipulated by the shark to wreak more havoc on the boat. When the shark, after falling into a giant hole, resurfaces inside Bob's Burgers, Teddy can't help himself, saying, "you're going to need a bigger restaurant." Bob, Teddy, and Mort go inside the restaurant to deal with the shark, and it becomes a space where men can share their vulnerabilities. Of course, in the world of *Bob's Burgers*, this means that they will reveal their bellies, not their scars. In the scene on the boat, Brody nurses a cut on his head. Quint tells him he'll be fine and invites Hooper to touch a lump on his head from a St. Patrick's day scuffle, leading Hooper and Quint into an apricot brandy–fueled show and tell. Brody observes, lifts his shirt, considers what is likely a surgical scar, and stays silent. Edith Cranwinkle, the perpetually grumpy owner of Reflections Arts and Crafts, takes on the role of bereaved mother Mrs. Kintner. In a meeting in the restaurant, she declares, "I lost a son!" She later clarifies that it was, "a sun quilt. It was beautiful!" In the film Mrs. Kintner slaps Brody; with this role taken up by Teddy, and since Larry Murphy does the voice for both Teddy and Edith, it is like a single, angry entity, trying to get the attention of the authorities before it is too late.

The episode shifts, as the film does, from a whole community facing a threat to just three men: Bob, Teddy, and Mort. The restaurant serves as their "vessel" on Ocean Avenue, underscored by Teddy using "restaurant" in his reprise of *Jaws'* most famous line, "we're going to need a bigger boat." Teddy embodies Quint, not just in replaying his famous chalkboard scrape, but also in his mien—skulking around the edges of scenes, just waiting to be asked what he knows about the situation, sure that he alone understands the potential of the shark. Mort makes a less than perfect corollary for Hooper, but he does resemble him in the most crucial aspect; like Hooper, he is a nerd. In fact, anyone unfamiliar with the show might grasp this role for Mort as soon as he announces his recent enrollment in a stand-up comedy course.

Tina's sympathy for the shark mirrors the confusion of the audience in the final moments of its life in the film. The shark attacks the boat and eats Quint alive in a manner that recalls his tale of a shark attack during his service in the navy. As its jaws close around his torso, Quint looks at Brody angrily, but says nothing. He's dragged into the water, a cloud of blood swiftly obscuring him from Brody's sight. It's an anonymous, ignominious demise for a character who had previously given table-pounding monologues. Brody, when he finally manages to kill the shark in a scrappy, non-traditional way—just like our heroes in the restaurant—gives Spielberg the opportunity to present the death of the shark as something powerful and majestic. Brody shoots a compressed air tank in the shark's mouth, causing an explosion, the blast piercing the horizon. Then, over a plaintive piano, Spielberg shows the shark's body falling through the water as if through space, gracefully hurtling down through a cloud of blood like a plane shot out of the sky in slow motion. It is the hero's death that is denied Quint, and, as film critic Amy Nicholson notes, it makes the viewer feel for the shark, which, unlike Quint, was simply accepting nature's bounty. Thus, the strange musical interlude between Tina and the mechanical shark works as both a commentary on Tina's unlimited desire to connect, even with inanimate objects, and the seductive powers of cinema, which, after all, allowed "Bruce," the name of the three mechanical sharks used in the filming of *Jaws*, to extract such a broad range of feelings from the audience.

Mort disappears early in the action in the restaurant. The beats *Bob's Burgers* wants to replay require his presence only at the start of the restaurant sequence, to participate in the belly exposure. Teddy, unfortunately, must enact the toughest part of the final scenes of the film, taking Quint's place within the jaws of the shark. However, where Quint is grizzled, Teddy is generously coated in fat. He hides this with his boydle, which keeps the shark from snapping him in half until Bob finally disarms the shark by throwing the broken ice cream machine down its mechanical gullet. Two machines that won't turn off take each other out.

In "The Deepening," we get three experiences of *Jaws*: that of the return viewer, who can't help but notice that there are more scantily clad young women than they remembered; the experience of identifying with the fictional characters; and the liminal space of being part of its creation, fictional and not-fictional, and incorporating it into your story, as Teddy did. *Bob's Burgers* revises *Jaws* to make a much a clearer indictment of those in power. Because it is a mechanical shark, the idea that this is a man proving dominion over nature can't even be explored. Instead, it's about the limits of greed, and when Mr. Fischoeder runs away at the end of the episode, this show for the family has made a resonant, relevant horror story about the price of capitalism.

E.T.

"The Deepening" gives us a reading of *Jaws* that ends up being a mission statement for *Bob's Burgers* as well. That *Jaws* resonates so deeply with *Bob's Burgers*, while *E.T.* feels more like a lark derives from the fact that *Jaws*, from its source's source—Peter Benchley's novel's inspiration, *Moby Dick*—critiques fundamental American values. How can this country support vibrant, healthy communities and imagine itself as a proving ground for rugged individualism? Where one exists, the other, inevitably, will be diminished, and that paradox is at the heart of *Jaws* and *Bob's Burgers*, while *E.T.* works within a thematic framework that *Bob's Burgers* simply reflects, but doesn't wrestle with. Being a child is difficult, children need space to explore, but loving parents maintain safe boundaries. Because there is less to wrestle with, the *E.T.*–inspired episode is loving but not revelatory.

Briefly, *E.T.* follows ten-year-old Elliott, the middle son of a single mom living in the San Fernando Valley with his adorable younger sister, Gertie, and jerky teen brother, Michael. E.T., short for extra-terrestrial, encounters Elliott after being left behind on what appears to be a specimen-collecting mission. Elliott, frightened at first, lures E.T. into his home with a trail of candy. They develop a friendship, mirroring each other and eventually developing an empathic connection, to the extent that when E.T. drinks beer in the house, Elliott—in the middle of frog dissection—gets intoxicated and kisses a girl. This bond grows stronger, as E.T. gets better at communicating with the kids, and shadowy government operatives investigate the evidence left behind from the excursion that stranded E.T. in the first place. E.T. fashions a communication device so that they can rejoin their community, the kids help, but E.T. begins to fade, and Elliott follows because they are so profoundly connected. The government gets more aggressive in their hunt, and Elliott is hospitalized, but the kids join forces so that E.T. can rendezvous with a rescue ship and return home.

2. *Spielberger of the Day*

Like *E.T.*, "OT" opens with our titular character lost in the woods. However, since OT is a $14,000 toilet, not an ambulatory being, OT falls out of the back of a truck. We then see Gene at breakfast, very excited to receive the flour sack that will be his baby—a common project for middle school kids. Unfortunately, Gene keeps dropping the babies, which split open and spill flour again and again. Dejected, Gene walks home from school by himself, where he happens upon the titular Outside Toilet, which speaks with Jon Hamm's single-barrel scotch-soaked velvet baritone. Gene gets to know the toilet. It tells him jokes, provides warmth, and is an ideal companion—nothing like a baby, or a bag of flour, but exactly what Gene needs in the moment. When Gene returns to the restaurant, the man driving the truck, Max Flush, insists that Gene reveal the toilet's location. Gene refuses, and Flush stakes out the restaurant, only to be tricked by the Belcher kids and their friends, ending up on a ferry to King's Head Island. When reunited with the toilet, Gene tenderly refills its tank, then realizes it's running low on power. The kids manage to get the toilet moving, rigging Gene on the toilet behind their bikes and big wheels. When a bridge is out, the kids stop suddenly, sending Gene and the toilet soaring in front of a full moon just like Elliott and E.T. in the film, but with a much harder landing, since, despite Gene's demands, the toilet does not have wings and cannot fly. They take the toilet to a coffee shop to recharge, where they are discovered by Flush, who turns out to have stolen the toilet from King's Head Island. King's Head Island, a land of privilege, might as well be another planet as far as the Belchers are concerned, and so while Gene is sad to part with the toilet, he, like Elliott, knows that despite their soul connection, they must both return home to their families.

The sentiment runs no deeper than the OT's bowl in the *Bob's Burgers'* version of *E.T.* While Gene is about the same age as Elliott, and, as the episode reveals, also looks jaunty in a red hoodie, he operates from a very different place. Mary, Elliott's mother, regards him with affection, but he can't bring her the joy that Gertie, the absurdly cute baby of the family, brings, nor can he offer the support of Michael, trying to stretch into the role of "man of the house," Elliott and Michael deeply miss their father, an emotion that is made visible as they go through the possessions he left behind in their attempt to assemble a phone smart enough to call space, but they are as fundamentally estranged by their stages in life, as Elliott is from Gertie, who doesn't seem to know enough to mourn their father's absence. Elliott finds the cure for his alienation in, well, an alien. Gene, by contrast, might be the least alienated eleven-year-old on his planet. Gene prefers being a solo act because he longs for total artistic control, and falls into successful partnerships by accident, not design, like in the Season 6 episode, "The Gene and Courtney Show" (6.7). Though he's always seeking his parents' attention, he doesn't embody loneliness the way Elliott does, which is why his *E.T.* moment must provide a plot point to explain why Gene might be in a position to become so attached to the toilet.

When they become psychically united they are eventually ill, side by side, in plastic boxes that resemble incubators, as if they were conjoined twins born prematurely and possible unable to survive on their own. Early in the film, Elliott mentions that their father is in Mexico with another woman, which clearly wounds his mother. Michael snaps at him for his inability to consider anyone else's feelings. Elliott feels so much pain at his father's absence that he has no room to consider what that comment would do to his mother. When Elliott and Michael dress E.T. in their father's clothes, it's clear that the alien has become not just a replacement for the companionship of peers but a vessel for his idealized relationship with his father. These possibilities allow him to Elliott to empathize with E.T. in ways he never can with his mother, as E.T. becomes his mirror, his father, his soul mate. The resulting bond nearly overwhelms the boy; a few days after that insensitive exchange with his mother, when he is told he has to think of others, Elliott becomes so consumed by another creature's feelings that he nearly perishes. The terms of Gene's relationship are set before they meet. Gene knows he was "born to be a mother"; he is denied the opportunity when he drops the flour sacks, so the outside toilet has a role to fill as soon as Gene meets it, but this role is far different from E.T.'s. Their relationship is always hierarchical, with the outside toilet acting as an ideal child. The outside toilet articulates its needs clearly from the beginning, asking for water and power, whereas E.T. must learn rudimentary English and form a symbiotic bond with Elliott before his needs can be met—honestly, a familiar scenario for many of us who have tried to communicate with our fathers. Gene gains strength as the outside toilet loses power, because their connection takes on a different valence.

The toilet never becomes Gene's soul mate. His relationship is always maternal, not mimetic. When he visits the toilet with Tina and Louise and refills the tank, he mentions trying to breast feed before switching to the bottle. Elliott knows E.T. is a boy because E.T. both reflects him and takes on, even parodies, the shape of a father. Gene genders the toilet because, gosh, it's hard to find a more masculine voice than Jon Hamm's. Where the connection to *Jaws* allows Bob's magnificent paternal powers to shine, tracing the connections between "The OT" and *E.T.* feels more like a bit—an impersonation for the sake of impersonation's sake—rather than an opportunity to shed more light on both these fictional universes. The greatest vulnerability in Spielberg, the fracturing of family life and the loneliness of youth, are themes that are rarely explored with much depth in *Bob's Burgers*, especially when it comes to the core family. *E.T.*, in beginning with a fatherless child, and suggesting that that bond can come from somewhere, first with an alien somewhere between a Shar Pei and giraffe, then with the mysterious Keys who begins as an enigmatic antagonist who so symbolically embodies manhood that for most of the movie his most salient quality and name derives from what hangs from his crotch. The kids who related so deeply to Spielberg's under-loved protagonists grew up to create a cohesive, functional two-parent family. The resonance of those themes means that when Spielberg's work is replicated, it's done within a universe that he himself never imagined, one with supportive siblings and parents who love each other.

The antagonists in *E.T.* are not money-hungry Max Flushes. They are attempting to better understand the world around them. While only Keys exhibits the kind of wonder we see in Elliott and his peers, they are all driven by curiosity, which, as much the family dynamics, places *E.T.* in a far different fictional universe from *Bob's Burgers*. Spielberg's vision lacks the benign, dependable support of the family, but maintains a level of faith in the powers that be that *Bob's Burgers* never gestures at. Keys can be reached and reckoned with; it's the kids who are incapable of understanding his position and how it might align with their own. There is no level of communication or mediation that will put Max Flush and the Belchers on the same team. He wants his stolen $14,000 toilet. There is no common ground to discover. Oddly enough, for a goofy family sitcom *Bob's Burgers* believes in a far darker version of humanity than Steven Spielberg, at least the Spielberg of the 1970s and '80s, who forms the major points of reference for *Bob's Burgers*. In *E.T.* the government operatives and scientists can be redeemed, in fact, as the shot of Keys and Elliott's mother suggests, they might even make this family whole. In the *Bob's Burgers* version, there will be no reconciliation between Max Flush and the Belchers, and the outside toilet, once returned to its home, will never return to Gene's orbit.

The fact that the alien planet is a wealthy suburb fits well with *Bob's Burgers'* overall distrust of any party truly thriving under late capitalism.

That Max Flush is one of them—which is to say, not from King's Head Island—makes a nice parallel with *E.T.* Spielberg never demonizes the aliens, even though a really obvious critique of the film is that the whole thing might have been avoided if this species advanced enough for manned space travel had also mastered the buddy system.

In Spielberg, a cohesive family, particularly one with a father, might be enough to resolve the central conflicts. The metaphorical fathers of Amity fail to look after its children, so people die by shark attack. Elliott's father fails to provide the support and understanding that might keep his son from becoming a lonely misfit. Instead of sulking in the woods with an alien, Elliott might have been watching a Lakers game, just as the city fathers could have prevented further attacks by immediately closing the beach. The conflicts in the Spielberg-influenced *Bob's Burgers* episodes derive from the dirty truths of late capitalism. Mr. Fischoeder's lack of regard for human life mirrors that of Mayor Vaughn and the business interests he represents, but *Bob's Burgers* closes with him ducking his responsibility rather than a celebratory final shot of the heroes, reminding the viewers that there are likely more horrors to come.

Duel

There might be no clearer homage to Spielberg in *Bob's Burgers* than Season 4's "Christmas in the Car" (4.8). Like most episodes, it has an A plot and a B plot. In this case, the A plot centers around a quest to get a Christmas tree that ends up becoming a deadly cat and mouse game between the Belchers and a semi-truck, festively decorated to look like a candy cane. This mirrors the plot of Spielberg's 1971 made-for-television thriller, *Duel*, which was also his first feature-length film.[7]

Duel stars Dennis Weaver as David Mann, who is heading out on a sales call. We start the film from the perspective of the car—pulling out of the driveway, blowing a stop sign, cruising through downtown Los Angeles, hitting the freeway and then taking a highway east into the desert, the only sound that of the radio (as heard by our initially unseen protagonist). Finally, the camera pulls back and reveals Weaver, chuckling at the radio, with only his Aviator frames and mustache for company. He passes a filthy tanker truck, only to be overtaken by it and pass it again, to the apparent annoyance of the driver. As anyone who has traveled for long stretches on two-lane highways knows, each pass carries with the driver the stomach-curdling possibility of suddenly facing another vehicle coming the other way, and commercial trucks sometimes play by counterintuitive rules, as their mass requires them to build up speed before hills. The film traces how this initially mundane encounter develops into a murderous multi-stage chase that critics like Nigel Morris read as an homage to everything from Victorian phantom rides to Warner Brothers' Road Runner cartoons (20–31). The source material, a short story of the same title by Richard Matheson, was inspired by the author's experience of learning about the Kennedy assassination on a long drive. Matheson made a tailgating truck the scapegoat for the anger and confusion brought on by the president's murder (Haskell 49).

Mann's impotence (could the name be more schematic?) characterizes many moments in the film, but perhaps none so acutely as the encounter with the bus driver. When he pulls over, he has a chance to take on a role that would allow him to live up to the model of his car, the Valiant. The name badge is particularly prominent during this encounter to play up the irony of the situation. Mann, ostensibly coming to help, has merely pulled over because he follows instructions. As soon as the bus driver explains what kind of assistance he requires—he needs a push—Mann blanches. Mann insists that his car is too low; his bumper will get stuck beneath the bus. The driver laughs off his concerns, and the school kids, who have been disregarding Mann's pleas to leave his car alone, obediently get on the bus when the driver asks. From the back of the bus, the kids yell and taunt Mann, as he tries and fails to push the bus, then gets his bumper stuck. The kids get off the bus again, and Mann, seeing the truck waiting in the tunnel, orders them back on. Though they readily follow the instructions of the bus driver, they have nothing but contempt for Mann, and don't just ignore him, but tease him.

In an interview with Edgar Wright, Spielberg calls *Duel*, "*Jaws* on land" but while both films are Xanax-worthy thrillers, they are not engaging the same anxieties (Green). As befits the relative size of the two operations, *Duel* exploits personal weakness whereas *Jaws* looks at the horrors of a broader breakdown of the sense of civic duty. They are contrasting in that where *Duel* is personal, *Jaws* is municipal. In the same interview, Spielberg reveals that he thinks of *Duel* as the redemption story of a bullied kid, coming out of his own early trauma.

Contested masculinity haunts *Duel*, and at first it seems like a great fit for the Belchers. Bob, like Dennis Weaver's David Mann, has a signature 'stache, a family, and a red car. Genre differences account for many of the changes between the film and *Bob's Burgers*. While both feature

47

middle-aged family men with distinctive facial hair, it's difficult to imagine Bob sighing with relief after basically murdering an anonymous truck driver.

As with its other Spielberg homages, *Bob's Burgers* brings some of the subtleties of *Duel* to the surface. The truck pursuing the Belchers has been dressed as a candy cane, a costume integrated into the loft on the front of the truck in a way that makes it look phallic not just from the side, as any tanker truck would, but also from the front, so that it seems like a candy-striped penis is bearing down on them. The contested manhood within the household also comes through. While we never see David Mann at home, his reaction to sexist jokes on the radio and his exchange with the gas station attendant suggest that he has ceded primacy in the home to his wife, and he does not feel good about it.[8] Bob's willingness to go along with Linda's ideas place them in the car on New Year's Eve, but Bob, unlike Mann, never seems bitter or squeamish about his masculinity. The episode of *Bob's Burgers* opens up possibilities that seem closed to Mann.

Mann's masculinity is under threat everywhere he goes. On the road he's threatened by the tanker, at home he is threatened by his wife. He can assert his dominance at the end of the film by tricking the driver of the tanker into going over a cliff, but this is a pyrrhic victory. In setting up the climactic collision, Mann sacrifices his car, again, the Valiant. Asserting his power leaves him more vulnerable to bullies than before, and definitely in trouble with his wife.

In the *Bob's Burgers* episode, Bob accidentally blocks the truck after trying to hide from it, then his car gets stuck (snow tires were going to be Bob's Christmas gift to Linda).[9] Once the car is stuck, everyone gets out, but—unlike Mann, whose orders fall on deaf ears—Bob easily corrals them back into the car. *Duel* never has a face-to-face showdown; every encounter is mediated through the vehicles. Because Bob doesn't have to win anything from his encounter with the driver—he understands why he's angry and is willing to go along with a fight, even a pretend one—the driver ends up saving the day for the Belchers. A push from the candy-cane tanker sets the Belcher car free.

Bob's Burgers gives us the encounter that never happens in *Duel*, and probably would have spared a lot of carnage, human and automotive. Bob, who knows he's been an annoying motorist, talks to Gary the truck driver. Rather than seeing life as a two-lane blacktop—i.e., a zero-sum game—Bob tries to seek understanding so that they can not only survive this collision but grow from it. Gary gets Linda's Dutch baby, her prize from their stop at the diner, and the Belchers get the push they need to get home.

In defining the Belchers against Spielberg's kids and family men, several generational contrasts emerge. First, *Bob's Burgers* shows much more willingness to take capitalism to task as fundamentally inhumane and anti-family. The mechanical shark is capitalism, unleashed by the craven Mr. Fischoeder, and enjoyed by its victims until it literally tears their home apart. We see similar echoes in *Bob's Burgers'* version of *E.T.*, where the show creates a greedy villain out of whole cloth in order to re-set the now-classic story within a world that would make sense to the Belchers. *The Goonies* and *Duel* become, through *Bob's Burgers*, anthropological studies showing the limits of gender roles and empathy in the Boomer imagination. These moments show us why *Bob's Burgers* makes better family viewing than these classics that mean so much to Generation X, because while the writers of *Bob's Burgers* obviously love these films, too, the episodes based on them provide valuable correctives, to the extent that it might help a parent decide that as much as they loved *The Goonies*, they might not have the energy to explain a developmentally delayed adult confined to a dungeon by his family. Goonies never say die, but "The Belchies" say, huh, maybe that's enough.

3

"We're not not-going to a toy-pony convention"

Bob's Burgers and Fan Culture

Bob's Burgers' fan culture could easily be the subject of a book twice this length. Thus, rather than any attempt at a comprehensive representation of the way viewers construct theories about the show and expand its narrative scope, this chapter surveys the community and its products. First, I explore the way the show makes itself particularly amenable to the imaginative flights of its fans, then I limn some of the more distinct threads they elaborate, winding through fan theories, fan fiction, visual art, tattoos, podcasts, and fan crafts.

The show has a lively relationship to its viewers, to the extent that the Season 8 premier episode, "Brunchsquatch," incorporated the work of dozens of fans, resulting in a vertiginous array of styles (8.1). Loren Bouchard engages so readily and openly with fans on Twitter that he has even hired animators on the basis of their fan art (Wellen, "*Bob's Burgers* Returns"). Even without the encouragement from the top, many elements of *Bob's Burgers* make the show especially accessible as a playground for fans seeking to use its fictional universe as the basis for creative exploration.

First of all, the distinct look of each Belcher allows for the characters to be legible when rendered in a wide variety of styles, at all levels of skill. The mustache and apron, the pink bunny ears, the yellow barrette; these are all cheap and accessible for a last-minute Halloween costume. A hasty version of a *Bob's Burgers* still reads as *Bob's Burgers*. In that sense the show is like a gateway drug to cosplay.[1] On the page or screen, these markers make, for example, a manga-style version of the Belchers instantly recognizable. The most mainstream demonstration of this phenomenon occurred in 2013 when *Archer*, also featuring the voice of H. Jon Benjamin, featured a crossover with *Bob's Burgers* in its fourth season premier (4.1). Drawn in a comic book–style reminiscent of Hanna-Barbera's action-adventure series *Jonny Quest* (1964–5), "Bob" was just Sterling Archer with amnesia and Bob's undershirt, apron and mustache. The rest of the Belchers were easily identifiable by the color of their clothes and accessories, even though the style of *Archer* meant that they all had, for the first time, some semblance of a chin. Anyone with a tangential awareness of *Bob's Burgers*—a familiarity limited to seeing the commercials on Fox during a football or baseball game, for example—could easily recognize the characters as their *Archer* counterparts.

The show also respects fan culture by incorporating it into characters' lives, most notably Tina's. A second season episode reveals Tina's passion for writing all kinds of fanfiction. A shot of her bookshelf reveals notebooks devoted to everything from "Sexy *Sesame Street*" to "Erotic Garfield" and "Sexy *60 Minutes*" (2.8). She spices up her nonfictional universe as well, with something she calls "Erotic Friend Fiction," in which Tina imagines steamy storylines for herself and her peers. In the second season episode "Bad Tina," Tammy threatens to expose Tina's Erotic Friend Fiction at school, and rather than subjecting herself to Tammy's control, Tina reads it out loud in the Wagstaff cafeteria (2.8). This potential humiliation is averted by chance—Tammy farts loudly during the reading—but also by the loving support of her family, who refuse to allow Tina to be ashamed of her imagination.

Bob's Burgers subtly suggests that Tina learns to fictionalize the world around her by observing her parents. Bob's childhood toys included a scouring pad named "Brilly," a rusty spatula he calls his World War II fighter plane, and Mr. Doglavich, a piece of soap (3.3). Bob's abilities to anthropomorphize remain, as he immediately starts talking to the upscale appliances in Felix Fischoeder's short-lived nightclub some eight seasons later (11.3). Linda creates elaborate stories for the thriving community of vermin residing in the alley behind the restaurant. Linda names one of the raccoons Little King Trashmouth. According to Linda, "he's gay! That's his boyfriend, Gary. They just got married!" (3.17). While Tina's elaborations on her life and fictional heroes require more commitment, the whole family lives in a world of enchantment, with stories and characters everywhere they look.

In the fourth season, Tina's collection of miniature horses plunges the series into the world of the fan convention. "The Equestranauts" depicts the conflicts that arise within a pop culture fandom (4.17). In that episode Equesticles—adult men obsessed with the Equestranauts, an analogue for My Little Pony fans who call themselves Bronies—swindle

Tina out of an incredibly rare figurine. This episode, like most install-ments of *Bob's Burgers*, never adopts a moralizing tone. However, the plot, pitting an adolescent girl against men in elaborate horse costumes, explicitly points out the dangers of fan communities, as an adult call-ing himself Bronconius wages a devious campaign to steal a toy from a child. He is thwarted, barely, by the combined efforts of Bob and the rest of the Belchers. Tina, reunited with her doll, has, to Bob's dismay, lost interest in the little horse by the time it returns. Thus, *Bob's Burgers* gen-tly critiques the collector culture of fandom by showing how the greed it inspires drives adults to capitalize on objects designed to inspire chil-dren's imaginations.

Louise finds her fandom through Tina when Tina inadvertently escorts her little sister out of her latency period by taking her to a Boyz4Now concert (3.21). Louise finds herself disgusted but helplessly enraptured by the youngest Boy4Now, Boo Boo. An argument could be made that these obsessions have a genetic component, as Linda bases the most crucial relationship in her life—her union with Bob—on his resemblance to Tom Selleck. In moments of confusion, Selleck's face gives counsel from her cup of coffee (2.3). As explored elsewhere, Bob's vision of himself as a father derives from his relationship to popular cul-ture, specifically the samurai series *Hawk & Chick*.

By showing its characters' passion for pop culture as well as their willingness to elaborate on that culture, *Bob's Burgers* implicitly invites fan engagement, even if that engagement entails dubious or dark read-ings of the show. *Bob's Burgers* fans' theories enlighten and disturb in equal measure, often revealing more about the imagination of the viewer than the show itself. *Bob's Burgers* generally takes a sunny view of small-town life despite the economically distressed circumstances of its protagonists. However, many of its viewers possess more gothic imagi-nations, expressed through their speculation regarding the show.

A popular fan theory from *Reddit* posits that each calamity in the opening credits takes the life of a Belcher, first Linda, then, one by one, each child, youngest to oldest. Geargirl, the author of this theory, leans heavily on the opening credits and the series of plagues rained down on the restaurant for her evidence: first fire, then rats, and finally, a downed telephone pole. Louise starts a fire, which kills her, and so she survives in Bob's memory as an agent of destruction. Gene adopts the rats, who give him a fatal infection, which is why Gene exists in Bob's fevered mind as a child of mysterious passions. Tina, the final child, sur-vives watching her father hallucinate the presence of her mother and her siblings while coping with her own grief. If she seems strange in Bob's rendering, it's earned by the grief of outliving almost her entire family as barely a teenager. By the time we get to the Re-Re-Re-Opening, Bob is the final Belcher. The proximity to the funeral home means that Bob can feel close to Linda, who was the first of the Belchers entrusted to Mort's Mortuary. Bob found the restaurant empty when he became Mort's semi-regular customer. Thus Mort, who seems like a pretty useless character otherwise, is actually checking on Bob as he tries to run the restaurant while in the throes of elaborate hallucinations of his dead family. The restaurant itself is a tribute to Linda, so Bob's strivings for culinary greatness are truly labors of love. Geargirl finds evidence for her reading in the first three episodes, finding surreal notes in each family member's behavior that she traces back to their death. This theory has found so much popular purchase, it even came up within an interview with Loren Bouchard (Brooks, "About That *Bob's Burgers* Fan Theory"). Bouchard attributed the theory and its popularity to fans' desires for serialized narrative. Geargirl's theory allows the Belcher children to remain the same age while still participating in a narrative progressing through time because they live only in Bob's imagination. This theory appeals to anyone who spent their teens trying to match shades of black, which is to say, many *Bob's Burgers* fans appreciate a darker take on this colorful show.

The notion that Bob has only a tenuous grip on reality surfaces in other theories as well. The second episode of the series finds Bob trapped in the crawl space, looking for Louise's beloved toy, Kuchi Kopi. *Reddit* user pphemerson13 ties that experience to Bob's habit of talking to inanimate objects, mentioned above, which pphemerson13 sees as a sign of acute mental illness.[2] The theory falls apart pretty rapidly, as Bob actually talks to a burger before he goes into the crawl space, so his eerie isolation within the walls of his home could not account for that behavior.

Many of these theories reckon with the same problem: how did Bob end up surrounded by these weirdoes? My favorite fan theory, another gem from *Reddit*, posits that everyone on the show is drunk save Bob, noting that the other Belchers always cut him off when he's talking and have very limited self control—familiar tells for anyone who's logged hours on either side of a bar (Djinnkj). The few times we see Bob drinking, he fits in with them much better. Each of these theories, however implausible they seem, shows us the same thing: an engaged fan reading the show critically. As someone who has taught literature and critical thinking for 20 years, even if I did not enjoy *Bob's Burgers*, I would celebrate the invaluable service provided by any text that inspires close reading.

Another popular vein of fan speculation involves Louise's signature accessory, her bunny ears. Even flashbacks show Louise with some form of ear-like headgear, and she's only seen without them in one episode: the Season 3 premier, "Ears-y Rider" (3.1). There's never any explanation of her obsession with the ears within the show, leaving it open, so far, for a variety of explanations. One links *Bob's Burgers* to *The Simpsons*, positing that Louise's bunny ears are an homage to Marge Simpson's rabbit ears. But does Marge Simpson have rabbit ears? She does, kind of. Marge Simpson was originally conceived as having rabbit ears beneath her bouffant. The vestigial ears live on in the 1991 Konami video game *The Simpsons* (Cronin). When Marge gets attacked by a vacuum cleaner or electrocuted, her ears are visible beneath that luxuriant blue tower of hair. HeWasAZombie introduces the possibility that Louise so takes after her dad that she, too, has a bald spot, which she covers with her hat. T-lasagna thinks Louise's ears connect her with another agent of chaos in animation, Bugs Bunny. Viewers also think of the ears as a kind of armor or safety totem, like Linus' security blanket from the comic strip *Peanuts* (FatDude6). My favorite among the theories is that without her hat, Louise looks just like Linda, and she just can't stand that reality (MDef255). Given the lengths Louise goes to to differentiate herself from her mother and define herself as her father's daughter, this explanation seems very consistent with the Louise of the past ten seasons. Explaining the ears is also a popular prompt for fan fiction. BobsBurgersStories writes at length (over 26,000 words) to give the hat an origin story, beginning with a fire that damaged Louise's ears as a baby. In another take, written with the headcanon that Louise is a transgender girl, she prizes her ears because they represent her femininity (sanibel). On February 22, 2019, Loren Bouchard responded to a fan's query on *Twitter* about the meaning of the ears with a single word: "movie." While some may be relieved, I'm saddened that this incredibly productive era of fan inquiry will come to a close.

Gene also is the subject of fan speculation. His musical abilities fluctuate between seasons. Fans paying close attention to his musicianship find wild irregularities. Gene scores and writes a musical in Season 3, yet in Season 5 he is fired from a band for only knowing three chords (Tomothy37). This seeming plot hole—which really comes from fans wanting *Bob's Burgers* to be a serialized narrative—is resolved, for some fans, by imagining each season existing in its own separate time-line (Lime_and_Coconut).

Gene's gender identity and sexuality supply a lot of speculation as well, as I note in the chapter on Gene. The *Reddit* thread on Gene's gender identity, which bleeds into sexuality, gets very contentious in ways that perhaps reflect the ethos of *Reddit* more than fans of the show. The main post, by Reset-363, introduces the conversation pretty gently, noting that many *Tumblr* posts take as a given that Gene is not cisgender, but there is some controversy around designating him as a transgender girl, nonbinary person, or genderfluid.[3] Responses vary, the most hostile minimizing Reset-363's inquiry by saying, basically, he's just a weird kid on a weird TV show. Other responses support Reset-363 by providing examples of Gene's dress and behavior, and the most thoughtful refutation, by shj1985, notes that attributing Gene's embrace of non-stereotypically masculine presentation to being transgender supports the gender binary that trans-inclusive feminism seeks to dismantle.

Gene and Tina are both mentioned as having high-functioning autism, while Louise is diagnosed with a wide variety of disorders by fans, including anti-social personality disorder and obsessive compulsive disorder (The Fangirl; Mtrembrulee). The tenor of the psychological analysis of *Bob's Burgers* is generally empathetic. Colin McLaughlin attributes many of Louise's selfish or cruel behaviors to an addiction to money and power, but finds that her position as the last-born girl in a family barely getting by means that she comes by her greed honestly, from a desire for security more than an acquisitive nature.

Bob's Burgers generates a large quantity of fan fiction. As I note above, Tina herself produces fan fiction, which can be interpreted as a kind of tacit approval from the show itself for fans to take the elements of *Bob's Burgers* and build a makeshift fort within them. Spurred by the internet, the past 20 years have seen fan fiction explode from a niche interest associated primarily with science fiction and fantasy fans into a widespread creative endeavor that regularly breaks into the mainstream. The most popular example, fiction and film series *Fifty Shades of Grey*, renames the characters from *Twilight*, strips out the supernatural elements and inserts scenes of light BDSM. However, fanfiction, depending on your cultural framework, has a long history. While most studies begin with Sherlock Holmes or *Star Trek*, Virgil's *Aeneid* could certainly be classified as Homeric fanfiction (Burt). Indeed, before the age of copyright, characters floated freely from play to play to play and novel to novel, resulting in jubilees on the London stage in which Shakespeare's Falstaff might pass his flagon to the titular protagonist of Henry Fielding's *Tom Jones*.

The background given and stories enacted within a fictional universe are canon. This can get very complicated when working with a sprawling multimedia entity like, say, the Marvel Universe or *Star Wars*. By comparison, fans can easily comprehend the *Bob's Burgers* canon. Fan theories form headcanon—the background and plots that exist within a fan's conception of the universe. While headcanon can become canon, it thrives on its own.

Often headcanons form around ships—relationships that are not romantic on the show but get fan support. In the case of *Bob's Burgers*, one of the greatest dividing lines between fan and fandom can be found in ship awareness. Related to shipping is the concept of OTP, an acronym for "one true pairing"—the fan culture equivalent of soul mates. OTPs generate controversy and writing prompts, not the least because they are often built by combining canon and headcanon. A fan claiming Tina and Jimmy Jr. as OTP can draw on hours of canon, but fans aren't necessarily interested in building more support for that relationship when they can use smaller moments with other characters to create something new. Anyone who watches the show might see some possibilities in the way that Zeke appreciates Tina, but one of the most popular pairings in *Bob's Burgers* fanfiction is Louise and Logan. Logan is the bully who takes Louise's hat, so the idea that he is posited as her ideal partner in stories that take place when Louise is in her teens, really shows imagination on the part of the fans (3.1).[4]

A tour of the Louigan kingdom really gives a flavor for how canon becomes shipping becomes headcanon and, finally, fan portraits of OTP. Louigan is a portmanteau of Logan and Louise, a common way of designating couples in fandom and in real life since the turn of the century—remember "Brangelina" and "Benifer?" As I note above, Logan antagonizes Louise in his first appearance on the show. Kurt Braunohler supplies Logan's voice. In real-life, Braunohler and Louise's voice actor, Kristin Schaal, have been writing and performing partners for years, collaborating on a bicoastal variety show, "Hot Tub," since 2005. This chemistry comes through even in two dimensions on *Bob's Burgers*.

The earliest fan fiction featuring Logan and Louise as a couple I discovered was a short story on *Fanfiction.net* by christian95 called "A Surprising Proposal."[5] The story, from April 2013, depicts Louise and Logan at some point in the future, getting ready and then going to a carnival to celebrate their two-year anniversary. Louise teases Logan about how long it takes him to get ready in the opening, which implies that they either live together or she spends a lot of time in his apartment. The events of the story are intercut with each character's thoughts about the depths of their love for each other. At the story's end, Logan proposes to Louise on the Ferris wheel. Louise responds, "Yes, Logan, a thousand times yes." The tears welling up inside her spill over as they kiss. This story shows a lot more investment in the romantic plot than engagement with the universe of the show, not only in the imagined dialogue, which is, in my view, not representative of Louise's personality, but in its setting. Wonder Wharf, the boardwalk amusement park, clearly should be the location for this date. It has all the elements mentioned in the story, which is to say, carnival games and Ferris wheel. That this proposal does not take place on the Wonder Wheel shows christian95 as somewhat indifferent to the broader universe of the show.

Logan pops up in a handful of episodes after his third season debut, but it is the fifth season that propelled him into the romantic imaginations of hundreds, likely thousands, of *Bob's Burgers* fans. In "Late Afternoon in the Garden of Bob and Louise," Bob hires Logan to work in the restaurant as an unpaid intern so that he can have access to the community garden run by Logan's mother (5.10). Louise and Logan clash immediately. After a showdown of spit-throwing stink faces, Gene observes, "I bet when you reconnect in your thirties you guys will get married" (5.10). This line is funny because it shows that Gene's understanding of human relationships has already been thoroughly corrupted by romantic comedies. In real life, being attracted to people who treat with you disdain does not lead to romantic fulfillment, but Gene doesn't know that. However, for Louise and Logan shippers, Gene's comment indicates not cultural brainwashing, but intuition. After this episode aired at the end of January 2015, Louigan began its reign as the dominant force in *Bob's Burgers* fan fiction, replacing the great Jimmy Jr. v. Anyone Else feuds of the early teens.

Sometimes the flavor of a Louigan story makes it clear that the author is simply not old enough to understand the context of Gene's joke. For example, a "hot" (the metric used for popularity) story on *Wattpad* takes its cue explicitly from that episode. Titled "Bob's burgers 3 months Later [sic]," it recaps "Late Afternoon," then speeds three months ahead, to a terrifying encounter where Louise is attacked in an alley by two "thugs." A stranger, eventually revealed to be a character invented for the story named Tommy, rescues her, then Logan comes upon them, sees Louise crying and tells the guy to scram—Logan's the one who gets to make Louise cry (Medinajezebel23). The initial installment ends here, setting up a *Twilight*-esque love triangle between Louise, Logan, and the unknown guy, the two boys striving to be her protector. By the final chapter, part ten, Louise has united with and dumped 18-year-old Tommy. She never forgot Logan. The story ends with an indelible scene that I profoundly wish I could forget in which Logan and Louise have sexual intercourse. Obviously, this only lands with *Bob's Burgers* fans of a particular disposition. Many of the comments note that Louise is nine years old on the show, which by any standard is too young for this kind of romantic entanglement.

Louigan not only rules *Wattpad*, which draws a younger, less grammatically committed crowd, but also *Archive of Our Own*, commonly shortened to *AO3*, and *Fanfiction.net*. Both sites have around 300 *Bob's Burgers* stories each, and in both cases the stories with the most hits are Louigans. This translates into other media as well. Fanart site *Deviantart* has dozens of portraits of the couple at different ages. The quality varies from sketches on notebook paper and crayon to compositions that painstakingly replicate the look of the show.

Because young people have romantic imaginations, generating romantic possibilities for Louise, the character that the youngest fans are most likely to relate to, seems plausible. But fan interests in that regard are surprisingly narrow. For example, Boo Boo, the member of Boyz4Now who is the only character Louise has acknowledged an attraction to thus far, has only been paired with Louise twice on *AO3*. Why is Louigan so dominant? The pairing of Louise and Logan harkens back to the plot of Shakespeare's *The Taming of the Shrew* (1592). In this comedy, Petruchio courts the headstrong Katherina. Petruchio breaks Katherina's will by abducting her, denying her food and clothing, and contradicting everything she says. Though gaslighting would not come into the English language for another three and a half centuries, Petruchio relies on the same kind of steady manipulation to make Katherina believe her version of reality is fundamentally flawed, and thus become utterly dependent upon, or if you prefer, "fall in love," with him.

This is not to say that the Louigan shippers are simply championing their favorite play, but that they are working within the same tradition Gene alludes to when he imagines Louise and Logan running into each other in 20 years. Because of her irascibility, willfulness, and overt self-interest, Louise fits into romantic fantasies predicated not on equitable partnership, but upon a woman being reformed by love. These fans see Louise as someone who will have to be tricked or bullied into caring for another person, so rather than dreaming a life where she simply acts on her desires and say, marries Boo Boo, they imagine that she must be subdued. Of the kids on the show who recur, Logan is the biggest bully, and thus the most capable of bringing Louise to heel.

Finally, conflict and rivalries are productive, both in terms of generating comments and hits and in generating stories. There are two distinct factions within the world of *Bob's Burgers* fanfiction: Louise/Logan shippers, and Louise and Regular Sized Rudy shippers. Unlike Logan, who is a high school student, Rudy and Louise are in the same grade. The early 2017 episode "Bob Actually" works this potential pairing into the canon of the show (7.9). On Valentine's Day, Rudy pricks up Louise's ears by buying a bouquet of "love weeds" and checking that she will be in the cafeteria for lunch. Louise construes these as signs that Rudy will be declaring his love to her, but it turns out he plans to court Chloe Barbash. Louise attempts to protect Rudy from Chloe, who pretends to return Rudy's affection because he feeds her the answers on quizzes. When Louise breaks the news to Rudy, she kisses him but insists that he never speak of it. Even before this episode, viewers saw Rudy as a potential suitor for Louise. Alasdair Wilkins predicted this union even earlier, noting in his addendum to his *AV Club* recap of "Dawn of the Peck" (5.4) that:

> Louise actively cheers Rudy when he stops the scrambler ride, and she sounds *almost* concerned when she informs him that he will probably die before the end of the adventure. Between that and every other interaction they've had to date, yeah … this is real, people. I mean, when you adjust for how Louise normally treats even people she theoretically cares about, it becomes almost *too* obvious.

From Wilkins' tone and placement of this remark at the very end of the recap, it's clear that while he writes in a very conversational style he also wants to distance himself from the fans who will jump into the comments and elaborate on this theory. This is a common move for pop culture writers who establish their authority by working within the canon and developing their ideas with as much direct connection to the events of the show as possible. A *Reddit* thread started in November 2016 asks if anyone else thinks that Regular Sized Rudy and Louise would make a great couple (Carnage678). In over fifty replies, only four people bring up Logan and Louise, making it seem as if the Louigan crowd is either not that dominant on *Reddit* or simply choses to ignore a pairing that goes against their OTP.

The Genius of *Bob's Burgers*

When imagining a queer future for Louise, pairing her with Millie Frock has gained some steam as a prompt for drawings on *Tumblr* and is the basis for a few short stories on *AO3* and other fan sites. In terms of exploring the Enemies-to-Lovers dynamic that makes Louigan so popular, Louise/Millie is far more promising, simply because their dynamic as friends/enemies resonates deeply as a kind of relationship young women have, both in adolescence and adulthood. Millie first appears in Season 4's Halloween episode, "Fort Night," in which she tortures the Belcher kids, the Pesto twins, and Darryl, while they are trapped in a cardboard fort (4.2). In the opening minutes, Millie chases down Louise in the hallway of Wagstaff, to Louise's deep annoyance. Louise complains to Tina that Millie wants to "be my friend, or be me or be a rap duo with me." Tina says, "that's nice," to which Louise emphatically replies, "no it's not nice!" Millie's eager face fills the screen menacingly, as she insists that she and Louise had planned to do a joint costume that day. Louise denies it and walks away, leaving a hurt and twitchy Millie in her wake. When Millie overhears the kids freaking out in the fort, she says she will go for help, but instead is haunted by Louise calling her a creepy stalker, and then does creepy stalker things—she pours plastic spiders on them and thwarts their chances to escape. In subsequent episodes, Millie takes political power in the school to bring herself closer to Louise, and uses the Hannibal Lecter–like technique of exchanging information for time together (5.12; 8.2). Louise's confusion about whether Millie wants to be best friends or take over her identity locates their relationship along the homicidal/homoerotic continuum commonly attributed to the nineties thriller *Single White Female* (1992), itself a reworking of the themes from *All About Eve* (1950). Violence between women often has an erotic component, particularly since these encounters are usually staged for the male gaze, so in that sense it's hard to do an homage to *Single White Female* without the frisson of a possible lesbian encounter, even when that homage features two animated children.

The Louise and Millie stories sometimes play down the more disruptive elements of their relationship within the canon to allow for romance. For example, "Psyched" on *Archive of Our Own* imagines Millie and Louise's relationship seven years in the future (DingoJingoJango). On Louise's 17th birthday, Millie begins to confront her romantic feelings for Louise. The story posits that their friendship exists beyond Millie's imagination, as they celebrate Louise's birthday with a trip to Wonder Wharf and a wrestling session in Millie's room that, for Millie, at least, becomes fuel for a fantasy where the fighting resolves itself in a make-out session.

That sensitively rendered story includes a detail that finds its way into the blunter expressions of Louise and Millie fiction: Millie deeply resents Regular Sized Rudy because she views him as a romantic rival. The stunningly unsubtle *Wattpad* tale, "Millie's Infatuation," takes place at around the same time, but the seven intervening years have sharpened Millie's edges (thatCutesyPie2). This Millie Frock sleeps in a room wallpapered with surreptitiously captured images of Louise. Every time she sidles up to Louise in the hallways of their high school, Millie wears a t-shirt with Louise's face on it under her clothes. This version of Millie expresses her feelings in violent outbursts, first directed at her mother, then, when she sees Louise share a kiss with Regular Sized Rudy at school, at the girls' bathroom. She plots to murder Regular Sized Rudy so that she can finally be with Louise. She stalks him after school, and then, when he takes out his inhaler, stabs him. Rudy dies regretting the future he would never know with Louise, while Millie lords over him, smug at extinguishing the "regular sized bastard."

The Louise and Millie stories tend toward the Rouise (Louise and Regular Sized Rudy)-oriented universe rather than Louigan because the Louise and Millie shippers scratch, in a queer way, the same itch as Louigan: the enemies-to-lovers dynamic. If Millie's rival for Louise's affections (not that Louise has ever seemed particularly affectionate) is Logan, then Louise must choose between a straight or queer path, since both potential partners are people who treat her badly. Millie and Logan, despite gender differences, both allow fans to imagine Louise "put in her place" by someone who has shown a similar capacity for cruelty and self-interest. Thus, Rudy presents the only alternative path. Louise's choice of Rudy is not necessarily a rejection of queerness, because he offers Louise more than just a heterosexual version of the same dynamic. Rudy cares about other people and tries to get along with them. He could teach Louise, while Logan or Millie might tame her.

A more encouraging theme in *Bob's Burgers* fan fiction is the pairing of Tina with Zeke. The Tina/Zeke pairing, like Louigan, demonstrates the way canon evolves into headcanon. A *Reddit* post from 2018 invites fans to catalogue every thread implying a growing attraction between these two imaginary eighth graders (diggitySC). Zeke's comments and overtures toward Tina are lovingly recorded in that forum and others. Great moments in their proto-courtship include Zeke pooping on the Wagstaff school grounds to benefit Tina's career in closed-circuit TV news, telling Tina "I got a story to tell on our wedding day. You think that's not gonna happen, but I'll getcha girl! I'm gonna getcha!," and telling her has a crush when she threatens him with a water balloon (3.12; 5.8; 5.21).

Tina, Zeke, and Jimmy Jr. form a love triangle with a broader range of possible pairings than most. Tina/Zeke and Tina/Jimmy Jr. both garner support from fans; each pairing has roughly the same number of stories associated with it on *Archive of Our Own*.[6] The deeply supportive relationship between Zeke and Jimmy Jr. fuels a smaller but still significant amount of fanfiction exploring their potential as a couple as well. "All I Wanted" projects their friendship into the near future, imagining Jimmy Jr.'s joy in having regular high school dances to attend and Zeke's melancholy as he realizes that he wants to be Jimmy Jr.'s date for the dance instead of his buddy (dawnheart).

However, the charming thing about fanfiction is how shallowly or deeply it can develop the universe. What some fans want to see in *Bob's Burgers* sometimes requires thousands of words and historical research, like an as-yet unfinished backstory for Jimmy Pesto called "Sympesto for the Devil: The Story of James Poplopovich" (HumanDictionary). Though it starts as a fairly pedestrian Tina/Jimmy Jr. story, when the aged-up couple reveals their engagement, Jimmy falls into a spiral of alcohol, depression, and rumination, prompting a flashback to his grandfather, Pavel Poplopovich, making his way on Ocean Avenue by making Italian food for bootleggers and Mafiosi. But sometimes these writers hunger for simpler pleasures, like a tale of Gene shitting himself in class (BoboftheDay). And, perhaps due to Andy Kindler's status as a venerated stand-up comedian, Mort lives far more robustly in fanfiction than he does on the show.

Hardcore Mort fans aside, Louise and Tina are far and away the most popular subjects for fanfiction. This reflects the writers of fanfiction, who historically and currently tend to be overwhelmingly female, and, in the case of *Bob's Burgers*, appear to be very young. My training is in literature and critical theory, not social science, but based on these texts, both in their adherence to standard English grammar and subject matter, I feel confident that their anonymous authors are within a few years of Tina's age. Still, though not representative, there are many other threads from the show that are lovingly enlarged and embroidered by creative fans.

When these outliers appear, they are often the product of a single viewer's fascination. For example, between January 2018 and March

3. *"We're not not-going to a toy-pony convention"*

2020, *Archive of Our Own* author allmilhouse published eight different stories exploring the erotic possibilities of Teddy and Bob's friendship. Sometimes Linda gets involved, as in "Feelings Under the Fridge," an extrapolation from "Christmas in the Car," in which Teddy, snared by the kids' elaborate booby traps for Santa, is freed from the fridge with a lot of meaningful looks and touching by Bob and Linda (4.8). It is specified in a note that allmilhouse has an alternate universe where Teddy, Bob, and Linda raise the kids together as a thruple. The allmilhouse stories find Teddy and Bob in unexpected embraces, enjoying their prominent secondary sex characteristics—one of them is titled "I Love You So Much (It's Hairy)"—and Linda's implicit approval, though her involvement is never direct. The writer feels a bit older than the standard fanfiction author, and this tends to be the case in the stories that involve Bob, Linda, or Teddy, at least in terms of adherence to grammatical convention and scope. These stories often enlarge moments from episodes or imagine scenes, rather than flashing years into the future, as Louise, Gene, and even Tina's romantic adventures require.

Of course, some fan art transcends the kudo, comment, and upvote economy of *Reddit, Tumblr*, and the *Wattpad*. In 2013, Cole Bowden was a college student, frustrated by his rudimentary culinary skills. *Bob's Burgers* inspired Bowden. He determined that the burger was the ideal foundation on which to expand his expertise, and that he would allow the show to lead the way. He began a *Tumblr* blog, called "The Bob's Burgers Experiment," charting his progress. After a friend linked to the blog in a *Reddit* forum, Bowden gained thousands of followers, eventually drawing the attention of *Bob's Burgers'* cast and crew members, including Kristen Schaal, Eugene Mirman, and Loren Bouchard (Courneen). At first, Bouchard avoided interacting with Bowden, as he likes to monitor fan activity, but was worried about interfering with the project (Rutsch). Finally, after Bowden asked if he could have some lead time on upcoming burgers of the day so that he could prepare burgers along with current episodes, Bouchard got in touch and let Bowden know that if there was going to be a *Bob's Burgers* cookbook, he wanted Bowden to be involved. Rizzoli International Publications took an interest in early 2015, and in 2016 published *The* Bob's Burgers *Burger Book*, with recipes credited to Bowden, who by that point was working as a manufacturing engineer for Honda.[7] All of this took Bowden completely by surprise. Reflecting on his blog and how close it brought him to one of his favorite shows, Boden said, "This is all just a wonderful set of events. The blog started as a silly project in my college apartment!" (Courneen). If only all silly projects started in college apartments could have such whimsical and delicious results.

The cookbook itself might be one of the most practical, beautifully realized pieces of fan art ever. The burgers are rendered by the same Bento Box animation team that creates the art for the show itself, so they feel entirely at one with the *Bob's Burgers* universe. This is a rare treat, as the burgers of the day generally appear only on the chalkboard, rarely between Teddy's meaty paws. The illustrations provide a point of comparison for the brave soul who actually attempts the burgers. Cole Bowden's website is still up and occasionally updated, so less hardy souls can easily compare his photos with the versions from *Bob's Burgers*. As an actual cookbook, the book is hardbound, so it's easy to wipe down after a spill, but the binding is standard, so it will not, for example, stay open on a counter as one follows the recipes.

Bob's Burgers–inspired visual fan art thrives on many platforms and media. Pop culture–themed galleries Spoke Art in New York and Gallery1988 in Los Angeles both put on shows exclusively featuring art inspired by the show. Commemorated in a beautiful galley on Juxtapoz.com, the *Bob's Burgers* exhibition was the first outing for Spoke Art in September 2016. It featured Belcher family nesting dolls and an installation building out the space of the restaurant. The Los Angeles show at Gallery1988, which ran for a week in May 2016, had fewer sculptural pieces but far more prints for sale (Jones). The show included air-brushed photo-realist portraits of the family and unlikely crossovers, like Julius and Vinnie, the hit men from *Pulp Fiction*, musing about foreign outposts of Bob's Burgers and Jimmy Pesto's Pizzeria (Brooks, "Uhh This *Bob's Burgers* Fan Art"). Of course, there's no need to leave your home; on platforms like *Tumblr* and *Deviantart*, thousands of alternate renditions of the Belchers are available for perusal, including painstaking elaborations on Aunt Gayle's "Animal Anus" series from "Art Crawl" (1.8).

Other visual expressions of fan loyalty come through cosplay. *Bob's Burgers*' characters, as I note elsewhere, have simple, readily available or easily fabricated clothing and signature accessories, making them ideal for last minute or low-cost costumes. Also, the simplicity of the characters' designs makes them legible regardless of the age size or race of the people wearing. Thus, you can find Black, Latinx, and Asian friends and families decked out in aprons and mustaches (BleekLondon). Singer Kiera Please, wearing blue shorts, a blue T-shirt, and square plastic frames, simply drops into Tina's signature dance for a few moments and gives a perfect rendition of one of *Bob's Burgers* most popular gifs. The broad appeal of *Bob's Burgers* in cosplay means that while none of us actually look like the Belchers, all of us can be recognized as Belchers, despite the color of our skin and the protrusion of our chins.

Of course, the greatest triumph for the fan artist lies not in merchandising, but in becoming a part of the show itself. In March 2017, Fox set up a now-defunct website for a *Bob's Burgers* Fan Art Competition, shortened to *Bob's* FART (Opam). The site solicited entries in three categories: title sequences, character sketches, and backgrounds. Sixty-two different artists were selected, eventually providing the visual basis for the eighth season premier mentioned above, "Brunchsquatch." Backgrounds were matched with character sketches, with the styles shifting every scene, so that each moment of the episode featured two fan artists at a time.

Was this disorienting for viewers? Yes, it was. Was a script selected to make these transitions easier to manage? Perhaps. "Brunchsquatch" takes place almost entirely within the restaurant, with only one significant new character, a blogger named Dame Judy Brunch. It begins with the young Belchers attempting to make their case for getting a dog, allowing Gene to share his drawings of the family's future with or without the dog. This notion introduces from the start the way that creating art builds an investment in the world the artist creates. It's a very subtle yet moving place to begin this episode, because the viewer is reminded at the very beginning that these constantly shifting styles are truly the result of fans like them making their own Belcher family portraits like Gene's. This is not to say that the story feels designed to hold this art, exactly. Brianna Wellen gives a backhanded compliment to the episode's writing team, laying out the storylines, noting:

> It's impressive that the show hasn't yet tackled the well-worn sitcom tropes of the kids wanting a pet or a chance to jab at millennials' favorite meal, so it makes sense that when these story lines are introduced, they're within an episode already pushing the creative boundaries.

Wellen accurately identifies the way that the episode feels a little rote, justifying it by saying that the familiarity of these narratives provides a solid foundation for the disorienting visuals.

Still, there are elements of the episode that, intentionally or not, resonate with the way fans bring fictional universes into their own lives. Gene's rendering of the happy, dog-having Belchers includes the addition of a second wife, Susan. Linda greets this news warmly, saying, "I like Susan," simultaneously justifying and catalyzing the production of dozens of "Linda and Bob are polyamorous" fan fictions. When Linda imagines brunch, she casts herself and the kids as the leads from HBO's *Sex and the City*—a scene that is a little hard to read with the Belchers drawn in the style of another artist. Gene muses that Felix Fischoeder might have been better off hiding in "the upside down," referring to the spectral universe from the science fiction series *Stranger Things*.

Some fan art is too intimate to incorporate into a network TV program. As a public service, I have done an extensive survey of *Bob's Burgers* tattoos. In order to avoid potential copyright pitfalls, as well as respect the privacy of the tattooed, I will give word pictures in lieu of visuals. Before I break them up into categories, know that I have nothing but admiration for the artists who create these and the human canvases who wear them.[8]

Many fans combine their love for *Bob's Burgers* with their respect for the traditions of body art. Thus, many fans imagine Linda as a pin-up girl, often with a bottle of wine held suggestively, or ketchup exploding behind her. Louise and Tina are also rendered this way, but Linda seems the most popular choice in that style. Portraits of all the characters are often adorned with roses, within hearts, or coming out of a compass, with traditional banners declaring catches phrases like "I'm a strong, sensual woman" or "I'll see you in hell."

Fan tattoos acknowledge the strength of *Bob's Burgers* as an ensemble, not just in panoramas featuring everyone from Hugo the Health Inspector to Little King Trashmouth, the raccoon, as worn by *Reddit*or alexh2458, but in group tattoos. The line, "We're Belchers from the womb to the tomb," is readily adopted by brother and sister pairs, along with complimentary portraits of Gene and Tina (2.8; phatdoom). By far the most popular group *Bob's Burgers* tattoo is the silhouette of Bob and Linda, a big favorite of heterosexual couples. Muddywaffles86 proudly displayed the tattoos he and his wife got for their anniversary within the *Bob's Burgers* Sub*reddit*. In the discussion, muddywaffles86 acknowledges that they discovered that the artist had just done a similar set for another couple 30 minutes prior to their tattoo, but they stuck with their plan. That admission was followed by commenters expressing their approval, showing pictures of their own Bob and Linda couple's tattoos, and letting muddywaffles86 know that he had excellent workmanship and placement. Indeed, what's so surprising about the popularity of the Bob and Linda couple's tattoo is that the woman always gets Linda and the man always gets Bob, when traditionally you use a tattoo as a tribute to your loved one, not yourself. In any case, if the love expires before the ink, these fans can comfort themselves by the likelihood that they may again be a part of a matched set, making the Bob and Linda set fairly low-stakes tattoos to memorialize a relationship.

Bob's Burgers inspires tributes that seem too niche to be repeated, and yet, the evidence of great minds thinking alike lives on the internet. For example, Regular Sized Rudy's inhaler emblazoned with "it ain't easy being wheezy" appears on at least two different lower legs and a ribcage. Little King Trashmouth, Moolissa, Mr. Business, and Louise's most beloved toy, Kuchi Kopi, are also popular choices for fans flagging particular areas of interest. However, the fan tattoo evincing the most dedication to the program adorns *Reddit*or nitsirklea's lower back. Nitsirklea wears the same botched, unfinished portrait of Bob that Bob received in Season 4's "The Equestranauts." In the episode, Bob infiltrates a group of Brony-like fans at a convention. His family rescues him as he's in the process of getting a tattoo of a horse with his face on it. This unfinished tattoo shows up in subsequent episodes on Bob's rarely exposed back, to the delight of fans still flummoxed by Gene's vacillating musical talents.

In the audio realm, *Bob's Burgers* has inspired a variety of podcasts. Many of these are standard TV podcasts: jovial recaps that allow fellow viewers to marinate in an episode well beyond the 20 minutes of its actual running time. In this vein, *Burgers and Fries: Your One-Stop* Bob's Burgers *Podcast*, has twelve publicly available episodes recapping and scoring episodes in no particular order. The hosts, Bryan and Ryan, have a good rapport and high production values. They clearly have a larger trove behind a paywall, but as of this writing the podcast, which started in July 2018, may be on hiatus.

AfterBuzz TV, an online network consisting of a *YouTube* channel and hundreds of podcasts, covered *Bob's Burgers* during Seasons 6 and 7. Since 2012, *AfterBuzz* has produced after-shows for hundreds of series, with a fairly standard mix of summary and opinion (Graser). The "*AfterBuzz Bob's Burgers* Aftershow" has by far the most polished sound of all the *Bob's Burgers* podcasts. Each of the three hosts has the breezy, professional affect one would expect from a network founded by actress and TV personality Maria Menounos. However, unlike *Burgers and Fries*, the hosts seem genuinely interested in how television is made. They not only comment on how well gags hit, but how *Bob's Burgers* balances jokes and characterization. It can be difficult to tell the hosts apart, but this show's appeal derives from the way it gives the audience new ways to interpret what they've just seen, and for that purpose, it's a solid podcast.

The most wide-ranging and widely available audio content in the recap-and-chat genre comes from *Pod's Burgers*, a delightful show made by sisters Jen and Briddany Land. Beginning, appropriately for *Bob's Burgers*, near Thanksgiving 2017, the Land sisters mix episode recaps that bounce around the series with special episodes ranking their favorite holiday moments and musical numbers. The rapport between the sisters gives this show a warmth and humor that most closely mirrors the sibling dynamic many viewers enjoy from the show itself. Though it's currently on hiatus, since *Pod's Burgers* doesn't tie itself to the current episodes it could be a real treat for viewers on their first or second, or seventh trip through the series.

Outliers include *Bob's Burgers Crime*. This podcast, a true independent without any network affiliation or even a listed author or producer, is apparently part of a series of podcasts taking a true crime approach to animated programs. The opening music recalls *Serial*, with its high-pitched piano chords, but the 19 minutes that follow fail to live up to the intro. The unnamed host simply brings up various crimes committed by the Belchers and explains the extent to which they might be prosecuted in the real world. For example, turning the restaurant into a casino in "The Kids Run the Restaurant," they explain, breaks many state and federal statutes, but would probably not be prosecuted since all the perpetrators are under 18 (3.20). I could only discover a single episode, which seems sufficient.

Two for T/JJ trains a similarly narrow lens on the show. Hosts Michelle and G break down episodes of *Bob's Burgers* from the perspective of deeply loyal Tina and Jimmy Jr. shippers. Each host says that their interest in Tina and Jimmy Jr.'s burgeoning romantic connection fueled their interest in the show, and they explain their ideas about how they might have interacted with one another when they were even younger. The debut (and, as far as I know, only) episode recaps "Sheesh! Cab, Bob?" (1.6). While the host mentions that the episode is controversial, they never state the reason why—namely, that trans sex workers play a central role, and are called "transvestites" throughout. Again, this seems like a podcast that wasn't meant for a longer run, and as far as I can tell, never got one.

In response to stay-at-home orders during the 2020 pandemic, cohabitating couple Max Miller and Skylar Harrison started watching *Bob's Burgers*. In September 2020, they launched a weekly podcast called

3. *"We're not not-going to a toy-pony convention"*

Bob's Credits, in which they discuss the end credits for *Bob's Burgers* episodes. They cover two episodes at a time, resulting in 20 to 45 minutes of genial conversation. They open with a segment called "Bobpun or Maxpun" in which Skylar tries to guess the source of a burger pun. After a précis of the episode under consideration, Max and Skylar note what makes that credit sequence unique. As any listener might assume from the premise, Max and Skylar are both incredibly detail-oriented viewers. Max points out a slight change in typeface that occurs, and Skylar closely follows the illustration of Jocelyn's hair in "Spaghetti Western" (1.9). Sequences are then rated on a scale from one to ten. This might be the most niche-sounding of the *Bob's Burgers* podcasts, but their assessments are often sprinkled with trivia about the episode or the show in general, and they have a rapport that makes it seem like their relationship will survive quarantine.

Somewhere between visual art and fanfiction lies the world of fan crafts, created for pleasure or profit, representing the show as it is or as artisans wish to see it. *Etsy*, the largest marketplace for artists and entrepreneurs on the internet, offers a vast assortment of *Bob's Burgers* fan art. Several shops sell custom caricatures allowing fans to see themselves on the show. Price points are low, starting at eight dollars for a digital portrait, with turnarounds as brief as a day. At the higher end are custom sneakers painted with *Bob's Burgers* characters. Jhericoco uses Pumas, K-Swiss, or Nikes as canvases for images from the show, painted by hand and available within a month for only $295. Other shops offer painted canvas sneakers for around $200. CaptainTomsCreations lights the silhouettes of the Belchers with color-controlled LED for $280. Artists create string art portraits, skate decks, candle holders, almost any household item adorned with characters and images from *Bob's Burgers*, along with a sea of T-shirts, enamel pins, stickers, and, most recently, cloth masks that come along with any fandom.

As with the tattoos, the handmade items that truly impress are the diegetic works: the creations of objects that live only within the show. For example, *Bob's Burgers* fan and *amigurumi* enthusiast Abby Sy sells patterns for crocheted plush dolls through her website, *Ollie + Holly*. Her site includes patterns for Louise's Japanese-inspired toys: obviously Kuchi Kopi, but also for the other characters who line her walls, like Mazuchi, Bakeneko, and Dodomeki. Most delightful are her patterns for Mr. Frond's therapy dolls, "Distracts-His-Friendzo Lorenzo," "Portion Control Joel," "Repressed Memory Emily," "Miss Understood," and sole positive role model, "Self-Care Claire" (https://www.ollieholly.

com/product-category/patterns/cartoon-characters/bobs-burgers).
Etsy seller Unicornhideout will happily send you "Repressed Memory
Emily" for eighty dollars, but if you want the rest, you will have to content yourself with a six-dollar pdf and a new hobby to occupy your hands
while you watch TV.

    Bob's Burgers has a comic book, a series of Funko Pop figurines,
and a licensed pink bunny hat available for purchase at your local Hot
Topic. Loren Bouchard spearheaded merchandising for the show, starting with t-shirt giveaways at Comic-Con and expanding from there into
apparel, books, and music with one double-album released in 2017 and
a second in 2021 (Otterson). However enthusiastically fans embrace the
show's official swag, this gear only tells us what the marketing and creative teams think fans want. Fans' desires reveal themselves not through
the T-shirts for sale at Target or Old Navy, but through the thousands
of words they write imagining a passionate embrace between Zeke and
Jimmy Jr., or the series of illustrations they generate so that the Belcher
kids will fit on their favorite anime. I began this chapter with a sheep-
ish caveat: capturing the entire spectrum of *Bob's Burgers'* fan culture
eclipses the scope of this project. As I end it, I hope that the sliver of
that universe I expose here encourages you to find your own corner of
fandom to explore, and perhaps use *Bob's Burgers* as a catalyst for your
own creative expression, as so many fans and artists—let's call them
"fartists"—have done.

4

Our Father Who Art in Apron
Bob Belcher, Model Father

During the winter term of 2019 at the University of California, Davis, a group of 15 students joined me for a seminar called *"Bob's Burgers'* Onion-tended Consequences." The opportunity to have structured discussions with fans of another generation yielded many surprising results. I anticipated that my students would be primarily interested in the younger Belchers, given that they might share more lived experience with them. Instead, they often broke into reveries about Bob. They praised him as a father, a husband, and, to my astonishment, a sex symbol. My students forced me to reexamine my assumptions about the show's reception. Bob seems to embody every valence associated with the term, "straight man": his major role in the show is to react to the bizarre antics of the larger personalities around him, an island of heterosexual cisgender masculinity within a tempestuous sea of fluid gender identities and adolescent sexual proclivities that can lean toward the supernatural. But in the eyes of my students, Bob is not a straight man at all: not in a comedic sense, as an audience surrogate for the wackiness around him; nor as an ambassador of heterosexuality.

Bethy Squires characterizes Bob as the rational mediator in the family. Bob will say no to a bad idea, but he will also grudgingly compromise when circumstances require cooperation ("Breaking Down the Role of Each Belcher"). This doesn't describe a man likely to inspire lust in college-aged adults. However, simmering beneath Bob's rational suggestions and unflagging loyalty is the passionate yearning of an artist trying to express himself. His creative fire overcomes him regularly in the Thanksgiving episodes of the series, which, not coincidentally, also provide the catalyst for the rampant fan theories regarding Bob's bisexuality. In the fourth season's Thanksgiving episode, Bob has to keep buying turkeys, as they keep mysteriously turning up in the toilet in the morning after being safely tucked in to brine each night. The butcher assumes that Bob is hitting on him. In response, Bob characterizes himself as "mostly straight," a disclosure that has resulted in a whole subgenre of fan fiction pairing Bob with men from Teddy to Mr. Fischoeder, to Dr. Sloan, Dick Van Dyke's character from the late nineties procedural *Diagnosis: Murder* (1993–2001) (4.5).

As became clear throughout the quarter, my students were drawn to Bob because beneath the surface, Bob has the yearning and curiosity of someone who is still figuring out their desires and how they might be satisfied, which he carries along with the steadfast love and support of the ideal, if not idealized, father. Thus, Bob inspires the young by reflecting the dreamer who fears that their art will never be good enough while also comforting them with the steadfast support he shows for his family. Through working with them, I can see how he is daddy and zaddy.[1] In this chapter I start with how Bob emerges as a father alongside the three crucial fathers in *Bob's Burgers*: Bob's own father, Big Bob; Jimmy Pesto, Bob's business rival and most notable peer; and Hawk, the fictional father who is both an inspiration and a cautionary tale. In tracing these other fathers, the zaddy-ness of Bob gradually emerges.

Part of Bob's emergence as a model father comes from a dearth of paternal figures on *Bob's Burgers*. On *The Simpsons*, Homer fails as a part of a world of parents. Subsidiary characters, like Chief Wiggum, show up not only in their professional capacities but as parents—at PTA meetings and various school programs. Part of this is simply the community focus of the show but part of it is also that, while the Belchers are the focus of *Bob's Burgers*, the show isn't necessarily about family life in the same way.[2] For example, many of the secondary characters on *Bob's Burgers* are childless, from regular customers Teddy and Mort to school personnel like Mr. Frond. *Bob's Burgers* has very little ambient parenting, so any other models for fatherhood seem like very intentional contrasts with Bob.

As I note in my chapter on *Bob's Burgers* as a workplace comedy, the specter of Bob's father, Big Bob, literally hangs over the entire Belcher family in the form of the picture of Big Bob's Diner centered over the Belcher sofa. When we as viewers have the opportunity to observe the characters staring into their television, the shadow of Bob's childhood stares back at us. As the Belchers give themselves over to the flashing lights, the viewer contemplates the bleak paternal legacy hanging over them all.

Of course, Bob works very hard to be a different kind of father from his own. Big Bob shut down so much of Bob's creativity that he refused to accept a partnership in Big Bob's Diner, instead striking out on his own. While his history with Big Bob isn't revealed until the third season, given Bob's tolerance for his children's passions, it's not surprising that he comes from a place where his innovations were actively discouraged (3.3). For example, while he may not understand Gene's music, Bob clearly bankrolls his triangle and the Casio keyboard Gene fills with fart samples. Similarly, hirsute Bob submits himself to waxing to support Tina, and continues to love Louise despite her tendency to conspire against him, even forgiving her for forging a check for $1,000 (1.10; 3.10; 10.6).

The other father Bob must face is Jimmy Pesto, often literally. Unlike the picture of Big Bob's Diner, which rarely draws notice from the Belchers, Jimmy Pesto's Pizzeria never fades into the landscape. In the first season, Bob stands in the dark, looking into the bright busy windows of Jimmy Pesto's, while Jimmy conceals his gaze through a forkful of pasta (1.10). Like Big Bob, as a father he provides a monitory contrast to Bob, but because he is Bob's peer, Bob looks right through his restaurant window at Jimmy, while Big Bob lingers behind him in his domestic retreat, permanently part of his past.

The conflict between Bob and Jimmy enacts fundamental personal and professional dilemmas. In the first two seasons of the series, Bob and Jimmy's mutual antipathy drove the plot, particularly in episodes like "Sheesh! Cab, Bob?," "Burger War," and "Burgerboss." In each of these episodes, Jimmy baits Bob into a feud that threatens the happiness of the Belcher family. If Bob has to choose between his pride and the happiness of his children, the kids win every time. In "Sheesh! Cab, Bob?" he tenders his mustache in order to get Jimmy to allow Jimmy Jr. to attend Tina's birthday party. Likewise, in "Burger War" he forgives his family for migrating over to Jimmy Pesto's to witness Gene's musical debut, and in "Burgerboss" Bob realizes that his attempt to triumph over Jimmy in a video game is taking him away from his family, so he pays a child (Darryl) to do it for him (1.6; 1.10; 2.4).

From Season 3 onward, Jimmy Pesto stands, arms crossed, in the reflection of the pest control van that pulls up in front of the restaurant, threatening every Belcher adventure from the beginning, even when he doesn't appear in the body of the episode. Season three uses the rivalry as a way to showcase Bob's generosity of spirit. In "Family Fracas," Jimmy conspires with a game show host to cheat the Belchers out of an opportunity to win a desperately needed new minivan. As they walk home, their miserable station wagon still in the shop, the Belchers encounter

Jimmy trying to change a flat on his new minivan. After insulting Jimmy in front of his sons, Bob looks to his own family and realizes that helping Jimmy is the only way he can "win": Bob's insults are terrible, and he lacks a hype man like Trev to laugh at them anyway. Instead, he puts his head down and goes to work on the tire.

The shadow of Jimmy Pesto opens all but the first 22 episodes of the series. He's the only character outside of the Belcher family who appears in the opening credits, a remarkable feat since he hardly seems central to the show in the way that, say, Teddy, or even Jimmy Jr. does. The integration of Jimmy Pesto into the opening credits as we see Bob's dream, the restaurant, open and close and open and close again, insists that the whole show be read as a response to the cocky would-be Italian. Bob's response to that shadow defines his development as a character who, at first, will enthusiastically engage in petty conflicts with Jimmy. Jimmy often triumphs because Bob realizes that letting Jimmy win will somehow benefit his family, a dynamic established when Bob shaves his mustache in Jimmy's first appearance, "Sheesh! Cab, Bob?" (1.6). As the series progresses, Bob finds a way to turn his disdain into a sympathy that serves them both.

If *Bob's Burgers* were an extended *bildungsroman*, with a goal of Bob coming to see and accept himself as an artist, then the natural end of the series would be "Drumforgiven" (10.11). More than any other episode, "Drumforgiven" depicts a very different Bob from Season 1, or even Season 3. This Bob has evolved to recognize the differences between himself and Jimmy Pesto and accept them with equanimity. The plot follows Teddy's attempts to conceal the fact that he is currently working at Jimmy Pesto's. Teddy's sensitivity about the matter is completely disproportionate to Bob's concern once the situation is revealed. Teddy keeps expecting Bob to explode at him for being disloyal, but Bob understands and even sympathizes with Teddy. Linda finally has to explain to Bob that if he doesn't get mad at Teddy for working for Jimmy Pesto, Teddy will feel like Bob doesn't really care about him. Bob's growth, though subtle, is so dramatic that he literally must perform anger and annoyance to satisfy Teddy rather than simply exposing it as his genuine feelings. Thus, Bob has come full circle, from forcing himself to act less annoyed by Jimmy Pesto to making himself act more annoyed by Jimmy Pesto. By the end of Season 10, the rivalry between Bob and Jimmy has congealed to the point that Jimmy's sidekick, Trev, enlists Bob to help Jimmy out while he convalesces from a hernia operation because Bob is the closest thing Jimmy has to a friend (10.22).

4. *Our Father Who Art in Apron*

In that episode, titled "Prank You for Being a Friend," Jimmy tortures Bob, making the process of buzzing into his high-rise apartment building truly tedious. Despite the way Jimmy treats him, once in Jimmy's domain, Bob finds reasons to connect with him. His slot car racers, video games, and inversion table make Jimmy's apartment into a wonderland for Bob, full of useless things that he can't afford, and, even if he could, he would have to share with his children. Jimmy lives like a spoiled child, and Bob comes to pity him for this, rather than just see his success as a threat. Thus, over ten seasons their relationship evolves from pure hostility to the kind of mutual dependence that holds many "friendships" together; someone has a better video game console, or a nice mom, or access to liquor and cigarettes, and suddenly you find yourself in a friendship.

Unlike Bob, Jimmy's restaurant is so successful that in Season 1, Jimmy tries to take over Bob's lease so that he can turn the burger place into a gift shop. Restaurants with gift shops inspire a particular kind of ire. Jimmy's ambitions evoke Cracker Barrel, and that chain's limited relationship to the culture and cuisine of the American South. The menu items at Jimmy Pesto's are as Italian as Jimmy himself, which is to say, not Italian at all. His last name is Poplopovich, not Pesto, and while he may wear Italian flag underwear, underneath those red, white, and green chonies he is likely of Eastern European extraction.

Jimmy Pesto's studied self-presentation—the Italian flag tie, the clean apron—makes Bob's shabby, disheveled look seem like a badge of authenticity. Jimmy's willingness to dress up, ironically, becomes an immediate liability. His comeuppance in his first appearance comes when sex workers reveal that he likes to dress like a baby. Of course, he's always in costume; he's not the Italian American he pretends to be, and even if he was, his food has a tenuous relationship to Italian cuisine at best. Bob, by embracing the burger, aligns himself with a proudly mongrel cuisine. While historians of the hamburger trace its roots to Hamburg, a German port city that sent a steady supply of immigrants to the new world, the consensus is that the burger as we know it is a wholly American culinary creation (Ozersky 6–7; Edge 12–15). The nebulous origins of Bob's muse match his own. Loren Bouchard describes the Belchers as "a Greek-Armenian-Italian-Jewish-German polyglot" but notes that the last name is meant to locate some French or French-Canadian heritage on Bob's paternal side. Of course, the main purpose of the name "Belcher," particularly in the pun-happy universe of *Bob's Burgers*, is to cut the family and its aspirations down to size, but in any case, it's certainly a more embarrassing a last name than the one Jimmy cast aside, Poplopovich. Bob's willingness to embrace the cuisine of his country along with his name means that his mere existence gives him a kind of moral victory over Jimmy Pesto. Bob becomes the true American dream, a role that contrasts with his inability to embrace capitalism. These qualities come up elsewhere in the show, but never so clearly as when Bob and Jimmy are both onscreen.

Jimmy's reflection hangs over so many episodes of the series to underline the tension between Jimmy's craven capitalism and Bob's searching authenticity. If anything, it is the centrality of this conflict that makes *Bob's Burgers* a program for children. The struggle between Jimmy and Bob recalls the clashes of the Ingalls and the Olesons on *Little House on the Prairie*. Only the weather exerts more control over the Walnut Grove economy than the owners of Oleson's Mercantile, Nels and Harriet Oleson. Nellie, their daughter, revels in this power to the constant annoyance of Laura Ingalls. Many antagonists pass through Walnut Grove, but in lieu of plague, drought, or runaways, the show relies on the Olesons to provide conflict for the Ingalls. And, in general, the Ingalls are always right, even if they rarely prevail. Similarly, there is never a moment in *Bob's Burgers* where Jimmy has moral force behind him.

Bob tries to keep his restaurant open in the face of a family that keeps trying to turn it into a nightclub, casino, or piano bar. His kids exhaust him and cost him business opportunities, but unlike Jimmy, he never seems indifferent to their feelings. Bob is simply better at fatherhood than he is at capitalism. By contrasting him with Big Bob and Jimmy Pesto, the show makes a clear statement that one is incompatible with the other. If those examples escape the viewer, Mr. Fischoeder lurks creepily in the background, as Louise says, "one white cat away from being a supervillain" (1.10). Mr. Fischoeder owns the entire nameless town, or at least the waterfront recreation area, Wonder Wharf, and the buildings that house Bob's Burgers and Jimmy Pesto's. As the undisputed winner of this seaside town's edition of Monopoly, Mr. Fischoeder owns everything, but must rent a family, as in the Thanksgiving episode where he rents Linda and the kids, with Bob busy in his kitchen.[3] The world of *Bob's Burgers* constantly sets business at odds with family life. But Mr. Fischoeder, childless and with motivations driven by whimsy and greed in equal measure, exists outside the recognizable family structures that Bob and Jimmy Pesto inhabit. Jimmy Pesto makes for a better contrast to Bob because they are peers. Their relationship dramatically shows how, in a marked departure from other animated sitcoms, the characters of *Bob's Burgers* actually change over time.

Jimmy Pesto emerges as an early villain, reflecting Bob's ambitions as both a father and a businessman, but unlike Mr. Fischoeder, his role is not static. Character development is not only optional for animated sitcoms, it seems to mitigate against the medium itself. Sitcoms, historically, reset at the end of each episode, giving audiences pleasure by allowing them to see the characters they know react to new stimuli— growth and change is typically the work of drama. Having voice actors rather than live action actors allows an animated sitcom to ignore the passage of time, allowing this format even more license to preserve its characters in amber and simply shift the backgrounds. Lisa Simpson lives in stasis, dreaming of her adult life without ever aging into it. In fact, this is the source of many of the critiques of animated sitcoms; because they never have to grapple with the changing faces and bodies of their actors, the characters are static, missing not only the third dimension of mass, but the fourth dimension, time. By developing its characters, *Bob's Burgers* cedes one of the advantages of the medium.

The relationship between Bob and rival business owner Jimmy Pesto evolves significantly, a creative risk that pays off by showing how Bob comes to understand the way his roles as father and business owner are at odds. But while Bob can inoculate himself against the toxic competitiveness that initially defined his relationship with Jimmy Pesto and forge a kind of friendship with his rival, he never finds a way to make it productive. Jimmy Pesto represents a model for successful entrepreneurship that Bob never really interrogates. Jimmy Pesto's whimsical specials succeed where Bob's fail; he even gets useful labor out of his children where Bob just accepts that they're "all terrible" (1.1).

Clearly, Bob's role as a father can't be disentangled from his approach to his business. As a restaurant, Bob's Burgers serves as both a tribute and a rebuke to Bob's own father. The portrait that emerges of Bob as a father becomes multidimensional because the show takes the time to devote episodes to his relationship with each child. Some of Bob's appeal as a dad comes from his willingness to support Tina, as she desperately, awkwardly, and, by necessity, slowly develops toward womanhood. In the third season episode, "Tinarannosaurus Wrecks," Tina devastates her family in slow motion. When Bob tries to teach Tina to drive, she finds the only other car in an otherwise barren parking lot and crashes into it—a car that, naturally, belongs to Jimmy Pesto (3.7). Gene represents the artist that Bob repressed in himself, with help from Big

Bob, and so Gene enjoys his father's support in his many artistic pursuits from music to tablescaping. However, none of these relationships carry the resonance of Bob's bond with Louise. Schematically, Louise and Bob's love represents the possibility of reconciliation between the forces for chaos and the forces for order: Marie Kondo embracing entropy.

Anyone who sincerely says, "oh, they're like my children, I can't pick a favorite" is either lying or has an only child. One of the family dynamics that makes the Belchers feel like a real family is the way that Linda and Bob clearly have favorites. While the whole family often rallies around Tina, Linda clearly favors Gene, her favorite duet partner and her coconspirator in schemes like turning the restaurant into a piano bar (8.12). Of course, as I note in my chapter on Gene and his relationship to gender, Gene actually aspires to be Linda, so their affinity makes sense. Bob, seemingly despite himself, adores Louise, the possible sociopath and agent of chaos. Although these bonds come up offhand in many episodes, "Tappy Tappy Tappy Tap Tap Tap" codifies them (10.18). This episode features Louise and Gene competing to make burgers of the day. Bob and Linda make their prejudices known as they wager on the outcome, recognizing that the kids must believe, for the sake of their self-esteem, that they tied, but each party showing a lot of certainty that their child will prevail. When Gene and Louise produce equally disgusting burgers, their parents are genuinely surprised.

Louise's position as Bob's favorite is not without its complications. The very first episode of *Bob's Burgers* positions Louise and Bob as antagonists. From changing the burger of the day from "New Bacon-ings (comes with bacon)" to "Child Molester Burger (comes with candy)" to starting the rumor that the restaurant uses human flesh in its burgers, Louise opposes everything Bob wants to accomplish in running both his restaurant and his life (1.1). However, as is also clear from the beginning, Louise's willingness to appeal to the darkest human impulses is not only a sound marketing strategy, it is an artistic impulse that resonates with Bob. Louise goes for the best joke, even if it's in bad taste, whereas Bob still deeply wants to please others.

In the first season, Louise and Bob bond over late-night television, playing a game called "burn unit" (1.9). They flip through the channels, casually insulting whatever they find. In response to a late-night sports report, Louise shouts, "I play soccer because I forgot I have hands," which earns a hearty "burn!" from Bob. In the episode that reveals this pastime, Louise feels threatened because Bob discovers the *Banjo* series of musical westerns, which engages Gene. Rather than judging what's on the screen, Bob and Gene earnestly connect with the story and its characters. The introduction of *Hawk & Chick* finally gives Louise a chance to enter a fictional world with her father rather than sit back and judge their own. It's the basis for *Hawk & Chick* that explains why this would be the fictional world that engrosses them both. The series that inspires *Hawk & Chick*, *Lone Wolf and Cub*, turns out to be a perfect mélange of their two personalities, featuring gratuitous bloodshed and heartfelt family drama in equal measure. Louise enjoys them without fear of seeming sentimental, while Bob embraces them for their emphasis on family bonds while reveling in the ludicrous fight scenes.

The show drew its inspiration for *Hawk & Chick* from *Lone Wolf and Cub*, an incredibly popular Japanese manga series that was swiftly adapted into six films.[4] The manga and films follow the adventures of Ogami Itto, a masterless samurai or ronin, and his son, Daigoro. The first film, with the American title *Lone Wolf and Cub: Sword of Vengeance*, opens in flashback, with Ogami executing a young child, maybe five years old. Then it shifts to Ogami pushing Daigoro, who looks about three years old, in a baby cart. A banner mounted on the cart reads, "Sword for hire; son for hire." As they enter a village, the villagers are clearly puzzled by what "son for hire" could possibly mean. Then, a young woman, looking deranged, picks up Daigoro, declaring that he is her child. Scampering behind her, the woman's mother apologizes to Ogami, explaining that her daughter lost a child to illness and has been mad ever since. Meanwhile, the younger woman forcefully presents her breasts to Daigoro. Daigoro exchanges a stern look with his father, then accepts the proffered nipple and suckles at the stranger's breast. Her features ease, as if she is releasing her grief along with her milk. This, then, is a son for hire. When the encounter ends, Daigoro returns to his baby cart. The woman's mother attempts to pay Ogami, who refuses, saying, "he was hungry." This incident recedes into a flashback explaining how Ogami and Daigoro found themselves in these circumstances.

It turns out that the opening scene of Ogami was from when he was still the shogun's executioner. Yagyu Retsudo, head of the Yagyu clan scheming to replace the shogun, and the shogun's inspector, Bizen, who wants the executioner's job for himself, scheme to ruin Ogami and consolidate power for themselves. Retsudo sends three ninjas to murder Ogami's wife and make it look like Ogami has been disloyal to the Shogun. Ogami discovers Daigoro, who appears to be about a year old, curled up near his mother's lifeless body.

The action shifts back to Ogami and Daigoro in the mostly empty village, allowing the audience to finally glimpse Ogami's nearly super-human skills as a warrior.[5] Ogami and Daigoro meet with a man desiring his skills as a ronin. Practically super-human, Ogami disembowels two ninjas creeping up behind him from a kneeling position, without so much as a glance over his shoulder, the negotiation in process barely interrupted. Now that they have a mission, father and son hit the road again. Ogami and Daigoro see puppies suckling at a dog who is otherwise engaged in sniffing at a log. Ogami grimaces, underlining the symbolic import of this tableau for the audience. Daigoro smiles from his baby cart, a smile that grows as they approach two girls, singing and playing with a ball. This confluence of images and the girls' song, which describes what happens when a hard turd falls from a mountain, triggers a memory in Ogami.

We are taken back to Ogami's family home, shortly after the attack. He looks at his son, about a year old, and says:

> Daigoro, the shogunate's men will be arriving shortly, but your father is resolved to defy the Shogun's will, and escape this place alive. To avenge the Ogami clan and to clear our name, to clear the dishonor I will abandon the way of the warrior, and live on the Demon way in hell. Listen, Daigoro, your father will walk the path of blood and death, the way of the assassin filled with slaughter and cruelty. Only by taking this way of the assassin can I avenge the Ogami clan and crush the Yagyu clan. Daigoro, you may choose your own way. Choose this Dotanuki sword and you'll join me in the way of the assassin. Choose this ball and I'll send you to your mother in the nether world. Daigoro, of course you don't understand anything. Not your father's words, nor what it about to happen. However, the blood of the Ogami clan in your body shall determine your destiny. [Daigoro forms his mouth into an "o"] Now choose.

Daigoro first crawls and reaches toward the ball, then backs up, looks quizzical and crawls toward the sword. Ogami lifts his son and says, "You would've been happier if you'd joined your late mother. My poor child. An assassin with a child. Remember Daigoro, this is our destiny." Shortly after, Ogami shows himself to be an incredibly capable assassin with a child, as he stabs and beheads dozens of people just to get himself and his son safely out of town. Thus, the father brings the son along on his path of vengeance and murder, a path that includes battles, beheadings, and for Ogami, sex at knifepoint with a sex worker—all in just the first of six films.[6] Daigoro and his baby cart turn out to be weapons unto themselves. Ogami straps a mirror to Diagoro's head to blind an opponent in a duel, and the baby cart is not only armored, but houses weapons like a *naganita*—a pole with a knife at the end.[7]

While this might, to some, seem like bad parenting, the author of the manga and writer on all but the sixth *Lone Wolf and Cub* film, Kazuo Koike, conceived of the story as a means of showing a strong bond between a parent and a child. The bond leaps readily from page to screen from the start, in Daigoro's searching look to Ogami when held by the disturbed young woman. His father's glance silently indicates, "yes, take the milk from this stranger's breast." But the significance of this in terms of *Bob's Burgers* resides in the way that *Lone Wolf and Cub* not only presents the possibility that a busy working father, like, say, a small business owner, or an assassin, might still be able to build a bond with his child, but that the bond might be strong enough to convince the child to continue in the father's footsteps. In the world of *Bob's Burgers*, the stakes are lower—Hawk and Chick are both barbers, so they cut hair, not throats. And, significantly, the show's version makes the child a girl, not a boy, and makes the actors portraying them a father and daughter in real life. This strengthens the resemblance to Bob and Louise, but both the fictional version of *Lone Wolf and Cub* and the genuine one are stews of gratuitous nudity and violence justified by their explicit message of family loyalty.

When Bob and Louise have a chance to interact with a grown version of the "cub"/"chick," Yuki, all of their ideas about the relationships between fathers and children are projected onto Yuki's estrangement from her father, Kojima (Hawk). They barge into Yuki's office, where she works happily—to Louise's disdain and disbelief—as an accountant. The Belchers try to get Yuki to attend the screening of the *Hawk & Chick* film, but rather than getting her to put aside her paternal anxieties, Bob and Louise expose their own:

> **BOB:** I'm sure it wasn't easy working with your dad all those years. I—I know. I've been there. I get it.
> **LOUISE:** Wrong. Wrong! Working with your dad is fun. I mean working with your dad was fun. Because he was a samurai and you killed monsters! [5.20]

They aren't succeeding in convincing Yuki to come to the screening, so they ask for a minute to reload as it were. Bob takes Yuki's side, clearly identifying with her as a son who rejected the family business, Bob tells his daughter, "Kojima needs to apologize to Yuki for driving her away. Yuki didn't want his life, Louise." Louise's lack of sympathy for Yuki comes from her inability to imagine a future without here father. Bob comforts her, telling her that this Hawk and this Chick will never have 30 years of silence between them.

When Louise and Bob see themselves reflected in the *Hawk & Chick* films, they are projecting themselves into a world of strict codes and clear enemies. Bob and Louise both have clearly defined nemeses: Bob has Jimmy Pesto, while Louise has Mr. Frond and Logan. The fantasy they enter together in projecting themselves into the world of *Hawk & Chick* is that they might unite against the same enemy, which just doesn't happen very often in their lived experiences. This is obvious from *Hawk & Chick*. However, the deeper relevance of the films for Bob can only be revealed by thinking through the basis for *Hawk & Chick*, the *Lone Wolf and Cub* films.

Ogami allows baby Daigoro to choose the path, and expresses the depths of his regret that this is the legacy he has to offer. Daigoro picks the family business: the way of the ronin. To be fair, his deliberation is brief—Daigoro is, after all, pre-verbal when he makes that initial choice. Louise is older than Daigoro, and knows more of the path than Daigoro could, and her free choice to follow her father means everything to Bob, as that was a choice he could not make for himself. In sharing these films, Bob sees a dream that went unfulfilled for his father but will be realized for him: he will see a child follow his path. That this child is Louise, who, unlike Tina, would never do so out of a sense of duty, affirms Bob. Louise responds to things that are cool and violent, like samurais fighting monsters, and yet somehow his restaurant resonates with her as well.

Louise acts primarily in her own self-interest. That she alone among the next generation of Belchers imagines herself taking over the restaurant, as first revealed in the third season, vindicates Bob's entire life path (3.22). Through Louise, the viewer and Bob have proof that he hasn't simply recreated the situation in which he was raised. His role in Big Bob's Diner was to serve food, not his muse. In contrast, Bob's own restaurant allows for self-expression in a way that drives Louise, a girl who rarely withholds criticism. Bob sees the way self-interest inspires Louise, which makes her tacit approval of his life's project deeply touching. If Tina or Gene wanted to take over the restaurant, it would have an entirely different valence. Rule-governed Tina would surely act out of obligation, while show-boating Gene would see the restaurant as a performance venue, and thus not really be continuing in the tradition of the Bobs, but enacting Linda's dreams as a frustrated entertainer. Louise does what she wants, and when she sees her future it has her willingly taking on the role that often seems impotent and burdensome to her father. Bob feels seen and validated by Louise's company and her ambition to take over the restaurant.

Even if the bond between Bob and Louise can be explained, she's still, like all Bob's children, terrible. As an adult who was formerly a child, it's thrilling to see a kid like Louise so deeply loved, valued, and admired by her father. When my students said that they thought Bob was sexy, I think part of what they meant must be that he seems like a person who can love them for who they are, even if they don't perfectly reflect their parents. It's easy for Linda to love Gene, and Tina so brazenly seeks approval that it would be cruel to withhold it, but for Louise to be so loveable to Bob makes Bob seem like someone who could love any child. Louise undermines him at every turn and can be fairly classified as a sociopath based on her behaviors, yet she is Bob's favorite. If Bob can love a budding super villain like Louise, he can love a gay child, a fat child, a nonbinary child, an anxious child, a depressed child—he can even love the child watching him right now.

5

Burger Boss

Bob's Burgers as a Workplace Sitcom

To see a life for what it is often requires a radical shift in perspective. When *Archer* briefly crosses paths with *Bob's Burgers*—easily done, since they share H. Jon Benjamin as lead voice actor—much of what is taken for granted as part of daily life at a family diner becomes new. *Archer*'s fourth season premiere begins with an uncharacteristically dour version of the shop, a very *Archer*-ish homage to its sister show's typical opening shot (4.01). Rather than bright primary colors, a gloomy drizzle obscures the yellow-on-green building, and only the lights beneath allow the red letters of the sign to pop. A mustachioed Archer prepares burgers for his family, only to be interrupted by four men in trench coats and fedoras, who lock the door behind them. When they threaten Archer and the Belchers, he expertly disarms and kills each man, demonstrating how Bob's daily tools—a spatula, a grill, a coffee pot, a bottle of ketchup, and an aerosol cooking spray—can become deadly weapons in the hands of a master spy (and sociopath). When Linda and the kids witness the carnage, they try to figure out what the men, apparently Russians, could be after. Linda asks if Archer/Bob has been gambling, to which he responds, "When would I gamble, Linda? The six hours a night I get to sleep? Because the other eighteen hours I'm slaving over this hot-ass grill!" Over Linda's objections, Archer leaves. He must, he says, to protect his family by finding out who sent the Russians and, in his words, "do a spa weekend. You know, between work and being a stepdad to Gene and Louise and, um … anyway, I'm just burned out."[1]

H. Jon Benjamin need not say a word as Archer as Bob to reveal the contrasts between the two; the chalkboard exposes one major difference right away. Though Archer shares Bob's passion for punning, he lacks his work ethic, thus Archer advertises a burger of the week rather than a burger of the day. Archer's laziness, a defining characteristic on *Archer*,

84

has few venues for expression in the diner, which, even ˈ
customers, supplies a seemingly endless stream of choˌ
plaints combined with the more realistic style of animatiˌ
plays up the daily misery of the diner in a way that rarely cˌ
on *Bob's Burgers*. In fact, *Bob's Burgers* slathers the harrowing reality of
the small family business in a secret sauce of whimsy, but when the sitcom becomes a workplace comedy, like *Archer*, it becomes uncharacteristically melancholy. To provide a context for the way *Bob's Burgers*
subtly critiques the conflation of work and family life on American television, this chapter takes a brief tour through the workplace sitcom, its
roots in the family sitcom, and the way *Bob's Burgers* mixes the two.

The television comedy developed two distinct genres in the 1950s
and '60s, the family sitcom and workplace sitcom (Putterman 90). The
logistics of making a weekly live action television program require the
re-use of a very limited number of sets, particularly if, like many sitcoms in the 20th century, it was filmed before a studio audience (Mills
·22). Thus, an office, garage, studio, or home makes a more cost-effective
setting for comedy than moving freely between such spaces. Though
there are exceptions, most notably *The Dick Van Dyke Show*, which was
explicitly split between work and home, most sitcoms settle into one of
these categories. The logistical realities of production determine the settings, which naturally impact the kind of stories that will be told there.

In *Reading Television*, John Hartley identifies two fundamental narratives for the sitcom developing from these practical requirements.
The family sitcom derives its drama from the tensions that arise in the
domestic sphere. Familiar examples of these include plots where a relative, often one or more in-laws or a "cool uncle," disrupts the home, a
child or spouse feels undervalued, or a secret is kept from a member
of the family. By contrast, Hartley attributes plots tied to sexual exploration to the workplace sitcom (97). Sometimes those plots are about
the frustration or denial of a sexual self, as in some of the earliest workplace sitcoms, like *Our Miss Brooks*. In more contemporary sitcoms, the
workplace allows characters to develop relationships that could lead to a
domestic (off-camera) comedy.

In both settings, the storylines must be essentially recursive. That it
is to say that each sitcom must return to its fundamental premise after
one, or occasionally two episodes. Though it lowers the stakes of any
given "situation," no plot can be allowed to permanently alienate a family member. Change can occur as dictated by the exigencies of production, but even the loss of a central actor does not so much change the

premise of a show as it does replace a name and a face in the opening credits. Valerie Harper's sitcom, *Valerie*, went on without her, first as *Valerie's Family* and then as *The Hogan Family*, while new actors can simply replace central characters, like Darrin on *Bewitched* or Becky on *Roseanne*.

The Mary Tyler Moore Show conflates workplace and family, as every member of the newsroom, even Ted Baxter and Sue Anne Nevins, acquires the sheen of lovability generally reserved for blood relatives and their consorts. *M*A*S*H*, *Taxi*, and *WKRP in Cincinnati* continued in this vein, to the extent that it is difficult to think of an era of television since 1970 that has not had a prominent workplace sitcom in which domestic affection was essentially replaced by the camaraderie of coworkers.

The year 1970 is not an arbitrary starting point. Many scholars consider *The Mary Tyler Moore Show*, which premiered in that year, the first workplace sitcom to integrate family dynamics.[2] *Mary Tyler Moore's* sadly still revolutionary premise, that a young woman can live a fulfilling life without organizing it around procreation, almost requires a certain domestic frame in the workplace. A father-daughter dynamic between gruff producer Lou Grant and associate producer Mary Richards develops quickly. By the series' 13th episode, Lou makes that bond explicit. When his nephew makes sexual overtures toward Mary, Lou warns, "let me remind you of something, and remember this forever. I think of this girl here as if she were my own daughter and that means she is your cousin, you get my drift?" ("He's All Yours"). Because this was the 1970s, this threat of incest does not prevent Lou and Mary from going on a date in the penultimate episode of the series, which is so uncomfortable it affirms rather than challenges the nature of their relationship. In the final episode of the series, Mary acknowledges the familial support she has enjoyed at the station, defining family as, "the people who make you feel less alone and really loved." Establishing the clearest familial tie between Lou and Mary allows *Mary Tyler Moore* to maintain its revolutionary bona fides while still allowing the traditional comforts of seeing a woman under the protection of a man, in this case, her father. The warmth of familial bonds obscures the cold realities of labor.[3]

M*A*S*H, debuting in 1972, went even farther with this concept. Its eleven-year run weathered many cast changes, which means it featured not just one, but two kinds of work-dads. It began with a hapless, overwhelmed dad, McLean Stevenson's Henry Blake, who would be replaced by Harry Morgan's stern disciplinarian, Sherman Potter.

5. *Burger Boss*

M*A*S*H, by deriving much of its humor from the coping strategies of Hawkeye, set up a version of the workplace that pivoted from *The Mary Tyler Show*. Rather than setting up its protagonist as an innocent newcomer, Hawkeye, a draftee, was a cynical burnout from the start. The father as boss, or work dad, for short, was critical in both. Mary Richards needed a father for protection, while Hawkeye needed someone to rebel against.

By the time *M*A*S*H* finally let its soldiers go home in 1983, several iterations of the workplace-as-family sitcom had come and gone, only to be replaced. As *WKRP in Cincinnati* and *Barney Miller* passed into the next life (syndication), *Cheers* (1982–93), *Newhart* (1982–90), and *Night Court* (1984–92) amused with the same formula in new settings.[4] The formula would stay pretty much the same throughout the 1990s, until *The Office* doubled-down on the familial aspects and the drudgery in 2005. Given its popular and critical success, it makes for an intriguing comparison with the way *Bob's Burgers* handles the workplace.

The American version of *The Office* has it both ways, making Michael Scott the butt of jokes because of his pathetic attempts to make himself the loving patriarch of Dunder Mifflin's Scranton office while structuring the series around these office drones literally becoming family. The transparency of Michael's aspirations reaches an early peak during the third season, when Phyllis negotiates six weeks of time-off for her honeymoon in exchange for allowing Michael to be part of her wedding party. Michael believes that he is "giving Phyllis away" but in fact ends up just pushing her father's wheelchair, which he exits to walk Phyllis down the aisle, stranding Michael at the rear of the church. Michael's attempts to assert himself as the beloved patriarch of an imagined work family are an integral part of the program. The idea of workplace as family distinguishes the show from its British predecessor; in effect, this trope is what makes the American version of *The Office* American (Beeden and De Bruin 12).

The central narrative that runs through the entire series is the flirtation, courtship and marriage of coworkers Jim and Pam, while many of the smaller plots involve the pairing off of other colleagues like Ryan and Kelly, Erin and Andy, and Angela and Dwight, whose marriage takes place in the series finale. In this sense, as much as Dunder Mifflin replaces family for Michael Scott, it literally generates family for our most likeable protagonists. Scott himself is a notable exception; though he meets and starts dating Holly Flax at work, he eventually leaves his job to be with her.

The Genius of *Bob's Burgers*

The Office was adapted from a British sitcom, but generated far more episodes, thus it could never be strictly a retelling of the original story.[5] What *The Office* genuinely preserved from its predecessor is its influential format; the program is shot like a documentary series, with handheld cameras, lapel microphones, and occasional talking head interviews. Though Michael provides much of the narration, the viewer shares the point of view of the affable, under-motivated Jim (Detweiler 730). Like *M*A*S*H* and *The Mary Tyler Moore Show* before it, *The Office* establishes a workdad but puts its protagonist in the "child" role. Jim and Pam are always treating the camera as their "buddy," giving the camera, and by extension, their audience, the exasperated looks and sly smiles that allow the viewer to laugh at Michael's antics, because they think it's funny, too. Unlike *M*A*S*H*, *The Office* never treats the workdad role as modular. When actor Steve Carell left in the show's seventh season, he was replaced by a series of actors in the boss role—Will Ferrell, James Spader, even British comedian Catherine Tate, but none tried to integrate themselves into the office as a father figure in the way Michael Scott did. In this way Michael structurally achieves his goal: like a true father, he cannot simply be replaced. As a boss, however, *The Office* demonstrates again and again that Michael's rise to power was rather arbitrary. Ryan begins as a temporary employee, but eventually rises far above Michael, becoming a vice-president and moving from the regional office in Scranton to the corporate headquarters in New York.[6] Throughout its run *The Office* revealed that the American tendency to pattern work relationships after domestic ones is artificial, while the show also clung to the domestic relationships that arise from the office as a major engine for plot.

The Office acknowledges the ridiculousness of the workplace as a substitute for domestic life when Michael Scott returns for the final episode. In his commentary from Angela and Dwight's reception, Michael wistfully shares, "I feel like all my kids grew up, and married each other. It's every parent's dream" ("Finale"). Despite the soul-numbing qualities of laboring in a dying industry, capitalism, as embodied by the workplace on *The Office*, still underlies, nay, enables the most foundational elements of the American dream. These hostages to capitalism begin to abduct one another into domestic servitude, like an office park adaptation of *Seven Brides for Seven Brothers*. The bleeding of the workplace into the domestic sphere when the workplace family becomes actual family contradicts the very notion of separate spheres. By marrying off our protagonists, *The Office* subtly and darkly suggests that even someone like Jim, who doesn't seem like a corporate drone, has, by ...ing in love at Dunder Mifflin, surrendered himself and his surplus labor by becoming even more dependent upon the benevolence of capitalism to support his growing family.

Conversely, a family sitcom adopting the tropes of the workplace allows the reading of family dynamics in stark economic terms. As a workplace sitcom, Bob obviously fulfills the role of the "hapless dad/boss," with Gene, Tina, and power-hungry Louise as his employees. Bob, like *Mary Tyler Moore*'s Lou Grant, or *M*A*S*H*'s commanding officers, often adopts an authoritative tone while accepting that he is unable to control his underlings. Thus, the beats between Bob and the kids echo moments from workplace sitcoms. However, *Bob's Burgers* gains unlikely poignancy from being more than a simulacrum of a family. Unlike *The Office*'s Michael Scott, the moments where Bob recognizes that he actually is a father in the workplace are among his saddest. In the very first episode, Bob addresses the kids and announces, "you're my children and I love you. But you're all terrible at what you do here, and I feel like I should tell you, I'd fire all of you if I could" (1.1). This establishes the lament that becomes a refrain within the series. Bob toggles between curses his children for their incompetence and himself for relying on their labor to run the restaurant.

The nature of the Belcher kids' responsibilities in the restaurant can shift from episode to episode. They wipe ketchup from menus, fill salt and pepper shakers, and, according to a recent episode, have the rather shocking, from a safety perspective, task of cleaning the bathroom (9.14). Bob also has tasks that are "special"—only Gene gives out samples in the burger costume, and Tina is the only one who helps him at the grill. These tasks—all of which seem like standard "sidework" to anyone who has worked at a restaurant—serve a purpose within the household identical to chores, in the sense that the kids trade them back and forth. Bob and Linda use these tasks as ways to punish and reward their kids. Of course, the major distinction is that unlike unloading the dishwasher or matching all the socks in the laundry, each task that the kids accomplish within the restaurant serves the business' bottom line by keeping labor costs low. As Ashlie Stevens explores in a 2017 *Salon* piece, real-life restaurateurs credit the show with being very accurate in its portrayal of the staffing difficulties faced by small restaurants. In the piece, Stevens notes the irony that 32 percent of restaurant workers face food insecurity. *Bob's Burgers'* commitment to realism means that the business is dependent upon under- or unpaid labor, which is

.place sitcoms won't touch. Because *Bob's Burgers* is
:dy, it can explore the issue of labor in the food indus-
,or of children can be positioned as chores instead of
clever trick on the part of *Bob's Burgers*. A standard sit-
ſ sustain a humorous tone while exploring this labor cri-
sı.. *Burgers'* blended format allows the depiction of under- or
unpaiɑ . ɔrers because they are children, so the audience never worries about their housing or ability to support their families.

Still, there are a few episodes where the realities of small business threaten to make the show more maudlin than whimsical. In the
third episode of Season 3, "Bob Fires the Kids," Bob confronts the legacy of mixing work and family life. A box of his toys arrives. As the kids
note, his toys are incredibly sad—a scrubber, a spatula, and a piece of
soap shaped like a dog that Bob calls Mr. Doglevitch (3.3). They remind
Bob that he spent his childhood working in his father's restaurant.
Later, Bob witnesses Tina "marrying" two napkin dispensers—a behavior that recalls the way he personified his restaurant implements as a
child. He fires Gene, Louise, and Tina and orders them to play outside,
in the hopes of giving them the happy childhood he never had. After
Bob exhorts them to "have a water balloon fight, play in a vacant lot, ride
bikes!" Tina, Gene, and Louise reluctantly head out to have a fun summer vacation, which amounts to a montage of bike accidents, a double Dutch disaster, and Tina being covered in ants. Eventually they find
their way to a blueberry farm, whose proprietors hire the children for
their primary agri-business: growing and selling marijuana. The kids are
content to harvest and run drugs for the blueberry farmers, who pay
them ten dollars a day, and it is not until a SWAT team breaks up the
operation that the kids find something that they would rather do than
make money: watch adults get arrested.

In order to replace his children, Bob hires Mickey, a bank robber
recently released from prison. As regular viewers know, the restaurant
is barely solvent as it is. Thus, Bob can only "pay" Mickey by providing
room and board—the same payment his kids received. Shortly after hiring Mickey, Bob discovers that he is digging a hole in the basement in
order to tunnel his way into the very same bank he tried to rob before.
Luckily, Bob fires Mickey at almost the same time that the pot farm gets
shut down, so the kids are suddenly available to work at the restaurant.
The necessities of running the business overpower Bob's guilt about
ruining his kids' childhood. Also, as the episode gently underlines,
because work is all the kids have ever known, they will find it wherever

they go, and it's safer for them to work with their parents than, say, a nice hippie couple with a farm.

The restaurant exerts so much influence on the kids that they will take any opportunity to make it their own. Later in the third season, in "The Kids Run the Restaurant," the young Belchers are left to their own devices, but this time within the restaurant (3.20). Bob cuts himself, requiring Linda to take him to the emergency room for stitches. Linda closes the restaurant, instructing the kids to stay upstairs in the apartment, with Tina in charge. Once their parents leave, they take very little interest in traditional leisure, rejecting games like "Torpedo" and "Surgery Sam." Louise insists that they re-open the restaurant, but despite new marketing efforts from Gene and Tina, traffic in the diner is slow. Louise realizes that the most profitable course is to make the restaurant a front for a casino in the basement. The Belcher children simply don't recognize a line between commerce and leisure, making them ideal capitalist subjects, as for them, all of their labor is surplus, readily given over to the capitalist, whether it's Bob and Linda, pot farmers Beverly and Cooper, or Louise herself.

In Season 5, Big Bob finally appears, revealing the origins of Bob's whimsical approach to fast food. In a flashback, Big Bob leaves little Bob in charge of the restaurant. During Big Bob's absence, Bob makes the "Baby You Can Chive My Car" burger for a regular. Big Bob returns, horrified that Bob wouldn't just give the man his usual order, and destroys it. Bob never forgets his father's rejection of the novelty burger. When Big Bob offers Bob a partnership in the business, he refuses, instead starting his own restaurant where he can sell the pun-based burgers that are flowing out of him, like the "Crispy Brinkley," "Richard Persimmons," and "Greed Is Gouda" burgers (5.6).

As introduced in "Bob Fires the Kids" and expanded in "Father of the Bob," Bob himself realizes the horror inherent in conflating work and family life, as his relationship with his own father is forever damaged when he refuses to be his business partner. He blames the family business for ruining his childhood, but only has enough imagination to create a more whimsical version of it for himself and his family. Bob has been so completely warped by his devotion to the family restaurant that he can only express himself through his menu, specifically his burgers.

Bob uses the burger as the medium for all his artistic ambitions. As his landlord, Mr. Fischoeder declares, Bob is "A beef artist. A beef-artist! Like a greasy, heterosexual Walt Whitman" (1.10). That his chosen medium is meat reflects the way Bob shaped his creative ambitions to the material available to him when he was first developing his aesthetic; thus, he works with produce, meat, and condiments rather than more durable art supplies. His pieces are designed to be mass-produced and consumed, almost a perfect marriage of capitalism and art. Bob's artistic aspirations put him in a liminal space, where he is misunderstood both by his business-minded father and by the local arts community, as represented by Edith and Harold Cranwinkle. The Cranwinkles own "Reflections," the local art supply store, and have nothing but contempt for Bob. In turn, Bob is always uncomfortable in their presence. Bob's discomfort implies that, on some level, he recognizes that he has turned his artistic ambitions toward a medium that is, at best, ephemeral. Edith and Harold represent more traditional modes of creative expression. More than just paper and glitter, the Cranwinkles sell the idea of art as something that exists for its own sake rather than a way of squeezing a little whimsy between beef and bun. Introduced in Season 1's "Art Crawl" episode, Edith Cranwinkle's affect alternates between judgmental and disgusted. In many of her appearances, she assesses a scene with a single word. Bob's readiness to be intimidated by them derives from his own insecurities as an artist who has never been able to take the traditional routes represented by the supplies sold at their store.

This is not to say that Bob's artistic efforts go unnoticed. When given the chance to succeed on a larger scale, as in the Season 6 episode, "Pro-Tiki/Con-Tiki," he shrinks from the opportunity as soon as he discovers that it will require him to transform the diner into a tiki-themed restaurant (6.15). At the start of the episode, Bob announces that his childhood friend, Warren Fitzgerald, will be coming to stay with them. Warren built and sold a successful business, making him the richest man Bob knows. Searching for a way to explain how cool Warren was in their youth, Bob finally resorts to *Happy Days*: "he made the Fonz look like Potsie." Warren arrives and is so genuinely impressed by Bob's burger that he offers Bob $100,000 on the spot to become a partner in the restaurant. Bob agrees, as the whole family is astonished by the prospect of such a large investment. Tina, in awe, says, "I never knew a check could have commas." Bob quickly sours on this partnership when Warren begins to redecorate the restaurant. As Teddy gets to work installing a new awning and Tina fusses over drink umbrellas ("To keep your ice dry if it rains."), Bob worries that the tiki theme will overwhelm his burgers. Warren explains, "the destination is still your burger but the restaurant is the journey there." Bob tries to go along as Warren and the rest of the Belchers enthusiastically embrace new features like a volcano and a talking pineapple. As the new concept brings new customers and the approval of Jimmy Pesto, Bob explodes, tearing apart the decorations and calling his customers stupid for liking them. Warren and Bob dissolve their partnership, and Bob returns Warren's investment. The episode ends with Warren telling Bob that despite his financial success, he envies Bob. In Warren's estimation, Bob's life with his family is "easily worth $200,000. Well, definitely at least $175,000."

When Bob acknowledges that he was far too aggressive in rejecting the tiki theme, he admits, "I would have hated any theme. I'm a burger man." The control of his burgers, and his ability to take them in every direction he can imagine, means more to him than financial success. The partnership with Warren dissolves, but the reason Warren gives for backing out feels oddly out of sync with the rest of the episode. Warren says that Bob already has the perfect business partners in Linda and the kids. As Alasdair Wilkins notes, this observation feels odd, given their total embrace of the tiki concept, not to mention their unreserved enthusiasm for the sudden infusion of cash into their business. Bob rejects the money for its potential to mute the impact of his burgers, his personal expression. Warren threatens Bob's creative outlet by suggesting that other elements might attract customers, which is very different from Big Bob's total rejection of novelty burgers. The only threat posed by the tiki theme is that patrons might have more than one reason to come to the restaurant, yet Bob rejects Warren just as he rejected his father. The most telling difference is that in this instance, Bob rejects the opportunity not only for himself but for his entire family. Though Bob may not consciously recognize himself as a tempestuous, narcissistic artist, he shows himself to be just that in the way he rejects this opportunity in order to follow his muse.

Bob's Burgers is very burger-centric—much of the drama of Season 7's Easter-themed "Eggs for Days" springs from making the restaurant ready to accommodate diners who gave up beef for Lent—but Bob himself is not above using other means to draw customers. In separate episodes during the second season, Bob installed the "Burger Boss" game and the soft ice cream machine as lures. Bob must, then, object to the source of the tiki theme, not the idea of a gimmick. The video game and the soft ice cream machine both sprang from his own desires, so he never thought of them as threatening his burgers. His hostility toward the tiki concept springs from hostility to the very idea of partnership.

When Warren suggests that he is already in a perfect partnership, he unintentionally implies that Bob's perfect partner is silence.

"Pro-Tiki/Con-Tiki" inadvertently reveals that Bob, in refusing to become his father's partner, has put Linda, and by extension, his children, in the role he refused: that of subservient, silent partner. The picture of Big Bob's Diner that hangs over the Belcher's sofa is a metaphor for the shadow that the family business casts over all the Belchers. Bob uses the business to control his family just as Big Bob used the possibility of a partnership to control Bob.

As much as Bob wants to free himself and his family from the drudgery of constant labor, he only goes as far as to allow for a bit more whimsy within the system in which he was raised. The breaching of the barrier between work and family and its legacy is perfectly symbolized within their home. They live above the restaurant with a picture of another restaurant hanging above them, like condiments between buns. The generational curse of the restaurant dominating the domestic space casts a shadow over *Bob's Burgers* bright primary colors. With its characters permanently on the precipice of poverty, the show imagines a generation so warped by the perils of capitalism that they are fundamentally unable to separate work from play. In the moments where Bob realizes that he is a product of a childhood of non-stop labor at his father's restaurant, like when he opens the box of toys in "Bob Fires the Kids" or visits his father in "Father of the Bob," his pathetic, thwarted attempts to have fun in Big Bob's Diner make him fear for his children. Bob sees his burgers of the day as a coping mechanism allowing him to tolerate what Archer calls in the opening clip, "18-hour days over this hot-ass grill." He sees himself, briefly, as a victim, not a boss, which forces him to reckon with the world in which he's immersed his children. But, as Gene says, he has raised "indoor kids." When set free for the summer, they find work. When given an hour without adult supervision, they construct a black-market enterprise.

If the children become figures of pity in the moments when the show makes it clear that they can't imagine a life for themselves outside of work, Bob is the most pathetic of them all. In Season 9 episode, "Roamin' Bob-iday," Linda spies signs of burnout in Bob (9.16). He sends the kids off to school as if they were customers, thanking them for coming in. Once he gets to the restaurant, he refills Teddy's coffee with ketchup instead of coffee, and eventually gets into a fight with a hamburger over the correct application of mustard. Linda realizes that he needs a day off, so she and the kids lock him out of the restaurant the next morning. Like the kids, when Bob is forced out of the restaurant, he simply finds another place to work, at Patricia's 77 Sandwiches. In the course of helping Patricia, he learns how her professional ambitions have limited her personal life. The moral message here is familiar from the very first episode of the show. Over nine seasons, Louise softens to the point that she is capable of showing sympathy for Mr. Frond, Tina expands her erotic imagination to include not just boys and zombies, but also a goose named Bruce, but Bob is stuck, learning the same lesson again and again. At the end of the episode, Bob sings an ode to his trade, "nothing makes me happier/than serving some food to some guy." He sings while a fantasy mountain of burgers forms behind him, but then, as he approaches the restaurant and catches a glimpse of his family, he comes to the end of his reverie, singing, "nothing makes me happier/than cooking again and again./But nothing makes me happier/ than them." It's a lovely sentiment, but also very familiar. When he sees what's happened in the restaurant on his day off—another biker has given birth, this time by the stools—he fires the whole family, which is another callback to the first episode, when Bob first says that, as employees, his children are "all terrible" (1.1). Bob, sagging under the yoke of being a father and a boss, ends the episode by trying to be a father again, but the hopelessness of this endeavor is underscored by the song that plays over the credits, a duet between Bob and Patricia celebrating sandwiches.

Archer's portrayal of the tensions that arise between being a family and being business has sharper edges and darker shadows than we typically see on *Bob's Burgers*. *Archer* itself is a workplace sitcom that mixes family, but the tone is, well, archer, than that of *Bob's Burgers*. Protagonist Sterling Archer works for his mother's spy agency, but family matters are generally played for laughs, not sentiment. *Bob's Burgers* handles its characters with far more tenderness and affection, so when Bob fails to put his family before his business, it can't simply be played for laughs as it is on *Archer*.

While a workplace sitcom in the tradition of *The Mary Tyler Moore Show* brings domestic comfort to the potentially frightening circumstance of embarking on a new career, inserting the workplace into the family sitcom normalizes the worst impulses of the Belchers—Gene and Tina's eagerness to follow orders, and Louise's eagerness to give them. Bob seems like a far superior boss than Michael Scott and a better father than Big Bob, yet his children seem far more capable of the pranking of

Jim and Pam than the kind of play generally associated with childhood. Thanks to Bob, the only home they know is defined by the whims and whimsy of capitalism, so they will choose labor and commerce over leisure again and again, one with a groan, one with a smile, and one with a malevolent grin beneath her bunny ears.

6

"Boys are from Mars, girls are from Venus"

Gender and Voice Casting in *Bob's Burgers*

Casual fans of *Bob's Burgers* may not realize that there is only one female voice among the five Belchers. Two of the principal female characters, Tina and Linda, are voiced by men. *Bob's Burgers* is certainly not the first animated sitcom to cross-cast, but it is the first animated sitcom to pair an exuberant drag performance (John Roberts as Linda) with the more traditional cross-casting of Dan Mintz as Tina. In fact, *Bob's Burgers* bucks many conventions of animated sitcoms in its voice casting, like using the adult Eugene Mirman to voice eleven-year-old Gene. These choices reverberate in unexpected ways throughout the fictional universe of the show. In all animation, a human voice becomes synonymous with a two-dimensional abstraction. The combination of the patently abstract with the distinctly human provides the opportunity to unleash something new. The form and voice create an avatar, which exists to carry the human into a fantasy setting, or, within a realist setting, can create a character that would not exist in our world. A drag queen can become an everyday mom. An adenoidal man can become a 13-year-old girl. A chubby middle-aged man can become a chubby middle-school boy. *Bob's Burgers'* voice casting allows these hybrids to flourish, but to what end? The voice can serve to add another dimension to that character, or the voice can make that character even more superficial. In this chapter I examine the impact of cross-casting on forming the character of Linda Belcher.

Animation has long-embraced cross-casting. June Foray originated Rocky the Flying Squirrel and his femme-fatale nemesis (femme-sis?), Natasha, Jokey Smurf, and hundreds of other characters of many genders and species over a career in voice acting spanning over half a century, from 1953 until 2014.[1] Animation, like so many corners of the media in this century and the last, is a male-dominated industry, so voice acting was one of the few ways in for women.[2] In her analysis of systematic misogyny in American animation, one of the few bright spots Katia Perea unearths is the following quote from William Hanna, of animation powerhouse Hanna-Barbera, who said of Foray, "she has contributed more to voice acting than anyone I know" (31).

Foray would not be the last great vocal talent to make a name for herself as a gender (and species!) not her own. Actresses Nancy Cartwright and Pamela Adlon perform two of the most iconic animated boys, Bart Simpson and Bobby Hill, respectively. As Adlon explains the practice to Terry Gross on *Fresh Air*:

> Well, the thing is about the phenomenon about women playing boys is that we're not going to age, and we're not going to go through puberty in the middle of, you know, a long-running series, what people hope will be long-running. And I used to, you know, take over for a lot of boys whose voices would crack and change.

Cartwright has been a ten-year-old boy since 1987, the year the Simpsons debuted as a segment on Fox's *Tracy Ullman Show*. *King of the Hill* allowed Bobby to age during its 13-year-run, but only from 11 to 14. However, Adlon managed any vocal adjustments required to keep up with Bobby's slow creep toward adulthood so adroitly that many viewers (like this one) may not have noticed.

Bob's Burgers casts for a particular type of voice actor. Unlike contemporary animated sitcoms like *The Simpsons* and *Family Guy*, or classics like *The Flintstones* and *The Jetsons*, *Bob's Burgers* features performers who bring a particular persona to each part rather than a flexible set of pipes. Performance scholar Starr Marcello would categorize the work that Foray, Cartwright, and Adlon do, whether cross-cast or not, as traditional voice acting. This type of voice acting is distinguished by versatility and transparency. Each, while primarily known for one character, takes on a variety of voices within a single episode, with Cartwright voicing not just Bart but many of his peers, including Ralph Wiggum and antagonist Nelson Muntz. In terms of transparency, Cartwright, Adlon, and Foray do not use their voices to refer to a persona external to the narrative. By contrast, the *Bob's Burgers* cast engages in "celebrity voice acting" (64–5). In making this distinction, Marcello refers to the kind of casting meant to bring fans of a particular actor's persona to a project, in the way that Robin Williams' performance in 1992's *Aladdin* was meant to signify that there would be humor in the film for adults. Though the cast of *Bob's Burgers* are hardly celebrities, each is clearly bringing a persona created outside of *Bob's Burgers* to the characters they portray on the show.[3]

Creator Loren Bouchard's chief value in selecting voice actors is particularity, which means he primarily casts standup comedians. For Bouchard, "'Standup is a crucible in which you bake your voice. You need to spend time in front of a live audience living and dying by your voice'" (Lindsay). Bouchard casts actors with personas hardened by repeatedly attempting to connect with people on the wrong end of a two-drink minimum. The extent to which Bouchard values distinction over versatility means that even though the central cast of *Bob's Burgers* were not household names, each was cast for the unique valence that their voice carried before their character had a name or even, in Tina's case, a gender. Exploring the impact of cross-casting on *Bob's Burgers* requires thoughtful consideration of what each actor brings from the stage to the program, and how that, combined with a cheerful chinless illustration, results in a character that audiences relate to just as much as a Roseanne or a "real" housewife—often more.

Is Motherhood a Drag?
John Roberts as Linda Belcher

Loren Bouchard's casting process for *Bob's Burgers* has no better exemplar than John Roberts' transformation into Belcher matriarch, Linda. Actor, musician and stand-up comedian Roberts was cast on the basis of a series of videos he made impersonating his mother. Linda Belcher's voice—cheerful verging on shrill, with a lot of Brooklyn behind it—comes directly from Roberts' drag performances in the first decade of the aughts. Roberts developed the character performing at a queer venue for drag queens, but the voice started even earlier, as Roberts explained in an interview:

> It's a voice that I've always had—you know, my mother, and my aunts are all from Brooklyn, so I've always done that voice really naturally since I was a kid. *Bob's* started as a demo, and I didn't audition for it. The creator of the show saw me performing at Comics, which was on 14th Street, and now is closed. My videos were out, and he just sort of picked me to do this [O'Donnell].

In the YouTube videos, Roberts wears a red wig and large glasses that give his head a silhouette similar to Linda Belcher's.

of content, the videos are sometimes eerily similar to the show, particularly the most widely seen clip, "The as his mother, raves about this year's Christmas tree, ᵤₚₑₒₚₗₑ to see it, directing family members in its care, and comparing it to previous trees. Each line has the enthusiasm familiar from *Bob's Burgers'* Christmas episodes, making the viewer feel like it is a series of outtakes from the show, even though "The Tree" predates the series by four years. Because his drag performance, as he admits above, directly led to Loren Bouchard casting him as Linda, the resonance between the early YouTube videos and *Bob's Burgers'* exuberant matriarch is built into the show.

In a touching clip from a local morning show, "Good Day, New York," Roberts and his mother, Marge, discuss the evolution of his performance. When a host asks Marge if her son's impersonations embarrass her, she echoes the sentiments of every stand-up comedian's mom when she says, "anything to get him going." Later Roberts reveals that he uses all of Marge's clothes in his videos, and Marge admits that she can't wear them once they're on YouTube. In contrast to the other members of the cast, who perform stand-up as heightened versions of themselves, Roberts was cast on the basis of this impression of his mother. While the performance is hilarious, it is also limited, as all impressions are, to Roberts' powers of observation and mimicry. Roberts' character is built from the loved experience of a child, not the lived experience of a parent.

Linda finds so much to love as a Belcher. In a family of frustrated dreamers, Linda stands alone, defined almost exclusively by her positivity. Bethy Squires writes that Linda's role is to say yes. In fact, Linda provides such constant encouragement that recently, a company seeking to avoid copyright infringement packaged a black wig and red glasses as "Supportive Burger Wife Costume" just in time for Halloween (Pomranz). While there is more to Linda Belcher than just her hair and glasses, in many ways there is less to her than the other characters on *Bob's Burgers*. In 21st-century America, having a mother's character defined almost entirely by her support of her husband and children feels retrograde in a way that makes me queasy. Linda is beloved for her mom-ish enthusiasm, but is that all she is?

Even the name, Linda, connotes an everymom-ness to a certain generation. Loren Bouchard and the writers of the show were, for the most part, raised by baby boomers, particularly women born in the 1940s and '50s. The social security administration confirms that

6. *"Boys are from Mars, girls are from Venus"*

Linda was the second most popular name in the United States for both decades. Bouchard was born in 1969, Linda's voice and co-creator John Roberts was born in 1971, and the majority of the show's writers were born in the 1970s, meaning that many of them were raised by women born in the '40s and '50s. As someone roughly the same age as many of the creators and performers on *Bob's Burgers*, I can attest, anecdotally, that as a child in the United States at least a third of all mom-type people (i.e., teachers and other people's moms) were named Linda. Thus, at least for a particular generation, even Linda's name can be understood as a generic term for "mom."

Linda consistently showers joy on the Belcher household. The enthusiasm she shows for the preoccupations of her very strange children is a reliable source of nostalgia or jealousy, depending on what kind of mom you had. She does her children's homework without complaint. She supports Gene's ambitions in competitive table setting. She's not afraid of Louise. She even chewed Tina's food for her when Tina had her tonsils out, according to Louise (2.3). Still, as an audience member, I'm not alone in wondering if there is more to Linda than just her momitude. When she parents apart from Bob, Linda seems constrained by gender in ways that Bob is not. There is a deep thread of irony running through this observation, since Linda is a creation of gender play.

The Linda-centered Season 3 episode, "Mother Daughter Laser Razor," shows Linda struggling for Louise's admiration (3.10). The way this struggle plays out illustrates the extent to which Linda allows gender roles to define her as a parent. A flashback reveals that Linda's dynamic with Louise has always been troubled, as a baby Louise calls out for "Dada." Linda gently, then less gently, encourages her to say "Ma-ma," until, frustrated, she gives up, telling baby Louise, "All right. You know what? Change your own diaper!"

In the beginning of the episode, Linda uses typical, fun-mom strategies to bond with Louise, trying to tempt her with family game night and then barging into a game that the kids have invented, "Stone the Witch," which Louise accuses her of ruining by "momming it up!" In desperation, Linda takes Louise to an eight-hour mother-daughter seminar run by her favorite mommy blogger: Dakota Applebaum, the Phenomemom. At the very beginning of the seminar, the Phenomemom, to Linda's shock, is revealed to be a man. Dakota Applebaum defends his expertise, claiming, "the female spirit flows through all of us. We are all estrogeniuses." Applebaum's statement and the seminar that follows very aggressively conflate gender with sex.[4] When he mentions the

101

"female spirit," he could easily be discussing gender. Cultivating the traits and habits a culture assigns to women is a practice accessible to all. It's likely that this is what Applebaum means when he invokes this universally accessible "female spirit."

Where this practice breaks down is in the tools he uses to summon the spirit, all of which derive from purely biological markers of sex. While everyone Applebaum addresses could well be an "estrogenius," the introduction of this charming portmanteau begins with his conflation of biological sex markers—which include estrogen levels—with the gendered (which is to say cultural, not biological) roles of mother and daughter. The uter-room, the umbilator, and the vagisack are all biological, even though the bond he is trying to strengthen is purely cultural. This is obvious because his credentials are purely cultural—he identifies himself as a man, after all. Focusing on biological realities of mothering completely undercuts any authority Applebaum could bring to the subject. Additionally, he allows a mother and son to participate in the workshop, so he must be open to the idea that someone born male could have a mother-daughter relationship with their parent, even as he leans on tools that suggest biological determinism. If the relationship requires symbols of biological motherhood to heal, how could Applebaum, who will never have first-person experience with the real-life analogs of the vagisack, umbilator, and uter-room, be qualified to spearhead this healing?

This confusion around gender or sex-based authority implicitly connects Linda and Louise's plot with the conundrum face by the remaining Belchers. Bob, Tina, and Gene mobilize around the removal of 13-year-old Tina's leg hair. This desire derives from an awkward incident in the diner. Tina overhears two cooler girls at the restaurant make fun of a classmate for her hairy legs. Mortified as she notes the hair on her own legs, she alerts Gene, who wraps himself around her legs, obscuring the offending hairs, for the remainder of the interaction. The significance of hairy legs in terms of both gender and class is made clear later, when Linda instructs Tina in the semiotics of women's grooming: "Just shave up to the knee. Only strippers shave above the knee. The good ones, anyway." The results of Tina's subsequent attempt at shaving are so gory that the audience sees only the horrified reactions of witnesses and not the bloody aftermath. With Linda occupied with Louise, Bob and Gene take Tina to the salon Waxing Philosophical, where Bob is given extremely gendered hair removal options, including his back and scrotum, before making it clear that Tina will be the client. Once Tina is set up for her procedure, she makes a frantic call for Bob, who agrees to get his legs waxed alongside her. Bob never hesitates or attempts to call attention to any sacrifice he might be making in terms of his gender presentation by subjecting himself to the painful trial of waxing. Bob only acknowledges the oddity of a man having smooth legs when he expresses how much he enjoys the silky feeling of his pants sloshing around them. Gender roles recede, rather than dominate this part of the episode, making the essentialist assumptions of Applebaum seem that much more ridiculous. Bob, by confidently ushering Tina into the world of female grooming, shows himself to be a true estrogenius.

Meanwhile, Linda struggles to connect with Louise, constantly bribing her to participate in the rebirthing-style exercises of the seminar. Eventually the kids escape the seminar for the laser tag arena next door, where Linda and Louise finally join forces against their common enemy, the Phenomemom himself. He shoots Louise for ruining his seminar, causing Linda to rain down lasers on him with the stereotypical fury and strength of a mama bear, or perhaps even a "fun" mama bear. In the end, Linda reverts back to a version of "mom" that is less self-conscious—i.e., doesn't require Louise to be reborn from a "vagisack" or fed from an umbilator (an allegedly umbilical cord–esque contraption that bears a suspicious resemblance to what an undergraduate might recognize as a "beer bong").

As Bob and Linda parent in parallel, their relationships to gendered expectations stand in contrast. Linda seemingly dives into a normative relationship by choosing a seminar specifically for mothers and daughters, but the legitimacy of the seminar is immediately undermined when the "Phenomemom" is revealed to be a man. All of the elements of the seminar are accompanied by goofy puns, not surprising to regular viewers of *Bob's Burgers*, but still, Dakota Applebaum's uter-room, vagisack, and umbilator deflate his authority by connecting his expertise to biological sex rather than gender. Unlike Linda, Bob forthrightly navigates the waxing salon, a consumer space defined by catering to gender norms in spite of biological realities, for Tina's benefit. Bob never grouses that it might not be his place as a father or a man to make sure that Tina conforms to the local standards for feminine gender presentation. Instead, Bob and Gene enthusiastically embrace the idea that hairless legs might provide pleasure for anyone, regardless of gender. This acceptance signifies that they are not attached to markers of gender, since hairy legs on their own are a purely cultural marker—biologically, all sexes are capable of accessorizing their stems with a lustrous coat of hair.

Bob's gentle accession to the demands of a misfit teenage girl makes Linda's insistence that Louise bond with her feel that much more desperate. When she finally earns Louise's respect, it is in an imaginary space, the laser arena. Within the arena Linda's reveals her true nature: neither violent, nor particularly masculine, despite the space, but purely mom-ish. Dakota shoots Louise, frustrated by the hours she has spent undermining his authority. Linda arms herself in order to protect her young, and in the imaginary space of the laser arena, blows him away. Linda's attack on Dakota is just as artificial as his vagisacks, so the conflict's resolution has a pleasing symmetry. However, Linda never stops momming, she just applies her momming to a common enemy, finally earning Louise's admiration.

While Bob is allowed to convey a kind of post-gender ease in his enjoyment of his own silky-smooth stems, Linda's overwhelming mom-ness eclipses any connections she might have made to her femininity, obscured first by the fact that the seminar is not a homosocial space, and second by Louise's refusal to allow shared gender or sex traits to be a source of closeness. Thus, the episode affirms Linda's limitations while giving Bob free reign to surprise and support the kids, outside of gendered expectations.

Linda, Un-Mommed

Perhaps the best place to seek a Linda that is not totally defined by her family is by examining contexts where she appears without the rest of the Belchers. Though rare, there are moments where *Bob's Burgers* allows Linda to branch out from her family, like flashbacks of her life before she met Bob, moments where she seeks opportunities outside the home, or times where she seems to have her own channel for artistic expression.

Explorations of her pre–Bob years are scarce. The very first episode of *Bob's Burgers* hints at her life before Bob (1.1). In "Human Flesh," a health inspector, Hugo, follows up on a rumor started by Louise that the diner serves burgers made from bodies provided by Mort's funeral home. Hugo and Linda were engaged when Linda met Bob. Linda has little to say about their relationship, save, "I was young, and my parents liked him because he always did the dishes." Hugo, inflamed by jealous passion upon seeing Linda again, shuts down the restaurant by publicizing the alleged cannibalism. Bob feels like he's failed himself and his family. The episode ends on an uplifting note when Linda ʟ despondent Bob back to reality by explaining that she loves Bob be͟ he has a dream. In fact, the whole pilot really centers around the extͼ to which Bob enlists his whole family in trying to realize his dream, whether they like it or not. Linda figures in primarily as way to show how little Bob is engaged with life outside the restaurant. Early in the episode Linda notes that Bob has forgotten their anniversary, which kicks off a brief, funny montage of Bob forgetting important dates as Bob and Linda grind the meat. Bob's dream is so important that he can't help but remind his children of their incompetence in bringing his dreams to fruition, telling the kids, "You're my children and I love you, but you're all terrible at what you do here and I'd fire you if I could." Bob's dream defines life for the family, and the extent to which Linda's past is important in the pilot episode is solely relegated to the impact it has on Bob's designs for the restaurant.

In Season 3's "Lindapendent Woman," Linda takes a job outside the home at an aggressively whimsical grocery store called "Fresh Feed"— clearly meant as an homage to Trader Joe's (3.14). At Fresh Feed, her enthusiasm for taking a disco minute, easy banter with costumers, and can-stacking prowess is celebrated in a performance review after only a week. When Linda's manager praises her, she quips, "Nobody ever said I rocked at my old job—and I was sleeping with the boss!" When she returns home, she tells Bob that he has never given Linda a performance review. Put on the spot, as Bob attempts to put together a review like Fresh Feed provides, it becomes clear that he takes much of what she does for the restaurant for granted. He can only muster an eight out of ten, noting that her hair falls out a lot, and she sneaks pickles all the time—both performance issues that should have been addressed far earlier. Feeling underappreciated, Linda starts working full time at Fresh Feed where she quickly rises to shift manager. Even with that recognition, Linda becomes disenchanted with the grocery store, because she realizes that everyone only works there for the money and will do whatever he or she can to get out of it. This reveals both how deeply unfamiliar Linda is with the working world and how much she conflates the business with her family. When the kids visit her at work, she introduces colleagues as members of her "work family" and indulges them just as she indulges her children, giving them permission to go home early for the flimsiest of excuses, including rehearsals for a Steve Miller tribute band.

The link between taking care of the diner and taking care of her family is clear. Although she tries to throw herself into Fresh Feed, she has no way to really understand working outside of the home. Linda loses the thread between cleaning up a spill on aisle five and nurturing her husband and children, as the relationship between her work and family life becomes too abstract for her to grasp. Of course, the irony here is that despite being praised as an "everymom," Linda fails to understand the connection between doing a good or even passable job at work and taking care of one's family, which the millions of women who work outside the home every day take for granted. The idea of "work family" is widely embraced in the U.S., but Linda never fully comprehends the limits of the work family—that is to say, Linda can't imagine a work family without the love that she shares with her coworkers in her other workplace, coworkers who are also her husband and children.

Fresh Feed disappoints Linda because it provides her with an inferior family. That she holds her workplace up to her domestic standards indicates how impossible it is for Linda to separate her roles. Teddy and Mort, the regulars, panic in Linda's absence because they doubt Bob can match her ability to perfectly regulate the temperature of the restaurant. She balances it gently like a womb, because in a sense that is how much the restaurant is a part of her. Also, that is where the restaurant is a part of her. She conceives of it as an extension of her family, which is why her industriousness and job satisfaction within the restaurant can't translate when she attempts to work outside it in "Lindapendent Woman."

Bob realizes that he doesn't want to run the restaurant without Linda just as she is freaking out as the shift supervisor at Fresh Feed. The grocery begins turning into a looter's paradise with her new staff of Tina, Gene, and Louise, the crew she recruits after letting her employees leave. Bob brings Linda back to the restaurant, restoring the status quo after 20 minutes of turmoil, as every sitcom must. Still, the episode's resolution feels even swifter than usual because it touches on something that doesn't often come up in the program. While several episodes explore Bob's dreams for himself and the restaurant, Linda rarely expresses any professional ambitions. She's given very little space in this episode, aside from a duet with Bob, to express what she finds nourishing about using her skills in a more public setting, where people are encouraged to dance and break out in song at regular intervals.

I argue that this is symptomatic of how fully Linda embodies her role as a mother. To put it another way, all of Linda's fundamental character traits—her desires, her ambitions, and her fears—relate back to her family. Pilot Viruet, writing in the *AV Club* about this same episode, notes that Linda is "hilarious in small doses, and she's optimistic and

endlessly patient with her entire family, but too often ι.
acter trait in any given episode seems to just be 'total puɔ
maybe, 'prone to breaking out in song'), and that's that." Viru
"Lindapendent Woman" as an exception, but in my reading it conɪ.
rather than expands the limits of her character by showing her failinɡ
outside the diner and returning without ever fully understanding what
she might have gained from succeeding on her own.

The expectations for the episode, and the side of Linda that might,
but does not, emerge from employment outside the home, derive from
Bob's Burgers' consistent success at embodying a particular slice of
American life. Again and again, *Bob's Burgers* distinguishes itself from
other animated sitcoms by being so firmly grounded. The program
details the economic reality of this working-class family unsentimen-
tally enough that "Lindapendent Woman" reveals that the restaurant
can't survive without Linda's creative bill-paying and phone calls to the
bank. Indeed, compared to the mysterious prosperity of *Modern Family*'s Dunphys—a single-income family of the same size, solely supported
by a realtor who could also be described as an idiot—*Bob's Burgers*
seems like a documentary. Though its premise shares much with the
socially conscious sitcoms pioneered by Norman Lear that rose in popularity during the 1970s, *Bob's Burgers* is aggressively silly. It's unfair to
critique the program for not giving Linda a chance to make the kind
of feminist interventions that were common (and necessary) to sitcoms
like *All in the Family, Alice, One Day at a Time*, and the original run
of *Roseanne*. Still, given how liberal *Bob's Burgers* is with the kids' personalities, ambitions, and the mostly unconditional support with which
Bob and Linda greet them, Linda's lack of characterization outside of
"fun mom," is troubling.

Even episodes exploring Linda's past struggle to reveal a Linda that
is not defined by her familial role. Season four's "Purple Rain-union,"
could ostensibly explore Linda's lost artistic ambitions (4.6). With her
25th high school reunion on the horizon, Linda gets an unexpected
call asking for her high school band, the Ta-Tas, to play at the event.
After working through the trauma of their last performance, where
they were overshadowed by a better, or at least competent, band (also
all-female) called Bad Hair Day, Linda reassembles the group. Including the rehearsal scene and their performance at the reunion, the Ta-Tas
only play two songs. One, by Linda's sister Gayle, is a keyboard-driven
slow jam with lyrics reminiscent of Prince's compositions for Sheena
Easton and Vanity:

The Genius of *Bob's Burgers*

> Derek Dematopolis,
> your neck hair makes me weak.
> Won't you enter my Acropolis
> and make my yogurt Greek? [Bouchard, Smith]

Gayle's song is so well received that she is shown making out with Derek Dematopolis in his car as the reunion winds down. Gayle's composition expresses a deep and very individual yearning. While her song might be based on her high school obsession, the version she sings at the reunion is at least updated, as it includes the refrain, "Derek, Derek, let's make a we-union." The only song Linda plays must be of a fairly recent vintage, as it expresses her pride in her body after motherhood. The title alone ("Not Bad for Havin' Three Kids") makes it clear that Linda's music, or at least this song, will not give us insight into who Linda is outside of her family:

> I've still got my sexy parts
> I've got two out of five
> I've got two out of five
> This is down here but it should be up there
> This is kind of loose and I think it might tear
> When I bend down I pee a little bit
> But it's not bad, not bad for having three kids! [Bouchard, Smith]

Rather than using the band's reunion as an opportunity to introduce young Linda's preoccupations, *Bob's Burgers* gives us more of the Linda we already know: a proud mom. She celebrates her body in her lyrics, but only in relation to what she has produced—namely Tina, Gene, and Louise. In giving viewers access to Linda's venue for artistic expression outside her family, *Bob's Burgers* once again exposes only the facets of her personality that relate to her children.

On *Bob's Burgers*, Roberts' tone never shifts into the modulated Jersey accent that inflects his regular voice, just as Linda is so fully absorbed into her mom-drag that she struggles to see the opportunities outside of it. In episodes where Linda is given opportunities outside the home, she only reveals the depths of her momness, returning to the family either in an attempt to remake the new space into a domestic space, as she does in "Lindapendent Woman"'s Fresh Feed, or reworking presumably non-mom material into a mom-anthem with her band in "Purple Rain-union." Why is Linda's momness so impenetrable?

Perhaps Linda shows the audience that motherhood is its own kind of drag. The mother as drag performer emphasizes the way motherhood is itself a performance. But what kind of drag performance is Linda

Belcher? In an investigation of Tyler Perry's wildly popular "Madea" character, Timothy Lyle defines two uses of drag in popular culture. The first is subversive drag—the kind of performance of gender that draws attention to the way, as Judith Butler explores in *Gender Trouble*, assigning a gender to a body emerges from a constellation of cultural signifiers and not the recognition of a biological truth. This form of drag forces the viewer to confront the shaky epistemological systems he or she uses to shunt people between the categories of male and female, and when done may well cause that viewer to confront his or her own performance of gender. Linda's drag never falters, but it is still very much a performance, no matter how cheerfully Linda submits to the act.

That cheerful submission, and the way *Bob's Burgers* refuses to break the fourth wall by introducing jokes and storylines that acknowledge Linda as a drag performance, suggest a non-subversive kind of drag, that the audience is meant to accept at face value. This form of drag reifies rather than disrupts gender as an essential category. The performer uses the garb as a way of affirming gendered expectations rather than shedding new light on them, often as a way of allowing misogyny to infect women's spaces. Timothy Lyle, in discussing Tyler Perry's work, explains:

> Nonsubversive drag acts do not work to expose the constructed nature of gender norms; instead, these drag acts highlight, sustain, and even perpetuate the construction, maintenance, and reiteration of gender norms, upholding hierarchal gender relations and normative power scripts that ultimately privilege the masculine political category. Therefore, drag can emerge as an appropriation of radically liberating practice by the dominant power structure. The practice of drag is thus "domesticated" and utilized as a tool to re-circulate conservative, normative logics and to sustain and even to perpetuate culturally sanctioned ideas about gender and its oppressive consequences for females (and those males who fall outside the gender binary) [946].

In his discussion of Madea, Lyle shows that Perry uses drag to enter female spaces but not female conversations. Instead, once admitted to the porch or the kitchen, Perry as Madea lectures women in a patriarchal mode, explaining how they can better fulfill their roles as women. Madea functions as a kind of Trojan horse, her conservatism weaponized by her subversive appearance.

Still, if Linda's not designed to call attention to femininity and motherhood as a performance, she is also not working in the mode of Madea. Roberts' drag persona, both in his videos and on *Bob's Burgers*, comes through conversation. In the videos he addresses the camera like a member of the family, a neighbor, or a friend. While Roberts' drag—usually consisting of a wig, big glasses, and sweater—allows the viewer to place the character in terms of age, class, and gender, Roberts uses it mimetically. Madea's drag allows a didactic man to enter women's spaces and command women to change their behavior. Roberts simply enters the conversation, lovingly attempting to reproduce the sounds and sentiments of his mother.

Now that the show has exceeded a hundred episodes, it's frustrating to have such a limited picture of one of its central figures, despite seeing her in many contexts outside the domestic sphere. However, I argue that expecting a layered portrayal of an adult woman in Linda ignores the inspiration for her character. Linda's one-dimensionality is built into the character. The limits of her interests and expression outside the home reflect her origin. Like a kind of Bizarro-world Athena, the mother on *Bob's Burgers* springs directly from her son's head. She is constructed from the perspective of a child, and as far as a child knows, a mother has no life outside her family.

Linda, despite these limitations, is a powerful figure within the universe of *Bob's Burgers*. Some of this power comes directly from her origins in drag performance. Jennie Livingston's 1989 documentary, *Paris Is Burning*, shows the alternative families created within the New York drag community of the 1980s. Livingston focuses primarily on queer people of color, a group terrorized at the time by a Cerberus: one snapping jaw of racism; another of homophobia; both dwarfed, finally, by the most immediately devastating fangs of the AIDS crisis. The drag performers organize themselves into "houses" to provide protection, mentorship, support, and structure. At the head of these houses is the drag mom—a figure like Angie Xtravaganza or Pepper LaBeija—who herds these misfits. While Tina, Gene, and Louise face nothing like the peril awaiting the young performers in *Paris Is Burning*—indeed, many of the young people Livingston chronicles never saw the far side of 40—Linda's status as a drag performer allows this queer trope to find a home in the most heteronormative space imaginable: the nuclear family. If it is disappointing to find very little dimension in Linda's characterization, imagining her as carrying the torch of matriarchs Xtravaganza and LaBeija lends depth and dignity to Roberts' performance and Linda as a character. *Bob's Burgers* re-frames a common queer trope, the drag mom, as the matriarch of a working-class nuclear family.

Out of the Mouths of Men

If motherhood is both naturalized and de-naturalized by Roberts' performance as Linda, Eugene Mirman's Gene naturalizes motherhood while utterly decoupling it from gender. Traditionally, adult women perform voices for prepubescent males in animated sitcoms. As a business decision, using an actual boy hinders production on many levels. First, children are subject to a different set of labor restrictions, which would be particularly onerous for a show like *Bob's Burgers*, which records the whole cast at once rather than piecing separate performances together. In addition, as any dedicated viewer of the *Brady Bunch*, recently fired member of Menudo, or former adolescent boy can attest, a boy's voice is subject to unpredictable changes as he grows. Thus, the safest route is to cast a woman, who requires no tutors, can work long hours, and will be able to develop and sustain the character's tone, pitch, and timbre. Loren Bouchard cast an adult man, Mirman, instead. In the voice of this adult man, Gene often ponders motherhood, not in the abstract, but as a genuine possibility for himself in the future. *Bob's Burgers* puts aspirational motherhood and actual (in the world of the show) motherhood in the mouths of men. If motherhood, as Linda embodies it, is not a performance but an expression of her nature, then it is equally an expression of Gene's nature. He declares in "OT: The Outside Toilet" (3.15) that "I was born to be a mother!" Gene has parenthood on his mind because his health class is about to issue flour sack babies. Unfortunately, when Mr. Frond calls Gene to the front of the class to "take responsibility for what he's done," Gene drops and breaks the baby. And the second baby. And the third. By the school day's end, Gene is so despondent that he tells his sisters he will be taking the long way home. So it is Gene, alone, who finds a $14,000 talking toilet in the woods (I discuss this as a reimagination of *E.T.* in the "Spielberger of the Day" chapter). The toilet, which never gets a name, becomes the object of Gene's maternal impulses. While lovingly filling the toilet's supplementary water tank, Louise asks, "why don't you breastfeed it?" to which Gene, ignorant or unbothered by Louise's snarky tone, replies that he has tried but the toilet prefers the bottle.

By contrast, Dan Mintz's Tina is very subdued. Mintz, like Roberts, also performs as a stand-up comedian, where his voice is equally nasal and uninflected. Mintz's performance as Daniel in the initial pilot for *Bob's Burgers* is nearly identical to his performance as Tina. Any shifts in his delivery are so subtle that they might be attributed to the superior recording quality of an episode that actually aired on network television.

Note the way Mintz's delivery shifts from playing Daniel to Tina, which is to say not much at all. *Bob's Burgers* is certainly not the first animated sitcom to cross-cast, but it draws more attention to that cross-casting than any other animated sitcom by pairing the low-key performance of Dan Mintz with the exuberant drag of John Roberts as Linda. Bouchard can juxtapose these very different performances of female voices because of the abstract nature of animated representation, but why?

In *Gender Trouble*, Butler proposes that gender be understood as "the repeated stylization of the body, a set of repeated acts within a highly rigid regulatory frame that congeal over time to produce the appearance of substance" (43–4). Animation, particularly the standards common to the situation comedy, could be accused of doing nothing but "repeated stylizations of the body." *Bob's Burgers*, like all animation, presents abstractions.

By cross-casting the humans behind these abstractions, the show puts two challenging representations of femininity side by side. The character of Linda, woven with a drag performance, defines herself explicitly in relation to masculine symbols. The hyper-femininity of drag, which shows, according to Butler, the extent to which all gender is an abstraction, is complemented by the character's attachment to masculine symbols. The sixth-season premiere of *Bob's Burgers* depicts a threat to the romance between Linda and Bob (6.1). Bob's discovery that his mustache is thinning forces the Belchers to imagine a world in which Bob and Linda never fell in love. According to Linda, Bob's mustache is "the friend that introduced us." Linda needs Bob, who in many ways is a far less traditionally masculine patriarch than most sitcoms provide, to keep his butchest signifier in order to imagine a life with him. In contrast, Tina is far less attached to labels, expressing sexual urges that go beyond just male and female to encompass zombies, ghosts, and possibly horses. Her attachment to gender expression is similarly fluid. Though she feels cultural pressure to conform to standards for women's appearance, like the removal of body hair, when inflamed by passion, Tina holds the objects of her desire to less rigidly gendered roles, actively pursuing dance-obsessed Jimmy Pesto, Jr., and the passive/inert shoebox named Jeff (5.2).[5]

The contrast of Tina's optimism and open heart and Linda's eighties-inflected obsession with mustaches and sugary vehicles for alcohol shows the gulf between two kinds of womanhood. Through the monotone of Mintz's low-key tenor, Tina demonstrates the range of gender

expression available for a girl who has not yet settled into the culturally gender-defined roles of wife and mother. Linda, for all her outland-
ishness, is also explicitly performing a role defined narrowly by gender,
underscored by Robert's homage to the drag queens who were the first
to separate the performance of gender from the female body. By putting
these performances side-by-side, *Bob's Burgers* allows us to consider
motherhood as an outlandish performance, while girlhood remains so
removed from gender roles that it can be represented by a man's voice.
Bob's Burgers exploits the tropes of the animated sitcom to feature a drag
performance and a cross-cast performance within a realistic animated
universe. This juxtaposition allows for a commentary on the performa-
tivity of gender roles that no other medium allows.

In Season 8's one-hour Christmas episode, "The Bleakening," Tod-
rick Hall appears as Miss Triple X-mas (not to be confused with her
usual *nom de drag*, Cleavage to Beaver) (8.6–7). Singing the song "Twin-
kly Lights," Miss Triple X-mas' performance awakens Linda to the
kinship she feels with the crowd in the holiday rave, a crowd she had initially regarded with some hostility. The show never breaks the fourth
wall by acknowledging that Linda is also a kind of drag performance.
Instead, the scene allows Linda to regard someone performing a particular kind of motherhood. She connects with the club because she
recognizes the maternal warmth it provides. Miss Triple X-mas brings
comfort, joy, and a sense of family with her song—exactly what Linda
attempts every day in the diner and the apartment above it. Linda and
Miss Triple X-mas both perform motherhood—the fact that they are
both in drag is not the point.

By letting Linda's drag go unmentioned, *Bob's Burgers* suggests
that all motherhood is a kind of drag performance. Season two's "Synchronized Swimming," reveals that Linda still does prenatal yoga, even
though more than nine years have passed since the birth of her last
child. Linda approaches motherhood as a series of roles to inhabit, inte-
grating the ones that suit her well beyond their usefulness, which is why
she still moves into "crowning otter" pose (2.3). In the course of a single episode, Linda impersonates her children by doing their homework
(including writing in Tina's dream journal) and becoming their teacher
by volunteering to be their synchronized swimming coach, turning a
ruse that the kids ginned up to get out of PE into a beautiful reality.
Predictably, the kids reject Linda's coaching, so she quits, only to be
drawn back to the pool by an image of Tom Selleck in her coffee, telling
her that the sexiest thing about her is that she's a fantastic mother. She

returns in time to lead the kids in performance. She takes the choreography directly from her prenatal yoga video, which unlike actual prenatal yoga, enacts the labor and birth of a child. She can lead this from memory (because she acts out these motions all the time). Linda's version of motherhood is a cherished routine she performs so regularly that Gene, who excels at it, says "I've seen her do it a million times."

In one of the few encomiums to Linda, Taylor Rapalyea commends her for being a "real mom," without mentioning that the bar for realism in animated sitcoms is pretty low. So low, in fact, that viewers empathize with Marge Simpson while still laughing when her baby is run through a grocery checkout scanner every single week. Still, Rapalyea notes that though Marge Simpson is occasionally held up as an "everymom," Linda Belcher trumps her in terms of embodying the many facets of American momdom, both physically and personally. Linda's long brown hair, worn loose, requires far less maintenance than Marge's towering blue beehive. Marge's uniform of red pearls and green dress seems hopelessly old-fashioned next to Linda's unfussy Henley or V-neck top and jeans.[6] Marge looks like a drag performer while Linda sounds like one.

Pop culture scholar Ciara Cremin notes, "the lowest form of humor is the laughter that a man is guaranteed to elicit by dressing (clumsily and exaggeratedly) as a woman" (168). While *Bob's Burgers* constantly resorts to punning, the show never uses its cross-casting for laughs. Instead, the vocal performances of John Roberts and Dan Mintz, like Pamela Adlon's Bobby in *King of the Hill*, are simply part of the fabric of the show. The two men bring very different performance styles to Linda and Tina, but the final impact is the same: it points out the extent to which every gendered identity is an abstract culturally determined performance, distinct from embodied reality.

7

Gene-der Trouble

Gene Belcher and Masculinity

In "I Get a Psy-chic Out of You," Gene reveals that he calls his testicles "two small coincidences" (4.16). For many regular viewers of *Bob's Burgers*, this is more than just a joke; it summarizes Gene's shifting relationship to masculinity. Gene Belcher's core identity is consistent, but his performance of that identity vacillates wildly. As noted in the chapter on birth order, Gene, at his core, is a performer, seeking attention and recognition for his creativity. However, the form he takes, like the media in which he chooses to express that creativity, varies.

Of the Belcher children, Gene is by far the most likely to dress up. While that is typical, middle-child-showboating behavior, Gene distinguishes himself by blithely disrupting gender norms while doing so. He not only dresses as a cowboy (and an eerily accurate version), but Gene also: casts himself as every character in *Die Hard*; dresses up as Queen Latifah for Halloween; performs as the sole member of his girl group, The Cutie Patooties; and regularly implies that he has female genitalia, referring to his vagina in one episode and threatening to hand over his sweaty lingerie in another.[1] Gene embraces these roles, not just through clothing, but in his speech and behavior as well. By Season 9, Gene and Louise trade gendered party favors—a straw boater hat for a feathered headband—with little more than a shrug (9.6). Gene brings up the possibility that he's wearing a sports bra just a few scenes later as if the show has simply absorbed this reoccurring bit with no need for commentary.

Perhaps the most concise example of Gene's willingness to embrace and discard identities is the infamous "this is me now" montage. In the ninth and final episode of the second season, Gene introduces himself at the family table as Beefsquatch, the promotional burger costume from the show's premier, topped with a Sasquatch mask. Louise sighs, and the scene cycles through versions of the same announcement with Gene dressed as a cowboy, as *Aladdin Sane*–era David Bowie, and as a Hare Krishna. Beefsquatch, the identity that prompts the sequence, becomes a popular fixture of Bob's fledgling attempt to become a celebrity chef, reliably appearing whenever the audience, or Gene, loses interest in Bob's careful meat management to violently consume burgers. Beefsquatch, as part mythological creature and part fast-food menu staple, resists gender categories, making it a unique choice, as Gene usually selects heavily gendered identities. This departure makes sense, since for Gene it takes Beefsquatch-level shenanigans to seize the attention of his audience. Much of his gender play passes without comment, but Bob must reckon with him as an abominable snowburger.

Within the universe of *Bob's Burgers*, Gene's parents and siblings mostly ignore him when he asserts that he has a vagina or identifies as a girl. The reaction from fans of the show is very different. This chapter follows Gene's exploration of his own gender and sexual identity, locates these identities within the broader context of the show, and asks what his willingness to embrace masculine and feminine models says about *Bob's Burgers* as a whole—and its fans.

Gene Genie

The "this is me now" montage explicitly connects Gene to David Bowie, an allusion that rewards interrogation on many levels, but particularly in connecting Gene with his mother, Linda. "Gene" is a homophone for "Jean," as in "Jean Genie," the first single from Bowie's 1972 album, *Aladdin Sane*. That album cover is the source of the lightning bolt look Gene adopts during the montage. Bowie's ascendance matches up with Linda's cultural milieu, in the sense that Bowie's cultural influence straddles the formative years of the baby boomers and Generation X.

The choice to use "Gene" rather than Eugene, the voice actor's first name, is instructive, not only because it links Gene with the Bowie track but because the diminutive version is also, at least to the ear, unisex. In fact, according to the statistics kept by the U.S. Department of Social Security, "Gene" as a boy or man's name has never approached the popularity of the feminine version, "Jean." "Gene" peaks in popularity in 1937, when it made up only .29 percent of the males born, while "Jean," at its height, accounted for over one percent of the girls born in 1929. With his name alone, Gene blurs the lines of generation and gender. The voice behind that name blurs these lines even further.

7. *Gene-der Trouble*

As I noted in the previous chapter, animation has a long history of casting women as boys. Women can replicate the voice of a boy or young man who has yet to go through puberty while being under no threat of going through puberty themselves, and, incidentally, are not hampered by child labor laws. The casting of Eugene Mirman as Gene puts a man's voice to a boy's thoughts. Many of these thoughts reveal Gene's aspirations to motherhood. The show accentuates Gene's comments flaunting traditional gender roles by having them delivered by a man.

When Gene asserts his maternal impulses toward the talking toilet in what is obviously, if you've read this far, one of my favorite episodes of *Bob's Burgers*, "OT: The Outside Toilet," he behaves just like a Jean. Jean, like Linda, was yet another "mom name" for Generation X. In that episode he breaks six flour sack babies, but still knows his destiny, and carries it out in his care for the toilet. He provides it with water, comfort, and even attempts to breastfeed it. The toilet is the rub releasing this maternal Jean from the genie's lamp.

The title of the episode and the bicycle chase at its close make the debt owed to Steven Spielberg's *E.T.* clear, as I explore in the "Spielberger of the Day" chapter. But rather than simply satirizing the earlier film, Gene's relationship to the toilet actually deepens the emotional resonance of *E.T.* The bulk of the film depicts Elliot's struggle to keep E.T. safe on his own—no one comments on the nature of Elliot's relationship to E.T. Unlike Elliot, Gene explicitly mothers the toilet, and Louise is there to tease him for taking on the maternal role, bringing the audience's attention to the nature of Gene's bond with OT. After seeing Gene's relationship to the toilet, Elliot's attempts to feed and protect E.T. suddenly take on a new cast. Elliot, a child of divorce who spends a lot of time alone or at the mercy of his older brother, embodies the mother absent in his own life as he cares for E.T. After Gene makes explicit his maternal relationship to the toilet, Elliot's protective, nurturing relationship to E.T. takes on a new pathos, particularly since Elliot, unlike Gene, is being the mother he does not have. Meanwhile, Gene, who has more than once implied that he has only recently stopped breastfeeding, can lavish maternal care on the toilet because he has known so much of it from Linda.

Gene's maternal nature stretches well beyond that single episode of nurturing a sentient appliance. Throughout the series Gene tosses out lines implying first-hand knowledge of childbirth. In the third episode of the second season, "Synchronized Swimming," he cries out while performing prenatal yoga in a swimming pool, "next time we do this, I'm going to need an epidural!" Season eight finds Gene commiserating with harried realtor Claire in an episode called "Mo Mommy, Mo Problems":

> **CLAIRE:** I'm only twelve weeks into being a mom but I'm loving it. I'm also not sleeping, my boobs hurt, and I'm up to my neck in poop.
> **GENE:** Been there! [8.19]

Gene's claims to motherhood connect his gender identity to his intense bond with Linda. They already share so much, particularly their love of music, that his insistence that he shares her experience of childbirth feels over-determined, outlandish, even. The reversal of tradition by having an adult man perform a boy's voice, and then to make that boy so deeply identify with his mom that he thinks of himself as a mother allows *Bob's Burgers'* audience to not only hear a drag performance of motherhood, but an adult man performing motherhood, decoupling one of the most gendered roles in our culture from gender. *Bob's Burgers* has two mothers: John Roberts as Linda, and Eugene Mirman as Gene. Gene's playacting at motherhood somehow makes John Roberts' performance feel authentic, even though both are illusions that challenge fundamental cultural conceptions surrounding who and what a mother is.

Genespreading

Watching Gene upend gender stereotypes in his embrace of motherhood can be oddly heartwarming. Through Gene's assertions of past and future maternity and his relationship with Linda, the show suggests that the nurturing care of a mother's love can come in many forms. However, some of Gene's gender play feels like a kind of "manspreading." Instead of showing admiration by playing a girl or woman, Gene sometimes takes uses these roles to assert his superiority.

In "The Kids Run the Restaurant," Gene forms a girl group after finding some wigs in the trash (3.20). The opening of a casino in the basement of the restaurant gives Gene's girl-group, the Cutie Patooties, the ideal venue for their first performance. Gene's confidence exceeds his patience. His band has never actually rehearsed, so he does not hear the girls sing until immediately before their debut, right beside the stage. Gene discovers that the only Patootie that can handle their first (possibly only) original song is a good sport whom Gene has given the stage name Girl #3. Unfortunately, just before they go on, the Cutie Patooties tell Gene that they are leaving the band, as a music career no longer aligns with their goals, which include learning to French braid and collecting glitter stickers. The scene ends with Gene, declaring for no one, "I don't need them. I can be a girl group all by myself! I certainly have the passion." Gene transitions smoothly from impresario to one-boy girl group when he performs the song he wrote for them, "Girls Being Girls," and wears his sparkly gown for the rest of the episode.

Gene never declares "this is me, now" when he becomes a one-boy girl group, but he might as well. Gene shifts his identities with all the unearned confidence of a teenage motorist. In this instance, Gene's readiness to replace the girls in his group indicates more about his megalomania than his gender identity. The most masculine thing about Gene might not be his "two little coincidences," but his belief that he can succeed in any role.

If Gene's willingness to take control, a traditionally masculine trait, seems uncomfortably close to a notion that anything girls can do, Gene can do better, *Bob's Burgers* allows Gene to grow beyond this. By Season 5's "Work Hard or Die Trying, Girl," Gene's self-confidence spins out of control, as he fires the entire cast of his musical version of the film *Die Hard* and takes on every role himself (5.1). However, at the close of the episode, he relents and combines his vision with ex-girlfriend Courtney's *Working Girl* musical, creating a hybrid that truly exceeds the sum of its parts.

"Work Hard or Die Trying, Girl" is the story of Gene making the stereotypically masculine film, *Die Hard*, into musical theater, a genre deeply feminized by its association with girls, women, and especially gay men. In merging that project with Courtney's *Working Girl* musical, Gene feminizes it even more, while reconciling with his reoccurring love interest, Courtney Wheeler. Gene collaborates with Courtney because putting on a show is, finally, more important to him than realizing his singular vision.

The contrast between this episode and the fate of the Cutie Patooties in "The Kids Run the Restaurant" shows Gene becoming more flexible in his creative vision, suggesting that perhaps his willingness to take on female roles in the first place says more about his determination to see them performed correctly than Gene's rejection of the gender he was assigned at birth. Thus, what might be read as genderfluidity on Gene's part indicates more about his ambition than his gender identity, at least in these instances. That his nemesis and eventual partner in this story is Courtney Wheeler connects Gene's flexibility with his gender presentation to his sexual orientation. While the two should not be conflated, Gene's affections and their objects (because sometimes he literally romances objects) must be introduced into any discussion of his gender presentation, simply because part of the way he embodies boyness, girl-ness, or middle-aged-ladyness is inflected by his sexual orientation.

Gene-der and Sexuality

While *Bob's Burgers* gives Gene many opportunities to frame his relationship to gender, there are few hints at Gene's sexuality, which is appropriate given that he is an eleven-year-old boy. Still, even nine-year-old Louise, openly hostile to most living things, gets a first crush, albeit against her will, when she sees Boo Boo from the boy band Boyz4Now (3.21). When *Bob's Burgers* addresses the possibility of Gene's burgeoning sexuality, it takes an even more unlikely course.

Gene's first romantic storyline, from Season 3's "Mutiny on the Windbreaker," is foreshadowed in the first few minutes (3.4). Captain Flarty invites Bob and his family on a cruise. Each member of the family, save Bob, gets a *Titanic*-inspired fantasy of life at sea. Linda, Tina, and Gene each imagine themselves sketched by a blonde young man (presumably Leonardo DiCaprio), while Louise fantasizes about watching the ship split and sink from a lifeboat. The suggestion that Gene's desires might mirror his mother's and his sister's is quickly complicated when Gene falls for Marilyn, a manatee puppet. Herman, Marilyn's "partner" uses Marilyn to flatter Gene into giving her $100 for, she claims, new head shots. Gene fails to come up with the money, but it doesn't matter, as Herman/Marilyn admits to the scam and apologizes. Heartbroken, Gene explains, "I know she was a puppet, but she put her hand right up my heart."

The introduction of Gene's romantic imagination treads a fine line, as the episode begins suggesting that he might be, if not homosexual, then at least something more than straight, as he imagines himself adored as a young woman by inserting himself into the scene from *Titanic* as Kate Winslet. As a corrective, the object of his desires once he reaches the boat is hyper-feminine. However, this object is also a puppet, operated by a man. Gene's first moment as a budding sexual being introduces layer upon layer of complication. Gene's romantic plot in this episode, foreshadowed by the *Titanic* interlude, then manifested in his clearly physical lust for the puppet, acts as a rebuke to any audience member who would attempt to assign a coherent sexuality to an eleven-year boy.

A few episodes deeper into the third season, Gene gets his first human love interest, the forementioned Courtney Wheeler (3.8). In describing her, Gene says, "she talks too much, she breathes too loud and she's always sucking on her necklace." Typical of middle school romance, Gene feels swept away by peer pressure, not by his awakening amorous desires. He consents to go steady with Courtney out of curiosity, not lust. Then, as he gets to know Courtney better, he learns that her father has many musical instruments and writes jingles, which is enough to keep them together until Courtney's birthday, when he nearly gives Courtney a heart attack by telling her how annoying she is on stage. At her bedside in the hospital, Gene admits that he does not like-like Courtney, but grants, "I like things about you. Like your dad, and his stuff." Unlike Tina and Louise's romantic storylines, Gene's erotic imagination remains, at least for the first five seasons, directed toward objects, like his Casio keyboard, his Sasquatch mask, the previously mentioned puppet and the automated toilet he finds in the woods. Still, there remains a certain "Wheel"-they or won't-they tension between Gene and Courtney that the show explores in later seasons.

Though Courtney Wheeler seems like a more obvious choice than say, a plush toy or an appliance, her use as Gene's romantic foil also complicates Gene's identity. I hesitate to presume that *Bob's Burgers* uses "sexual chemistry" as a metric in casting love interests for the Belcher kids, since they are children and *Bob's Burgers* is not trying to enter the Shondaverse. Still, in another example of *Bob's Burgers* gender blind casting, writer/director David Wain provides Courtney's voice. From the sound alone, Wain's performance builds on Courtney's trifecta of annoying habits—mouth-breathing, talking too much, and sucking on her necklace. Eugene Mirman never sounds threadbare or strained, and so putting Wain next to Mirman makes all of Courtney's deficiencies that much more glaring. Nasal and high pitched, Wain's Courtney never sounds like she has quite enough air or room in her mouth to effectively communicate. Several seasons later she becomes a broadcaster in the "Gene and Courtney Show" (6.7). Zeke declares them, "the Siegfried and Roy of our school, and their songs are their white tigers." In this episode, her deficiencies from earlier appearances are present but minimized. While she still has the necklace in her mouth, the audible sucking noises have ceased, partially aided by Gene's readiness to remove the necklace from her mouth. This intimate act is a by-product

iking Courtney, though their creative partnership, it
exist with their love, and the episode ends with their

who maintains on ongoing flirtation/near romance
ong with an endless series of secondary love inter-
Gene's age-appropriate (and species-appropriate)
objects of desire begin and end with Courtney. Yet, because of the way
Courtney's voice has been cast, this pairing feels as grating and awkward as Gene's crush on Isabella, the substitute lunch lady who teaches
him how to love dark chocolate in Season 7's "Bob, Actually" (7.9). Mirman's naturalism as Gene exposes how forced and artificial Wain is in
voicing Courtney Wheeler. And yet, only Gene can subdue Courtney's
most annoying traits, both by collaborating with her and by literally taking the necklace out of her mouth. *Bob's Burgers* turns Gene's potential
romance into yet another caretaking situation, thus reinscribing Gene's
maternal qualities. In a context where other characters might discover
their sexuality, Gene explores a role that is, historically, de-sexualized,
but very gendered: that of the mother.

When Gene is not attempting to be a middle-aged mom, he performs boyhood with little concern for gendered traditions. In Season 8,
Gene directly comments on his willingness to challenge gender stereotypes, welcoming summer by putting a basket on his bike—traditional a
girl's accessory. Gene has every intention of starting a trend—he calls it
a boy basket or a "masket," and sings its praises to an intrigued Zeke and
Jimmy Jr., noting that with it he can move freely with his "wax lips, extra
socks, a free yoga magazine, prednisone!" (8.18). By the end of the episode, Zeke and Jimmy Jr. have adopted boy baskets as well, and neither
seem emasculated. Gene's influence does not feminize Zeke and Jimmy
Jr.; rather, his efforts expand what is masculine.

This encounter with Zeke and Jimmy Jr. brings up the ways that the
show itself challenges contemporary conceptions of adolescent masculinity. Jimmy Jr. often challenges gender norms in his behavior. Jimmy
Pesto seasons his rivalry with Bob with macho bluster, but none of his
three sons—Jimmy Jr. and the twins, Andy and Ollie—take after him in
that regard. Jimmy Jr. loves nothing as much as dancing, hearkening back
to the heroes of eighties romances like *Footloose* (1984), *Girls Just Want
to Have Fun* (1985), and *Dirty Dancing* (1987). While certain corners of
the internet, particularly *Tumblr* and *Reddit*, use Jimmy Jr.'s desire and
talent as a dancer to scaffold arguments about his sexual orientation,
they overlook the context and style that Jimmy Jr.'s dancing takes. When

Jimmy Jr. dances, he kneels, leaps, and spins, recalling Kevin Bacon (or his double) working out his frustrations in the barn or Patrick Swayze as he builds toward the famous lift. The homage extends to the characters' names: both the diminutive "Jimmy Jr." or the full, "Jimmy Pesto," sonically resemble Patrick Swayze's "Johnny Castle," from *Dirty Dancing*.

In the movies referenced by Jimmy Jr.'s movements, there is nothing effeminate about men taking pride in their dancing abilities. On the contrary, in the 1980s, heartthrobs like John Travolta and Patrick Swayze dance as a demonstration of virility, living fountains of testosterone.[2] In describing a scene from *Dirty Dancing* in which Swayze practices on his own, George Rodosthenous nails the classically masculine attributes of the spectacle Swayze performs as Johnny Castle:

> His solo dancing has a "wild horse" quality: rough, untamed, imposing. It is a self-indulgent number that he is practicing in front of the mirror, like a new Narcissus flirting with his reflection in the water. His athletic body is on display ... it is an exhibition of strength, energy, and masculinity [301].

These qualities are especially apparent in scenes where no women are present, as they show the dancer expressing himself not as a part of some kind of mating ritual, but as a way of asserting himself, of discovering his own physical power. Jimmy Jr.'s dance often takes this form. He often dances solo, and early in the series seems to be wishing away observers by dancing with his eyes squeezed shut. Over the credits of the Season 2 premiere, "The Belchies," Jimmy Jr. performs a dance inspired by *Footloose* (2.1). In the original, Kevin Bacon as Ren using dance as a way of expressing hostility and frustration is made very explicit by intercutting a montage of earlier scenes of characters disappointing him. Ren begins by slamming his car door, smoking a cigarette and drinking a beer. Finally, he can't take it any longer, and rises onto his toes, swinging his hips to the beat. Fueled by anger, Ren runs, spins, kicks, and takes out his hostility on a rhythmic, rump-shaking tour of the warehouse. Jimmy Jr. takes on these same moves, with a similar rebellious spirit behind them.

Bob's Burgers uses dancing ability as a metric for masculinity in adult contexts as well. One of the ways Jairo, the capoeira instructor in Season 1's "Sexy Dance Fighting," poses a threat to Bob, is through his dancing ability. Many seasons later, Bob finds the courage to take up dancing himself, as a Valentine's Day gift to Linda. Bob and Teddy end up in a hip-hop dance class.[3] Bob immediately squares off against the teacher's son, establishing that dance prowess is the currency for expressing masculinity, at least in the space of the studio. Forged through conflict, Teddy and Bob present a beautifully coordinated dance for Linda at the end of the episode, so that Bob's dancing ability comes to express aggression and heterosexual romance.

While singing and dancing abilities have plenty of historical and cultural precedents as indicators of masculine virility, Gene's passion for decorative tablescaping has no such history. In Season 3's "Boyz4Now," Gene enters a tablescaping competition with the full, if not particularly attentive support of his parents (3.21). Their attention is merely dutiful until the obnoxiousness of another parent sparks the heretofore-dormant competitive fire in Bob and Linda. When Gene makes it to the second round of the tablescaping regionals, he realizes that he had no idea he would have to do another setting. Bob and Linda pressure him, as Gene's initial success has left the taste of blood in their mouths. Gene turns to the contents of Linda's purse for inspiration. The final product, a tablescape Gene calls, "The Menstru-rant," makes ample use of Linda's cache of pads, tampons, and condiments in a way that makes a dramatic impression on the judges but does not win the day for Gene. In creating the scene, Gene shows that he is in fact more comfortable with the realities of women's bodies than the judges of the competition, using the applicator as a straw, showing the pads open and artistically coated in strawberry jam, and offering the judge a pad for her lap in case of spills. She emphatically refuses to engage with the tampon straw. Still, Bob and Linda are proud, since Gene's rival also loses.

Throughout the episode Gene keeps correcting his parents. They keep calling his endeavor table setting, but Gene prefers the term "tablescaping." This links Gene with Food Network personality Sandra Lee, who brought tablescaping to the mainstream. Lee's signature program, *Semi-Homemade Cooking with Sandra Lee*, was a platform she negotiated fiercely with the cable network. She thought of herself more as a decorator than as a cook, but the Food Network allowed her only one segment on each show to devote to the presentation of the food, even though anyone who has sampled Sandra Lee's creations will attest that she definitely puts the majority of her effort into the aesthetic component of the program. Thus, each episode has a themed table-setting, or tablescape, to suit whatever conglomeration of processed foods Lee throws together in creating her meal. Gene's allegiance to Lee over the woman often perceived to be her rival (Martha Stewart), aligns Gene ever closer to the harried mom he aspires to embody. Lee's shortcuts include sins that go well beyond what Stewart would find acceptable.

If Stewart would side-eye Betty Crocker cake mix, witnessing Lee's desserts, often constructed of store-bought cakes and packaged icing, would move Stewart to Oedipus-level ocular trauma. Some of her recipes include melting ice cream, adding tea, and then re-freezing it to make a new ice cream, a concoction directly from the minds of bored, under-supervised children in the middle of summer. In her television persona, Lee positions herself as the anti–Stewart: her projects (calling the "No-Bake Love Cake" or "Heirloom Noel Cake" *recipes* seems inaccurate) rely on premade cakes and frosting and very little of the perfectionism and WASP restraint Stewart is known for.

While Gene's interests, particularly tablescaping, might seem effeminate, he is not so unusual for the broader gender landscape in which the Belchers live. In fact, Gene is not the only boy at the tablescaping competition. While there are no other cross-dressed kids when the Belchers go out trick or treating, Gene's regal Queen Latifah costume does not make him a target—Gene's a target because Halloween turns all of the younger kids into targets. While Gene claims many trappings of womanhood—including a vagina—no one interacts with him as if his presentation makes them uncomfortable. Part of it is a matter of age—Gene is eleven—but part is also how these declarations are understood within the world of the show.

Louise's refusal to give up her big wheel for a bicycle despite being nine years old and thus well into her bike years, shows how willing Bob and Linda are to allow their children to develop at their own pace. That Gene's enthusiasms have not been redirected into "boy stuff" shows that Gene's willingness to follow his passions regardless of their alignment with gendered cultural expectations stems from the tolerance of his household. In fact, Tina and Louise take a much bigger interest in sports.

Gene's scene-ending exchange at the beginning of "The Like Likeness of Gene" is particularly instructive. It is not only another example of Gene cutting a scene short with a surprising anatomical reference, but also shows him relating to his peers as if he is a much older woman—say, Linda's age.

> **COURTNEY:** I will take a chill pill, I will. Because I have a congenital heart condition and I take them every day.
> **GENE:** I had shingles once.
> **TINA:** I have a cut on my leg.
> **RUPA:** Those things aren't congenital.
> **GENE:** Show's over! We gotta get our congenitals to class.

"Congenitals" is a classic *Bob's Burgers* malapropism, but it is Gene's casual reference to shingles that is very typical of Gene's relationship to gender. Shingles is caused by the same virus as the chicken pox, a much more likely malady for someone Gene's age. Infection rates for chicken pox are the same for males and females, but shingles statistically impacts more women, for reasons not completely clear (Fleming 4). Gene claims a virus that has likely struck him and shifts it so that he becomes victim to a disease that generally strikes women over 50. The joke is a quick but unmistakable example of Gene once again choosing to identify as an older woman.

What's So Funny About Gene's Vagina?

Bob's Burgers is a comedy. Humor and social change can (and in my view, should) coexist, but it's tempting, in the search for role models and cultural representation, to overlook the possibility that Gene's idiosyncratic approach to boyhood is more about making the audience laugh than making the audience rethink their attachment to the gender binary. Gene's rejection of gender norms can, of course, be revolutionary and funny at the same time, but some interpretations of Gene's gender identity require a radical reinterpretation of his humor that seems out of character for the show.

The *Bob's Burgers* sub*Reddit* hosts a lively ongoing debate about Gene's gender (Reset-363). Some of the anonymous participants in these exchanges lack a nuanced understanding of the distinctions between, gender, sex, and sexuality, but for the most part they discuss the extent to which Gene fulfills masculine expectations. The following post initiates the discussion under the heading, "Gene is genderfluid?":

> So, it's my first post in this sub and I wanted to talk a little about this head-canon[4] that I saw on Tumblr, I think it makes sense since Gene's work in the show always was kick [*sic*] gender roles, it's a pretty feminine boy and we've seen him dessed [*sic*] as woman many times, he also calls himself a girl and Belchers are everything but straight, what do you think?

The discussion veers back and forth between fans who see Gene as simply a goofy kid and those who champion a more defined gender and sexual identity for Gene as a means of expanding the representation of sexual and gender minorities on television.

This debate has concluded on *Tumblr*, at least partially. Bloggers like airplanesoda post illustrations imagining the Belcher kids seven years in the future as "The Belcher Sisters," picturing Gene, hair grown out, wearing a feminine-cut tank top and cut-off denim shorts (airplanesoda). Cartoonist Steve Twisp makes an even more explicit statement regarding Gene's gender identity by publishing a comic strip on his *Tumblr* of Gene coming out as genderfluid ("Brainstorm"). These posts receive thousand of notes—*Tumblr*'s version of likes—and seem to generate very little controversy. To be fair, the differences between the *Reddit* and *Tumblr* fan response to Gene's gender identity might mostly come down to the differing mechanics and appeal of the two platforms. *Reddit* encourages conflict with its up and down voting scheme, while *Tumblr* fosters more passive appreciation by keeping its comments in a simple, chronological list. In any case, the activity on both platforms suggests that *Bob's Burgers* has a core group of fans who are very much invested in Gene's sexual and gender identity.

Interpretations of Gene's gender identity find expression beyond fan art. Dana Sayre cites Gene's carefree relationship to gender norms in an essay exploring the possibility that Gene might be prime-time animation's first genderfluid character.[5] Sayre cites Gene's tendency to classify himself as a girl, including his insistence in one episode that he has a vagina. She presents this along with several references throughout the series to Gene's penis to show that Gene never disavows his assigned sex, but is instead open to imagining himself as a girl or woman just as much as he identifies with himself as a boy or man. Sayre's assessment is correct: Gene's blithe relationship to gender, particularly the ease with which he identifies with roles that do not align with the sex assigned at his birth, sets him apart from the legions of wisecracking, scatologically inclined boys who populate both animated and live action sitcoms. However, Sayre never reckons with the way the show uses Gene's genderfluidity. First, while Gene, as a Belcher, gets the most airtime, is his portrayal out of line when compared with the other boys on the show? *Bob's Burgers* never pretends to be a prescriptive, didactic work, but certainly there are moments when the series uses what Sayre's identifies as Gene's genderfluidity exclusively as a punch line. In those cases, if Gene is read as a transgender youth, laughing at his attempts to assert that identity seems cruel. Aside from examining moments where Gene flaunts and challenges gender norms, I also want to explore the way the show relies on its audience's own discomfort with a boy identifying as a girl to generate quick laughs.

Bob's Burgers is often praised for the specificity of its characters.

This allows the show to derive much of its humor from seeing how they respond to each other. For example, Louise's burger of the day, "The Child Molester (comes with candy)" gets a laugh not only for being an extremely dark joke from a nine-year-old girl, but also from Bob's reaction to it (1.1). Unlike Louise, Gene's humor rarely develops out of conflict with the other characters. Instead, Gene orchestrates reenactments of popular culture pastiche. As noted earlier, Gene resurrects the fantasy of *E.T.* in "OT: The Outside Toilet." Gene consciously admires the work of this period. He sees himself as the star of eighties-era films and television shows, writing himself into the 1980 motion picture and television series *Fame* (1982–1987) in "The Frond Files" and creating a musical version of *Die Hard* in "Work Hard or Die Trying, Girl." Elements of Gene's performance of masculinity spring from his admiration for the pop culture of another era, including his embrace of music and dance as ways to highlight his value, much like his doppelganger Bruno Martelli, from *Fame*.

Gene's other comedic mode is the one-liner. These comments are often used as "buttons"—ways to end a scene on a laugh before breaking for commercial or going into another scene. Perhaps the purest example of this occurs in "Bob Fires the Kids" (3.3). Bob attempts to hire the kids back at the restaurant to replace Mickey and learns that they are otherwise employed:

> **GENE:** We're working girls now! Deal with it!
> **MICKEY:** You're a girl?
> **GENE:** Yes, I am!
> **BOB:** No, he's not.
> **GENE:** Tell that to my vagina!

Immediately afterward, the screen goes to black for the episode's final commercial break. The next scene picks up in exactly the same setting. No time has passed, but no one responds to Gene's insistence that he has a vagina. Instead, Linda asks, "you got other jobs?" Breaking the climactic scene of the episode in half allows the show to maintain its viewers' interest during the break. Ending on Gene's line secures a laugh, but the source of that laugh, Gene's insistence that he is a girl, is utterly forgotten when the scene continues. Furthermore, we don't get any reaction shots from Gene's disclosure, making this truly feel like a "throwaway" line.

Unlike other Belchers, Gene's jokes regularly end scenes. Because of their placement, these jokes must work without reaction shots, which means the surprise must hit the audience at the most fundamental level of humor. Under these circumstances, Gene tells a lot of fart jokes. He also tells poop jokes and their elder cousin, dick jokes. Thus, the problem with embracing the jokes that excite fans on *Tumblr* and critics like Sayre is that they are essentially in the same vein as Gene's fart megaphone. Using these moments as evidence for Gene's gender identity ignores their context—and the culturally embedded beliefs about gender that make these jokes so funny they don't require context.

Gene's insistence that he has a vagina, along with his conviction that he will be a mother, are jokes, but why? Ciara Cremin notes, as I mentioned in the previous chapter, that the least sophisticated, most essentialist, amusement derived from drag is the mere spectacle of a man pretending to be a woman as a kind of voluntary humiliation (168). Are Gene's one-liners simply verbal drag? Like horror, comedy derives much of its visceral power from skillfully deployed surprises. When Cremin bemoans the staying power of drag or cross dressing as a source of comedy, she critiques not only the creators who are relying on an easy laugh, but also a broader culture that is still so invested in the gender binary that men in women's clothes still have the power to shock an audience. Many of Gene's assertions work within that model. For example, in "The Kids Run the Restaurant," Louise, frustrated by her siblings' impoverished diabolical imaginations, cries, "This is going to be the longest hour of my life!" Gene replies, "wait until childbirth, girlfriend!" and the scene ends. Gene's one-liner sits outside of the dialogue, as his lines challenging his gender identity (and, in this case, age) often do. Thus, the line itself, not the other characters' reactions, brings the laugh. The show never abandons this well. In the *AV Club*'s review of Season 8's "The Hurt Soccer," commenters kept bringing up another drag-style throwaway line. In this case, Linda, who in collaboration with Gene is turning the diner into a piano bar, orders her son to get all of her costumes and wigs. Gene's response, "but what will you wear?" ends the scene on a note that gives the now predictable charge of Gene breaking a gender norm in the same way he always does (8.12). Later in the episode, when mother and son are shown running the piano bar, Linda wears a red dress while Gene looks surprisingly dapper in a dinner jacket.

In these moments *Bob's Burgers* tries to have it both ways: the show can be understood as progressive and inclusive by virtue of Gene's fearless embrace of traits outside his presumed biological sex, while at the same time the shock value of a boy declaring that he has a vagina gets a quick laugh. This laugh comes from the deeply embedded cultural taboo of observing breaking gender norms, thus it depends on the audience's investment in those norms for its humor. Thus, the laugh, in many ways, is the same laugh produced by drag, as Cremin describes it. Still, these one-liners are not the only ways in which Gene transgresses traditional gender norms.

Even when Gene doesn't refer to himself as a woman, his jokes are still based in the disjunction between his eleven-year-old male body and the strangely maternal commentary that comes out of it. In "Mazel Tina," the opening scene, with Tina anxiously awaiting an email invitation to a bat Mitzvah that promises access to boys from other schools (BFOS), closes with Gene declaring in phrasing familiar to all children, "you'll take the butts you're given and you'll like it!" (4.13). A few minutes later, Gene gets another scene-ending joke, this time about circumcision. Dressing up often develops from or into larger plot points, but the jokes about gender identity sit in uneasy company with the rest of Gene's humor, as part of a larger category of one-liners that seem directed toward the lowest common denominator.

Bob's Burgers clearly expects its viewers to find Gene's claims of womanhood funny; that is why so many of his declarations of womanhood punctuate the ends of scenes. They work on shock value, as verbal drag. That doesn't make the viewers who claim Gene as genderfluid wrong, exactly. Within the world of the show, the Belchers do not laugh when Gene says, "tell that to my vagina." Furthermore, though Bob corrects Gene when he categorizes himself as a girl in the same scene, Gene's family rarely reacts to his cross dressing, verbally or otherwise. Gene's one-liners rely on our culture's reflexive discomfort with gender ambiguity, a discomfort the Belchers apparently do not share.

Implicitly and explicitly, the role Gene seems most drawn to is that of an older woman, specifically a mom. Gene, more than any of the other Belcher children, admires and emulates their mother, Linda. He builds on her improvisatory singing with his constant sampling, as if trying to capture her creative spirit for himself. His admiration for his mother runs deep. Gene and Linda share such incendiary enthusiasm as they plot to turn the restaurant into a piano bar that it's clear why they are so rarely left alone together. Gene deeply admires his mother, who is, as I note in my chapter on Linda, not just his mother, but a drag mother.

The verbal drag Gene dons in the one-liners that make *Reddit* and *Tumblr* dream of a radically inclusive Belcher clan might not make Gene genderqueer, but the way it connects him to his mother might make it more significant than just a dick joke in women's clothing. Gene, as he observes his mother, lives the epiphany Butler describes in *Gender Trouble*. He sees himself as as capable of woman-ness as his mother. Gene intuits that, in Butler's words, "there is no gender identity behind the expressions of gender; that identity is performatively constituted by the very 'expressions' that are said to be its results" (33). Gene's verbal drag has his mother's exuberance behind it, as he recognizes her performance and selectively mirrors it. Gene's one-liners that contradict his apparent gender identity further identify him as the middle child, constantly on stage. Gene often carries a Casio keyboard with a rudimentary sampler function. This accessory masks the true sampler, Gene himself. Gene records and repeats snatches from his mother without context or self-consciousness. While the show has not explicitly created the first genderqueer child in primetime, *Bob's Burgers* has given its audience a version of the family where there is room for the only son to not just adore his mother but to follow his interests without the constraints of gender norms.

Fans' excitement about Gene's gender nonconformity still reveals more about the rigidity of gender norms in our culture than uncovering any "truths" about this beloved character. His interactions, when they don't line up with what our culture sees as masculine, are used as punctuation, so that a scene can end with a laugh. For an audience used to bright lines delineating the boundaries of masculinity and femininity, Gene's slips into verbal drag produce a tension that can only be relieved by laughter. For audiences looking to blur those lines, Gene's cheerful invitation to converse with his vagina feels like a radical acknowledgment of gender diversity, all the more astonishing for taking place in primetime on Fox on a Sunday night.

8

The Marshmallow Test
Bob's Burgers and Complex Identity

When it premiered in 2011, *Bob's Burgers* seemed an unlikely vehicle for the thoughtful exploration of complex identities. The animated travails of the Belchers in an unnamed seaside town fit in so well with the other members of Fox's Animation Domination lineup that many critics didn't bother to differentiate the program from the stalwart *The Simpsons* and Seth McFarlane's trio of family sitcoms, *Family Guy*, *American Dad!*, and *The Cleveland Show*. The scatological humor, not to mention the surname "Belcher," led some to assume that *Bob's Burgers* was merely another vehicle for fart jokes and pop culture references. Writing in the *Washington Post*, Hank Stuever dismissed it as "pointlessly vulgar and derivatively dull," which seems kind when compared with Matt Roush's review for *TV Guide*. Roush embraced the restaurant metaphor, asserting that *Bob's Burgers* is "as appetizing as a salmonella outbreak." However, even in its very first season, *Bob's Burgers* brought up issues of gender identity in ways that were far more nuanced than its brethren, particularly in its portrayal of transgender identity. This chapter focuses primarily on *Bob's Burgers'* depiction of transgender people of color, specifically a beautiful Black woman named Marshmallow, who introduces Bob and the rest of the Belchers to a world lived in at least two dimensions.

Transgender Representation and the Animated Sitcom

Animated sitcoms have a fairly dismal recent history in their depiction of characters with non-normative identities, particularly transgender characters. The portrayal of transgender characters on *South Park* and *Family Guy* provide context for what *Bob's Burgers* accomplishes in its treatment of the plasticity of gender and sexuality. In the U.S., live action narrative television introduced recurring transgender characters in the short-lived 1977 series, *All That Glitters* (Anderson). Since the turn of the 21st century, transgender representation has dramatically increased, on daytime television (*All My Children*), prime-time television (*Dirty Sexy Money, Glee*), and streaming television (*Orange Is the New Black, Transparent*). While many scholars have analyzed the depiction of transgender or genderqueer characters in live action television, animated series are not treated with the same degree of scrutiny, despite animation's limitless capacity for depicting human transformation.

As is often the case, *South Park* got to transgender identity politics before many other narrative programs.[1] Mr. Garrison, a third-grade teacher at South Park Elementary School, was initially portrayed as a closeted gay man, in contrast to the openly gay "Big Gay Al." Mr. Garrison eventually comes out in Season 6. In *South Park*'s Season 9 premier, "Mr. Garrison's Fancy New Vagina," Mr. Garrison becomes "Mrs. Garrison," experiments with heterosexuality and lesbianism, then transitions back as a man in the Season 12 episode where he gets a new penis, grown on the back of a mouse. That episode is called "Eek, a Penis." Mr./Mrs. Garrison's journey is not particularly sympathetic, but then, he is one of the shows' principal antagonists. Despite the signature vulgarity and crudeness of the show, Mrs. Garrison's plot opens up possibilities for the other characters that, in just 20 minutes, exposes the way transgender characters challenge the stability of any identity.

"Mr. Garrison's Fancy New Vagina" develops two plots that quickly intertwine. Kyle learns about Mr. Garrison becoming Mrs. Garrison right after he fails to make the fourth-grade all-state basketball team. He is told, first by Cartman, then by the coach, that as a short Jewish kid, he never had a chance. All the players on the team are tall and African American. Kyle, disappointed, tells his parents about Mrs. Garrison. His mother explains that sometimes people are born into the wrong bodies. This explanation gives Kyle hope. He loves basketball so much that Kyle assumes that he has simply been born into the wrong body. Mrs. Garrison's surgeon, Dr. Biber, accommodates Kyle's wishes, giving him a "Negroplasty" which darkens his skin and lengthens his limbs. Kyle's father, Mr. Broflovski, threatens to sue Dr. Biber for operating on a minor without parental consent. Dr. Biber, noting Mr. Broflovski's t-shirt, offers to turn him into a dolphin. Mr. Broflovski warmly accepts, and returns home hopping on a tail, a dorsal fin protruding from his back.

These new bodies eventually disappoint each recipient. Kyle learns that he can't actually play basketball on his new limbs because his knees are made from Mrs. Garrison's testicles. Kyle discovers this in the most dramatic fashion possible, when his knees explode during a game. Mrs. Garrison's celebration of her new life as a woman is tarnished when she learns that her operation has not made her capable of menstruation, pregnancy, and childbirth. When Mrs. Garrison asks to be returned to her former sex, Dr. Biber notes that he has not only recycled Mrs. Garrison's testicles, he has used her scrotum to fabricate Mr. Broflovski's dorsal fin. By the end of the episode, Kyle and his father have returned to normal, but Mrs. Garrison claims that she accepts her new self, saying "Even though I'm not truly a woman I think I still like the new me. I'd rather be a woman who can't have periods than a fag."

Mrs. Garrison's final sentiment puts an exclamation point on the flaw in this character's shifting self-conception: it conflates sexuality and gender identity. Mrs. Garrison's options are based entirely on her sexual attractions. Mrs. Garrison wants to remain a woman so that she can be heterosexual. Internalized homophobia as the catalyst for gender transition has been widely disparaged by both transgender rights activists and the psychological community. The depiction of Garrison's journey to become a woman totally misunderstands the possibilities of that identity. During the two seasons Garrison transitions, *South Park* focuses on exclusively on the romantic complications that arise rather than treating Garrison as a character with desires that supersede gender identity. By the time Garrison resumes a male identity in 2008, *South Park* had managed to incorporate very little insight about the lived experience of a trans person into the character.

Garrison's superficial understanding of gender and inability to conceive of it as separate from his or her sexuality reveals less contempt for transgender people than for that particular character. Kyle and his father both agree to surgery because they assume it will make their external selves match their beliefs about who they really are: in Kyle's case, a great basketball player; in Mr. Broflovski's, a dolphin. Thus, when they can't fully inhabit these new identities, they abandon their new bodies. By contrast, Mrs. Garrison undergoes her sex change seeking broader cultural approval, so she clings to the idea that she will no longer have to live as a gay man.

In 2014, *South Park* staked out a clearer position on transgender rights with an episode called "Cissy." The most unpleasant ten-year-old in the known universe, Eric Cartman, puts a bow in his hair and claims,

"I'm transginger, I looked it up: That means I can use the girls' shitter." As *Slate*'s Cristin Milloy notes, the program uses the situation to illustrate how ridiculous the bathroom issue has become by showing that only a total asshole like Eric Cartman would abuse the privilege of an all-gender bathroom, and that those who identify as men or women should expect and be allowed to use the restroom that conforms to that identity. The characters who exhibit transphobia are clearly buffoons, as shown in the subplot when Stan briefly questions his own gender identity. Rather than throwing Stan into a whirlwind of confusion, as conservative activists fear, the opportunity to consider his own relationship to his gender strengthens Stan's conviction that he is, in fact, an animated boy.

Family Guy does not share *South Park*'s reputation for timeliness and agility in addressing topical social issues. In 2010 Seth McFarlane defended his programs *Family Guy, American Dad*, and *The Cleveland Show* from allegations of homophobia by noting that he had come out against Proposition 8, the 2008 measure than banned same-sex marriage in California, and pointing to an upcoming episode of *Family Guy* called "Quagmire's Dad," assuring AfterElton.com that:

> I can safely say that the transsexual community will be very, very happy with the "Quagmire" episode that we have coming up in a couple of months. It's probably the most sympathetic portrayal of a transsexual character that has ever been on television, dare I say [Hartinger].

McFarlane should not have dared. Quagmire's father, Dan, is first introduced as a gay character. Upon meeting Dan, Peter and Joe surreptitiously text back and forth in his presence. Joe asks "how gay is this guy?" to which Peter responds, in Fox-appropriate language, "so ducking gay." Peter tells Quagmire his suspicions about his father, which Quagmire dismisses because his father is a decorated Navy hero. What follows is a gala celebrating Dan's service. Dan's brothers in arms assure Quagmire in a hearty stream of one-and-a-half entendres that his father "was really in his element surrounded by seamen," "took more loads than anyone," and "really stroked those privates."

Dwelling on the homophobia of the episode's first ten minutes might seem beside the point, since it is the "transsexual community" that McFarlane promised to gratify. However, the episode never veers from the tone established in those first scenes. When Dan becomes Ida, the Griffin family casually misgenders her, with the matriarch settling upon "it" as an acceptable pronoun. After dinner with the Griffins, Ida needs a drink and meets the family dog, Brian. Ida and Brian hit it off and have sex in Ida's hotel room. Brian returns home bragging about his new conquest, showing his family a picture of Ida. They can't stop laughing, and when he retreats upstairs, baby Stewie explains that Ida is not a "real woman," and Brian vomits profusely.

While Ida, the transgender character, earns the audience's sympathy throughout the episode, the sheer volume of humiliation heaped upon her by the Griffins and their friends make this far from a sympathetic portrayal of transgender life. Instead, by starting the episode with the threat of homosexuality and ending the episode with Brian's visceral revulsion to Ida, "Quagmire's Dad" affirms the point of view expressed by Quagmire himself. When his father comes out to him as a transgender woman, Quagmire's momentary relief that his father is not gay is immediately eclipsed by disgust. Finally, Quagmire says, "come on, just be gay." While Seth McFarlane did not write "Quagmire's Dad" himself, he was certainly familiar with the episode's content, since he voices Peter and Brian. Thus, McFarlane not only read aloud the scenes where Ida is called an "it," but also acted out Brian's horror and subsequent vomiting when he discovers that Ida is a transgender woman. *Family Guy*'s attempt to present a positive portrayal of a transgender woman failed, despite McFarlane's assurances. While it can be argued that the Griffins are meant as cautionary rather than monitory examples, they are so central to the program that, for the 21-minute duration of the episode, their values dominate the story.

Bob from the Block

Bob's Burgers shares more with *Family Guy* than just a Sunday night programming block. Both series follow working class families in small towns on the Atlantic coast. *Bob's Burgers* and *Family Guy* focus on patriarchs who are explicit about their lack of formal education and primarily interact with people from similar backgrounds. The fact that *Bob's Burgers* takes a far different approach to its transgender character, Marshmallow, belies the notion that *Family Guy* could be excused for its insensitivity because it simply realistically represents the way people like the Griffins might behave.

Unlike the Griffins, an explicitly Irish American family living in Rhode Island, the Belchers are difficult to place. Swarthy Bob corrects people who assume he has a Mediterranean background. When creator

Loren Bouchard claims that they are of "a sort of Greek-Armenian-Italian-Jewish-German polyglot," and that their last name is French, he may be obliquely responding to critical attempts to identify the family's ethnic background, like Hank Stuever, who suggests that the Belchers might be Greek or Armenian before deciding that the program itself is too dumb to merit his curiosity. In terms of class, *Bob's Burgers* is far more specific. The Belchers live from paycheck to paycheck. Flashbacks confirm that Bob and Linda have logged even less time in college than Homer Simpson. Their closest friends are Mort, a mortician, Teddy, a carpenter and handyman, and Gretchen, a hairdresser, all White, though their larger circle includes non–White characters like Mike, their Black mail carrier.

The social canvas of the program quickly expands to encompass a far wider range of people. Marshmallow was introduced in the first season episode, "Sheesh! Cab, Bob?" as a friend of three gender nonconforming sex workers Bob meets during his brief stint as a cabbie (1.6). The episode opens with a typical confrontation between Bob and Jimmy Pesto. Bob trades insults while hosing down the sidewalk, a visual pun on "pissing contest" that underscores the pointless, testosterone-infused nature of this kerfuffle. Jimmy yells that Bob's missed a spot, and quickly corrects himself, saying, "oh, no, that's your mustache." Bob's attempt at a snappy comeback, "at least I can grow one," falls flat. When Bob asks Louise for a better line, she foreshadows the episode's major themes by contributing the misogynist classic: "nice shoes, do they make them for men?"

Despite the opening scene, Jimmy Pesto is not the source of Bob's woes, at least not directly. The family is once again in dire financial straits. Tina wants her 13th birthday party to be a glamorous affair that will set the stage for her first kiss. To afford it, Bob takes a night shift driving a taxi. The intended recipient of this kiss is Jimmy Pesto, Jr., son of Bob's fellow pissing contestant.

On his first night behind the wheel of his cab, Bob meets Glitter, Marbles, and Cha-Cha. Bob assumes they are women when he picks them up. When Marbles tells Bob, "most cab drivers are too brutish to pick us up," Bob takes a closer look. After a montage of close-ups of their Adam's apples and facial hair, Bob says "and that's because you are...." Cha-Cha finishes Bob's thought with a raucous, "fabulous!" breaking the tension in the cab as Bob and his passengers actually see each other for the first time. Bob greets them warmly, helps them with their business, and eventually socializes with them.

Meanwhile, Louise trains Tina for her first kiss with lots of yelling and slapping. By the end of the week, everyone is ready for the party but Tina and Bob. Tina can't bear to go without Jimmy Jr., whose father is withholding permission to attend unless Bob shaves his mustache and gives it to him as a trophy. Bob sleeps through the first half hour of the party because he got drunk (and possibly smoked crack), celebrating his last night driving the cab with his new friends—the gender nonconforming sex workers. When Bob finally arrives, Tina sees that his "nighttime friends are there," but not Jimmy Jr., and hides under a table. Bob decides that Tina's birthday means more to him than his pride, and he shaves his mustache. As Bob prepares to tender his manhood to Jimmy Pesto, the sex workers explain to Tina that her father is a good man. They convince Tina, but it's too late for Bob's mustache. Bob emerges clean-shaven with a plastic baggie full of dark hair, a sacrifice underscored by Linda's cry, "you made yourself ugly to save Tina's party!" In that moment Bob is the father that Marbles, Glitter, and Cha-Cha have been telling Tina about. Within that baggie is the proof that Bob's desire to be a good father eclipses his need to assert his superiority to Jimmy Pesto with symbolic displays of masculinity. Thus, the meaningless pissing contest from the first scene becomes a marker for Bob's growth over the course of the episode rather than another example of Bob's failure as a man.

The sex workers' role in Bob's triumph at the end of the episode goes well beyond comic relief. From the moment they are introduced, Bob's "nighttime friends" challenge him to be a better man, even if Bob can't always find the right words to identify their gender identity. Like *Family Guy*, *Bob's Burgers* fails in using the correct terminology in reference to gender-nonconforming characters. After initially calling them ladies, Bob switches to transvestites or transvestite hookers. Linda follows Bob. When Glitter, Marbles, and Cha-Cha enter the restaurant, she refers to them as ladies, and then in an aside to Bob, calls them "transvestite prostitutes." However, on an individual basis, Bob knows Glitter, Marbles, and Cha-Cha's names and uses them without any inflection suggesting that they might not be "real" names. Bob lacks the vocabulary to explain how these women identify, but he never allows his initial uncertainty about their gender to prevent him from enjoying their company. For the week that he drives the cab, they are colleagues. When they blow off steam at the end of the workweek it's not about dressing Bob in drag or taking him to an underground club, but just having a few beers, and maybe some crack. Bob may not be able to accurately describe who they are (transvestites) or what they do (hookers) but he does embrace them as his friends.

Bob shares Peter Griffin's class and educational background, but in the world of *Bob's Burgers* that does not necessarily mean that a cisgender man will find his masculinity threatened by interacting with a transgender woman. In Bob's case, the example set by Glitter, Marbles, Cha-Cha, and, as the show continues, Marshmallow, makes him identify less with masculinity as an end in itself—the mustache—and more with the roles he can fulfill as a man, specifically his role as a father. The visual cues that show Bob realizing his passengers might not be exactly who he assumes them to be—flashes of Adam's apples and facial hair—become so insignificant to Bob over the course of the episode that he surrenders his mustache. For Bob, facial hair was significant enough at the beginning of the episode that he used it to define his own masculinity in relationship to Jimmy Pesto and that of his passengers, Marbles, Glitter, and Cha-Cha. Bob's willingness to shave his mustache shows that these symbols no longer exert the same power over him.

Bob uses his mustache as a proxy for manliness in the opening ("at least I can grow one!") but by the episode's close the trappings of gender have less significance for Bob. Unlike Brian Griffin, who feels betrayed when he discovers he has misgendered Ida, Bob's moment of confusion in the cab allows him to loosen his attachment to his own gender signifiers. This carries over to the portrayal of Bob's new friends, who are no longer observed in pieces as bits of facial hair or Adam's apples but as members of his community. Marshmallow makes her debut framed by the door of the diner, centered in the threshold wearing a sumptuous white fur coat that she hands to Bob to reveal her skimpy white monokini beneath. Marshmallow does not get atomized; rather than closing in on blemishes that might undermine Marshmallow's glamour, she sits at the center of the frame in her debut. The visual message of Marshmallow in her entirety combines with Bob's nonchalant "oh, hey, Marshmallow," to demonstrate the depth of Bob's comfort with his new friends.

Bob's Burgers' initial portrayal of transgender characters in "Sheesh, Cab, Bob!" is not without its problems. Calling trans women "transvestites," and portraying them as sex workers plays into stereotypes that are not only disgusting, but deadly. As Elena Blank notes, there's a double meaning in Tina's quest that comes up at the end of the episode, when a man flirting with Bob's nighttime friends suggests to Tina that they have both kissed their first boy. While the man doesn't seem angry, this points to the dark reality of life on the margins of the margins. Lacking the protection of Whiteness and cisness, trans women of color are dispro-portionately subject to violent crime. As the Human Rights Campaign notes, 2020 saw the highest murder rate for trans people in the United States yet. A month away from the year's end, the murders totaled 39, up from 25 the previous year. Even more disturbing, of 50 states in the U.S., 40 allow the "Gay Panic" defense, which doesn't make murdering some-one as a result of homophobia or gender confusion legal, but certainly makes it excusable.[2]

The underlying message is that while someone like Bob may not have the language to discuss complicated gender identities, he is capable of treating gender minorities like human beings. Moreover, Bob actu-ally learns something from the way gender nonconforming people treat symbolic markers of masculinity that shifts his relationship to his own symbolic masculinity, namely his mustache.

Marshmallow and Bob:
A Love Story

Marshmallow becomes a familiar face in the community and as a regular in the diner, is always greeted by Bob with, "oh hey, Marshmal-low." In the third season, she gambles at the kids' underground casino and receives a pot delivery from Tina. In her first few appearances she is almost a sight gag, glimpsed as a part of a montage or panorama show-ing how vices like pot and gambling weave disparate parts of the *Bob's Burgers* universe together. By the eighth season, Marshmallow becomes part of the Belchers' Christmas celebration in "The Bleakening," both by attending Linda's impromptu holiday bash and chastising Bob when they see each other at an underground rave on Christmas Eve.

Bob's friendship with Marshmallow develops without turning her into one of the oldest clichés of minority representation in media: "the magical negro." Though the employment of African American char-acters as selfless helpmeets obviously has a history that predates film and television, the "magical negro" specifically refers to characters in films who, in the words of Krin Gabbard, "prominently feature impos-sibly gifted black characters who only want to put their special pow-ers at the service of attractive white people" (143). The saintly African American character appears, as Danny Glover does in Lawrence Kas-dan's *Grand Canyon* (1993), seemingly out of nowhere to provide sup-port for the White protagonist, without a glimmer of self-interest (Hicks

28). As Gabbard notes, these characters are often dressed, as Marshmallow often is, in white, like Morgan Freeman's God in *Bruce Almighty* (2003) or Cuba Gooding Jr.'s angel in *What Dreams May Come* (1998).

As I trace Marshmallow's appearances and her importance to Bob, it seems plausible that she might exist, in Bob's fantasies if not in fact, as merely a prop to support Bob's self-actualization. Though this reading is tempting, Marshmallow is not, in fact, terribly helpful to Bob. Marshmallow's cameos in episodes like "Bob Fires the Kids" and "The Kids Run the Restaurant" show her joining the Belcher kids in enterprises that are explicitly against Bob's best interests, specifically drug trafficking and gambling. "I Get a Psy-chic Out of You" includes a rare moment where Marshmallow tries to come to Bob's aid by cracking his back, but the scene resolves with the suggestion that Marshmallow's ministrations may be doing Bob more harm than good. Instead, it is Marshmallow's friends, Glitter, Marbles, and Cha-Cha who actually help Bob, yet they do not become regular parts of the series. Marshmallow certainly carries symbolic weight for Bob, but doesn't actually help him, instead modeling what an unconventional life lived boldly could look like.

Bob's admiration for Marshmallow remains constant as her role expands in the later seasons. Though "Sheesh, Cab, Bob!" includes many nervous laughs, misgenderings, and the use of outdated terms like "transvestite," the later episodes make clear that Bob feels genuine affection toward his new friends. He manifests that affection more and more as Marshmallow returns to the series. In the previously mentioned fourth season episode, "I Get a Psy-chic Out of You," Linda believes that a bump on her head has given her the gift of second sight. When Linda predicts that someone "tall, dark, and handsome" will be next to enter the restaurant, Marshmallow appears. Rather than allow Linda to use the incident as another example of her psychic abilities, Bob corrects her, saying, "Marshmallow isn't handsome. She's beautiful." Marshmallow casually acknowledges Bob's compliment, saying, "blush." While this might seem flirtatious or give the appearance that Bob is overcompensating, as the scene develops, Bob and Marshmallow's ease and joy in each other's company becomes clear. Later in the scene Marshmallow lifts Bob to crack his back, then throws him to the floor and walks on it as Bob cries out. Marshmallow's readiness to pick Bob up and throw him on the ground, as well as Bob's protests, give us a moment of genuine warmth and friendship between them. Marshmallow frightens Bob because Marshmallow is walking on his back, not because Bob is confused about where he can place Marshmallow on the gender binary.

141

The reoccurring gags attached to Marshmallow emphasize Bob's admiration for her. *Bob's Burgers'* Season 6 finale—also the program's 100th episode—finds Bob in a terrible quandary (6.19). The episode has a valedictory feel common to landmark episodes of television. One hundred is not just a round number, but also the traditional number of episodes required to make a program saleable for syndication, which, in the era before streaming, was a major income source for all parties involved.

Coasters, a free dining and lifestyle magazine, is coming to interview Bob and check out the restaurant. Bob's nerves send him to the restaurant toilet, which Louise had covered with a mysterious substance that turns out to be a super-strong spackle. The episode reintroduces characters from earlier in the series: Bob's friend Felix, who is responsible for the sleek bathroom remodel that included the seatless toilet; Skip Marooch, the celebrity chef who tips off *Coasters*; dentist Doctor Yap, who attempts to extract Bob like a tooth; Mr. Fischoeder; even Bob's nemesis Jimmy Pesto has a role to play. Within this context, surrounded by friends and familiar faces, when Bob fantasizes about leaving the toilet, the first thing he imagines is hugging Marshmallow. For Bob, the return to normal at his restaurant means greeting a friend who, in demographic terms, dramatically deviates from the norm.

The Season 6 episode, "The Hormoniums," positions Marshmallow as a combination of Godot and Cinderella. She lives at the center of Linda's story taking on all the parallels of a fairytale princess while remaining regal enough that she never has to appear. Linda successfully peddles one of Marshmallow's shoes, abandoned at the diner and never reclaimed, as it is "out of season," as a wine cozy to Gretchen for 15 dollars. Excited, she tries to get in touch with Marshmallow to produce more (6.14). Bob admits that he doesn't have her phone number, saying, "all I know about Marshmallow is that she comes and goes as she pleases, she answers to no one, and she is truly free." Though Linda dismisses Bob's reverie, the moment underscores the deepening admiration Bob, who was named after his father, who works in a restaurant named after himself, with people that he made himself, feels for someone who resists definition. The plot is resolved when it turns out that large women's high-heeled shoes are prohibitively expensive when used for wine storage, which makes the fact that Marshmallow could so easily leave it behind all the more impressive to the perpetually broke Belchers.

Marshmallow never appears in this episode. In fact, the storyline with her shoe is only the "B" plot—the main plot involves Tina's ambivalence when she joins a group that sings compositions warning about the dangers of teen kissing. Still, Marshmallow hangs like an apparition over the caper, as if the Belchers were the cleaning staff after Cinderella's famed ball. In its reference to this classic story of transformation, our Cinderella, Marshmallow, doesn't even care about reclaiming her shoe.

That Marshmallow never appears in the episode despite being both the explicit and spiritual analogue to the heroine demonstrates how completely *Bob's Burgers* reappropriates the tale. The episode leaves out the classic beats of Cinderella, denying the audience Marshmallow's transformation as well as the circumstances under which one might leave a diner wearing only one shoe. The episode elides these questions, depicting Linda's creativity and entrepreneurial spirit instead. The potential for transformation comes not from a fairy godmother, but from the flotsam Cinderella, the large-scale transformation, leaves behind.

In a sense this episode is a perfect synecdoche for Marshmallow's role on the program overall, in that she is a tertiary figure who consistently inspires other characters on the show while her backstory, which is defined by many of the themes that versions of Cinderella reliably draw out, is never brought into the main narrative. Rather than reading this as Marshmallow being shunted to the margins, I want to read it instead as Marshmallow playing the role for which she is named—she tops the sweet potato of the Belchers' wider community, and with her shade (and she shades) and protection, the Belchers are inspired to develop, even transform, into their truest selves.

Cinderella's transformation is purely instrumental—she must show herself as a princess so that she can claim her birthright. Marshmallow's transformation, by contrast, is just for Marshmallow. She can leave her slippers behind. When the clock strikes midnight, the Black, transgender sex worker has nothing to fear, and Bob, our straight, White male, sees that freedom and gasps. Marshmallow's confidence reveals the fragility of Bob's identity, dependent on the success of his restaurant and the thickness of his mustache.

Marshmallow Is Not a Condiment

The development of Bob and Marshmallow's friendship has never merited a special episode. Instead, it is simply accepted as part of their lives, whether that means Marshmallow comes to help Bob work the farting noises out of his new counter seating or Bob's casual acknowledgment that of course Marshmallow would be among the crowd at the casino in his basement.

Marshmallow is Bob's respite from his role as the exasperated straight man in the Belcher family. In that sense, Bob, literally a straight man (although open to the possibility of being "mostly straight" [see Season 4's "Turkey in a Can"]), could find no better complement than Marshmallow. Unlike Bob, who is constantly reminded of his indeterminate (but White) ethnicity, Marshmallow is Black. Derrick Clifton, writing in *The Guardian*, laments that her portrayal plays into a "trite transgender prostitute stereotype," by featuring her in revealing attire and using her as window-dressing in situations that are already outlandish. However, Marshmallow, unlike many recurring characters on the show, gets more than one outfit—while her white monokini leaves little to the imagination, her green crop top and denim cut-offs, while not demure, will certainly allow her service in a restaurant. In any case, Clifton misses the point. Rather than treating Marshmallow as an opportunity for the characters to learn a lesson, she is part of their broader community. In this sense she's more in line with the transgender conspiracy theorist Lola (played by Shakina Nayfack) on *Difficult People* than the sometimes-saintly character Laverne Cox plays on *Orange Is the New Black* (Peeples). For Marshmallow to be part of the social landscape against which the story of the Belchers takes place represents a level of inclusion that outshines even *South Park*'s thoughtful "Cissy" episode. Unlike "Cissy," in which characters challenge their gender/animal identities for only the duration of the episode, Marshmallow's liberation from cultural norms is a living possibility for Bob, one that he can return to again and again.

As minorities, particularly sexual minorities, gain wider representation in popular media, they tend to follow a path familiar to the integration of other minority populations in film and television, appearing first as villains or figures of ridicule, then in similarly one-dimensional, but positive roles, as saviors and confidants. *South Park*'s introduction of Mrs. Garrison falls into both categories, as Mr. Garrison is both one of the series' longest running antagonists and subject to Cartman's worst schemes. *Family Guy*'s assault on Ida begins before she comes out, as Dan, her previous identity, is subject to a torrent of gay slurs. When she begins living as Ida, Brian (a dog) vomits when he realizes that he has had sex with a trans woman, an act that goes beyond ridicule into visceral disgust. *Bob's Burgers* not only avoids these clichés, but dodges the other trough of minority representation, the angelic other who exists only to support a White, cis, straight or otherwise marked as conventional protagonist.

Perhaps the best example of the way Marshmallow has been integrated into the show is from her appearance in Season 8's Christmas episode. In *Bob's Burgers* first hour-long episode, "The Bleakening Parts 1 and 2," Linda throws a Christmas party at the diner. Marshmallow brings her friend, Art the Artist, and grouses about the closure of the local gay bar, the Wiggle Room. After the party Linda can't find her Christmas tree, and the focus of the episode shifts to a mystery plot with Linda looking for her decorations, which the kids attribute to the mythical "Bleaken," a kind of anti–Santa. Eventually the Belchers end up at a rave in an abandoned warehouse. Linda finds her decorations and calls the cops while sending Bob to retrieve her tree. As he ascends, he sees Marshmallow, who responds to his "hey, Marshmallow," with a dismissive, "mmhm mmm." Art admits to stealing the decorations and explains that the Wiggle Room always looked amazing for the holidays. When he tells Linda that he did it to bring people together for the holidays, she realizes that she has the same dream. Bob draws the police away from the party and Linda and the kids celebrate with Marshmallow on the dance floor. The episode ends with Linda passing out on Christmas morning, full of cheer and possibly drugs.

Through Marshmallow the Belchers find their way to a livelier, more diverse community, without Marshmallow exerting any particular effort. She brings Art to the diner, he steals Linda's tree without her knowledge, and the Belchers spend Christmas Eve at the rave, listening to drag queens and DJs with fake British accents. Though heartbreaking, when Marshmallow blows off Bob's "hey," it shows that Marshmallow holds Bob to the same standards most of us apply to our friends: if you call the cops on the party, don't expect a hero's welcome. All is forgiven as Bob runs half-clothed in antlers and a harness to lead the police away from the warehouse, but before his redemption Marshmallow justifiably crushes Bob in true Marshmallow fashion, with minimal effort. Marshmallow doesn't even bother to form words, letting the effortlessly legible "mmhm mmm" stand in for "why did you ruin our party by calling the police?" Because of Marshmallow the Belchers celebrate a holiday tradition that is far more familiar to queer and gender-nonconforming people: dancing under tacky lights to terrible music. Marshmallow never invites them, but because she is in their life, they have access to these spaces, and each character seems deeply grateful as they dance with Marbles (remember Marbles?) and Marshmallow.

Unlike many relationships between White male protagonists and people of color, or cisgender male protagonists and transgender characters, Bob and Marshmallow's connection isn't defined by unceasing support or ridicule. Instead, Bob sincerely admires Marshmallow, and if he derives inspiration from her, it is purely from observation—not through any deliberate efforts on her part. The Belchers stay at the rave because Marshmallow's presence signifies safety to them. Linda explains to the partygoers that when she called the cops "I didn't realize how wonderful this party was. I couldn't see you. I thought you were dumb kids." It is Marshmallow who answers her from the crowd, because naturally in the over 100 episodes that have passed between Marshmallow's first appearance and this scene, a tall Black trans woman in a white monokini is a comforting sight for Linda and the rest of the Belchers. It's hard to imagine a more sincere argument for inclusivity than this vulgar, working-class family, full of holiday spirit, dancing with their friends at a queer rave.

Though the first appearance of trans characters on *Bob's Burgers* may have used Glitter, Marbles, and Cha-Cha as fairy godmothers to mentor Bob as he becomes the father of a teenaged girl, the show positions Marshmallow as the princess. The Belchers, particularly Bob, demonstrate with her every appearance that they admire Marshmallow's regal bearing as she is, and are grateful for her friendship.

However, as many note, as much as the Belchers esteem Marshmallow, the show itself has a blighted history of respecting women like her. In the writers' room in 2011, the decision was made to have Linda and Bob repeatedly use the term "transvestite." While that offense has not been repeated, the decision to give Marshmallow's voice to a White cis man, David Herman, means that the lack of a Black trans voice in the writers' room was echoed on the screen and has been for years. In the wake of Jenny Slate's decision to stop voicing a biracial character on the *Netflix* animated series *Big Mouth*, Loren Bouchard was confronted on *Twitter* regarding Marshmallow, and replied that he was "on it." At the time of this writing, no new casting information for Marshmallow is available, but I believe that Bouchard is sincere.

Marshmallow, as a Black trans woman, exposes the show's lack of interest in understanding intersectionality. As Kimberlé Crenshaw, the originator of the term, first brought to light in 1989, discrimination is as complex as identity.[3] When someone like Marshmallow is subjected to discriminatory violence, be it physical or structural, it is impossible to neatly assign its cause. Her woman-ness, her Black-ness, her trans-ness: each category plunges her into a past and future of prejudice in the United States. The show elides the dark side of Marshmallow's identity by ensuring that nothing bad ever happens to Marshmallow. Though she is an object of admiration, her perspective never defines the stories in which she appears. Thus, the viewers of *Bob's Burgers* never reckon with the struggles that birthed intersectional feminism despite having the ideal vector for doing so. In worshipping Marshmallow, *Bob's Burgers* ignores the narrative possibilities and lived experiences of people like her. Within the show, Marshmallow is beloved, but the weaknesses in "Sheesh! Cab, Bob?" cannot be overcome by recasting Marshmallow's voice. The limitations critics see in Marshmallow's portrayal will only be corrected when the show, embraced by so many people with complex identities, is also produced by people with complex identities.

9

"You're so good at touching strangers"

Bob's Burgers in Uncertain Times

I write this from a county with one of the highest per capita infection rates of COVID-19 on the west coast of the United States, a place that has exhausted the capacity of its hospital, a place that experts say will get worse before it gets better. I have not gone to a bar, restaurant, party, or my office (which is across the street from my house), in months. My country is also in the middle of unprecedented civic upheaval. Two months after much of the U.S. took lockdown measures to control the spread of COVID-19, on May 25, 2020, Minneapolis Police Officer Derek Chauvin murdered George Floyd, compressing his throat by kneeling on him until he died. Chauvin detained Floyd on suspicion of using a counterfeit 20-dollar bill to buy cigarettes. George Floyd joined a long list of Black Americans killed by White police in recent history, including Breonna Taylor, Tamir Rice, and Michael Brown. Floyd's murder, captured on cellphone video footage that was widely disseminated, galvanized millions of Americans to insist that our country reckon with its history of systemic exploitation, degradation and murder of Black people. How is this relevant to *Bob's Burgers*? These events, one on the heels of the other, may have a profound, even existential impact on the show going forward. In the next few pages, I trace COVID-19's impact on *Bob's Burgers*, and why that impact is inextricable from the movement for racial justice in the United States.

The year 2020 has been fatal to many industries, but one sector that is thriving is home entertainment. Since March of 2020, an enormous percentage of the consumers of English-language entertainment has been in exile. Cinemas, theaters, and stadiums have been empty, giving television an uncontested grip on the imaginations of billions of people. *Bob's Burgers*, with a setting both familiar (a family restaurant) and

148

suddenly exotic (a family restaurant!), can feel like the animated equivalent of a weighted blanket: warm, but not cloying; realistic yet comfortably inoculated against the ravages of time.

James Poniewozik, television critic for the *New York Times*, mentions *Bob's Burgers* as a source of comfort in a column written early in the pandemic before calling binge watching "a kind of emergency shelter." Poniewozik reflects on watching the Season 9 premiere in quarantine. In the B plot, Bob must care for Teddy's baby rat. This is a pretty big favor to do while running a restaurant, so Bob reassures himself by talking about how carefully he will wash his hands. At the start of a pandemic, this moment takes on a new valence for Poniewozik, who winces at Bob's attempt to follow the basic hygiene required during a global public health crisis. Poniewozik explains that television like *Bob's Burgers* can be both a balm and an irritant. As we escape to 20-minute conundrums sketched in bright primary colors, we can't help but focus on what we've lost: the perpetual frustration of a shared office refrigerator; the ability to watch people touch their faces without wanting to smack them.

Poniewozik spends little time explaining his choice to use *Bob's Burgers* as a central example of that escapism—he simply notes that it's a program he can enjoy with his son. Perhaps Poniewozik thought of *Bob's Burgers* because, as a network animated program with a fairly broad appeal, it might be an unlikely source for the anxiety that is the focus of his essay. However, in ways Poniewozik doesn't bring up, focusing on *Bob's Burgers* at the beginning of this global pandemic presented an opportunity to think about how both the content of our entertainment and its context may be forever impacted by COVID-19.

Television production requires a great deal of labor and coordination under any circumstances, but making it safely while following public health protocols is a formidable task. How much should actors get paid to risk kissing a coworker, particularly if they, or members of their household, are part of a group at great risk of suffering complications from COVID-19? Of course, the actors are only the tip of the iceberg in terms of production workers put in forced proximity to one another. Hair and make-up artists, drivers, caterers—it's daunting to consider how many elements of production must be accounted for when thinking about how live action television production might go forward without a vaccine. Tyler Perry, with his own production empire near Atlanta, was the first to announce a return to live action production. His plans require that the entire crew reside on set—only possible because his studios are located on a decommissioned military base.[1]

Of course, while Atlanta has become an entertainment hub, it's not Hollywood. California Governor Gavin Newsom announced that production could resume on June 12, 2020, but given all the new standards and precautions, studios did not go right back to work (Faughner). Soap operas, the programs that produce the most episodes on the shortest timelines, were the first live action series to go back into production in Los Angeles. Of these, the first to return to production, *The Bold and the Beautiful*, convened on June 17, 2020, after exactly three months dark (Bahr). Executive producer Bradley Bell noted that at first, the writers tried to pitch in by designing scenarios where the characters would not have to touch each other, but, given the program and, moreover, the genre's focus on romantic intrigue, that would not be possible. Instead, they would use camera angles to make it seem as if the actors are much closer to each other than they are, and, for embraces, kisses, and caresses, Bell said they would bring in mannequins. When possible, they would even use the actors' spouses as doubles.[2]

Despite these precautions, production closed on the second day due to several positive tests for COVID-19 (Vary). Though Bell assured the public that these were false positives, if the mechanism for determining who should and should not be going to work is this flawed, any return to production seems premature. Los Angeles began shutting down again in light of skyrocketing infection rates, while other potential shooting hubs are in states with a reputation for closing too late and opening too soon, like Georgia, the aforementioned home of Tyler Perry's production company. As Michelle King, the creator of *The Good Wife*, notes, the locations with the most data-driven approaches to addressing the pandemic, like New York City and California, aren't particularly warm to the idea of having a production shoot on location, while the other option, using a soundstage, creates an environment that is much more conducive to the spread of the disease (Vary). The general feeling among executives is that every production planned before COVID-19 will be far more expensive to create during the pandemic, noting the time and money that will be expended on testing, new cleaning protocols, equipment, and the digital effects required to simulate the large crowds once supplied by background actors (Aurthur and Vary).

In light of this new reality, animation seems like the only way forward. For the most part, animation takes place in three settings: the writers' room, the recording booth, and the computers that animators use to add dimension to those words. All three seem eminently possible under quarantine conditions. In fact, at the same time that *Deadline* and *Variety* were publishing articles about the future of television production, the *New Yorker* gave a little portrait of a day in the life of an animated show during a pandemic. Writer Laura Lane sat in on the first table read over Zoom of the Netflix series *Big Mouth* and talked to the writers about how the writers' room has changed now that they are part of a grid on a screen rather than gathered around a charcouterie tray and a whiteboard. Work on the next season took on a new shape, but creator Nick Kroll expressed no doubts that the season would be completed.

Given how relatively bright its futures look in comparison to live action production, it's not surprising that animation has seeped into live action shows whose seasons were interrupted by the virus. *One Day at a Time* (2017), a multi-camera sitcom, became animated for a special episode scripted, but not shot, after production shut down. Executive producer Gloria Calderón Kellett came up with the idea, partly because she is married to a cartoonist, and partly because the episode consists mostly of hypothetical situations and flashbacks (Andreeva). While the special was greeted with mixed reviews, the negatives had less to do with the medium than with the writing, so it's certainly possible that other programs may take this route in order to maintain popular interest in a property during the production shutdown (Leeds). In the case of *One Day at a Time*, the show may never return to its original format, as it was one of the few contemporary sitcoms shot in front of a live studio audience.

Thus, the pragmatic television viewer looking for a binge with no end in sight might invest heavily in animated programs, as they have the best chance of maintaining their production schedules. Unfortunately, *Bob's Burgers* is not one of those programs. Though many viewers might not be aware, *Bob's Burgers* differs from most animated shows in that its core cast records episodes in person. Some lines come not from the writers, but from the voice actors riffing in the same room. Though viewers might not be consciously aware of the difference this makes, it's a very real presence on the show. Not only does *Bob's Burgers* have the kind of wacky throwaway lines that can only come from improvisation, it also has characters talking over each other and cutting each other off in ways that sound reactive. It's unlikely that these effects can be replicated by voice actors recording their dialogue alone, in the comfort of their own homes. Consider how much more lively and chaotic sounding the interplay between the kids on *Bob's Burgers* is when contrasted with, say, the kids on *The Simpsons*.

Loren Bouchard had been very frank about the impact recording together has on the show. Bob's exasperation, according to Bouchard, flows naturally from voice actor H. Jon Benjamin's personality. When asked about his approach to recording actors in 2011, he explained:

> We're religious about trying to get people together. It's sacrosanct and it's much harder to schedule, but in our opinion, it's worth it. Having the actors together is one of the most important things that we can do. They feed off each other. They get a kick out of each other, and again, that goes back to that tone that Benjamin brings as Bob. It's like it's partly real. He loves working with Eugene [Mirman, who plays Bob's son Gene], then he gets annoyed with everyone because he's a misanthrope, and then he gets amused again. Trying to put some of that energy into a cartoon has just been this thing I've been trying to do [Keller, "Loren Bouchard"].

Bouchard generously credits his voice actors with shaping their characters in interviews—compliments that often hinge on the way that the show is built with live actors in the studio.

The repercussions of Bouchard's belief in the chemistry between his performers driving the comedy of the show manifests in his casting. In many instances, Bouchard casts for guest roles based on pre-existing relationships between actors. Bouchard cast Kurt Braunholer as Louise's nemesis, Logan, because Braunholer had worked as Kristin Schaal's partner in comedy for many years (Adams, "Bouchard Breaks Down" [1 of 5]). Similarly, H. Jon Benjamin's original comedy partner, Sam Seder, recurs as Hugo, who, as both Linda's former fiancé and a health inspector, is Bob's chief antagonist in early seasons of the show (Adams, "On Sympathetic Leg Hair" [2 of 5]). Though Bouchard doesn't claim to know how long Seder and Benjamin have known each other, he credits their long relationship with allowing for a kind of rapport that he finds entertaining, not only because of what it brings to the writing, but because of the possibilities for the actors to improvise with each other. Thus, while there will be more episodes of *Bob's Burgers*, the texture of the show might be very different under circumstances where the actors will no longer sit together in the same room as they record.

Loren Bouchard responded to a piece imagining what the Belcher family would do during a quarantine shutdown by tweeting that the writers are still working on Season 11, but there is no plan to address COVID-19 within the show. Despite the intent of Bouchard's tweet, according to his own assessment of what makes the show unique, this will not be the *Bob's Burgers* that has made us all feel safer at home, simply because there is no way, right now, to make more episodes of that show. The quality that differentiates *Bob's Burgers* from other animated sitcoms must be sacrificed for the health and safety of everyone involved. Compared to the impact the COVID-19 crisis has had on other programs, it seems like a pretty minor adjustment, but it will be difficult to parse if the show feels flat because the voice cast can't record together or because the writers can no longer gather in-person to develop their ideas. If the audience fails to notice, then perhaps the lively aspects of *Bob's Burgers* really did come from the writers all along.

Getting attached to *Bob's Burgers* in quarantine represents a poignant, charming choice to remain invested in the past. Unlike *Big Mouth* and other animated programs, *Bob's Burgers* was designed to incorporate the interplay of people in a room into its animated world. Obviously, putting people in a room together might not be possible for future seasons, as the show, like all of us, must forge a new path during this pandemic. These challenges will finally reveal the true measure of what Bouchard thinks of as *Bob's Burgers'* secret sauce.

If the new episodes prove Bouchard to be mistaken, it could be a great benefit to the show, as it might allow for a broader group of actors to work on *Bob's Burgers* and in animation in general. Anyone of any race or gender who can speak could provide a voice, but *Bob's Burgers* skews horrifically White and male, to the extent that its most popular non–White, non-cis character, Marshmallow, was originated by a cis White man, David Herman. Along with COVID-19, the first half of 2020 launched another threat to *Bob's Burgers*, one that many people have seen coming for a while: the threat that a show so dominated by White male voices might not be a show that audiences have an appetite for in a world striving for equity.

Bob's Burgers has faced criticism over the years for the lack of diversity in its cast. Among the actors portraying core Belchers, all are White, and only one is a woman. Though he wasn't specifically addressing these criticisms, in a 2013 interview Bouchard responded to the question of why so many female characters are voiced by men by bringing up the ineffable qualities that come from an incongruous pairing of body and sound:

> For me it's similar to having an adult play a kid: You get a weird energy from that voice that doesn't quite fit. And it's not the joke. It's not that a man is doing a woman's voice. It's just how to get that energy on the screen and in the track. Sometimes, the way to do that is to have a woman play a woman and have a man play a man, but other times cross-gender casting will get you that. We're not trying to take work away from funny women—it's another way to get an interesting voice coming out of a character's mouth [Adams, "On Sympathetic Leg Hair" (2 of 5)].

Bouchard's process brings incredible results. The comment above comes out of a consideration of the third season of *Bob's Burgers* which is, if not the show's peak, then the beginning of a plateau. The problem, of course, is that these voices that play so well together tend to resemble each other in ways that make the world of the show, like the U.S. entertainment industry as a whole, far less diverse than its audience. This is the conundrum: some of the charm of the show is built on the exclusionary hiring policies that have produced a seemingly endless stream of White faces expressing White points of view.

When actors of color appear on the show, they are inevitably playing characters who are BIPOC. Tim Meadows, a Black actor who, as of the tenth season, has the most appearances on the show of any non–White person, plays Mike Wobbles, better known as Mike the Mailman.[3] Known better by his uniform than his last name, Mike has never been at the center of even a B-plot, and functions mostly as background. Aziz Ansari's Daryl has fewer appearances, but is more memorable because, as a fellow student at Wagstaff, he gets embroiled in plots involving the kids. He even becomes the subject of one of the show's few discussions of race when the following exchange occurs, in the Season 2 episode, "BurgerBoss," while Bob is high on painkillers:

> **BOB:** Let's be honest, there's a race thing going on here. Darryl, you're … something, Black?
> **DARRYL:** That is not the issue.

Some viewers see this exchange as evidence that Darryl is Black, along with the similarity between his coloring and Mike's ("What Ethnicity Is DRL?"). In any case, the character hasn't appeared on *Bob's Burgers* episodes conceived since accusations of sexual misconduct by Aziz Ansari surfaced in early 2018, so it seems very possible we have seen the last of Darryl, who as a fan favorite and love interest for Tina, might have eclipsed Mike the Mailman as the most visible person of color on the show.

The idea that a frisson of interest is created by casting someone who doesn't necessarily resemble the character they are playing applies only to cisgender White people on *Bob's Burgers*. As I noted in an earlier chapter, men provide the voices of women, from Linda and Tina, to secondary characters like David Wain's Courtney and H. Jon Benjamin's Ms. LaBonz. Black guest actors like Wanda Sykes, Jordan Peele, and Keegan-Michael Key play only Black characters. Of course, there are so few people of color in the *Bob's Burgers* universe that using actors of color to bring more diversity to the show is tough to argue against. In recent seasons incidental characters, like Nat the limo driver's estranged wife, are cast with and portrayed as people of color, which is a great step for the show both in terms of getting a better variety of voices and making the *Bob's* universe more like our own.

In terms of cross-racial casting on *Bob's Burgers*, the most prevalent examples are Melissa Bardin Galsky's Ms. Jacobson, a teacher at Wagstaff, and David Herman's Marshmallow, one of the most beloved recurring characters on the show. The casting of White actor, writer, and producer Melissa Bardin Galsky as Black teacher Ms. Jacobson is less surprising after reviewing her history with Loren Bouchard. Galsky starred in his earlier series *Home Movies* (2002–2004) and was a part of his team on *Dr. Katz, Professional Therapist* (1995–2002). Galsky's character, a hopeful but often exasperated middle school teacher, generally appears as a way of introducing a challenge for Tina and her classmates—letting them know that a dance is coming up, or assigning Tina and her classmates a report on "a place that inspires them" (10.21). Though no overt reference to race is ever made—people often comment on her beauty—Ms. Jacobson is rendered in the same shade of brown as Mike and Darryl. By representing Tina's teacher as a person of color, the show makes the world of *Bob's Burgers* more inclusive. Teachers can be pretty and Black, like Ms. Jacobson, or stout, White, and grumpy, like Ms. LaBonz. Unfortunately, in the case of *Bob's Burgers*, this diversity is literally two-dimensional; behind both characters are two people who have been working with the show's creator for over a decade.

Marshmallow, the other notable example of racial cross-casting on *Bob's Burgers*, debuts in an episode that opens up a myriad of questions about how underrepresented groups show up in pop culture and how pop culture should have shown up for them. As I detail elsewhere, Marshmallow first appears as part of a clique of transgender sex workers in the first season episode "Sheesh! Cab, Bob?." Among her friends were Steve Agee's Glitter, Jack McBrayer's Marbles, and Oscar Nuñez' Cha-Cha. Unlike Marshmallow, the other sex workers lack a definitive gender identity. Depicting them in short skirts and heels, with distinctive Adam's apples, the show underlines the way their femininity contrasts with typically masculine identifiers but does not make it clear whether they identify as women. Unlike Glitter and Marbles, Cha-Cha— depicted with shiny black hair—speaks with an accent. Nuñez, best known for his many years as beleaguered gay accountant Oscar on *The Office* (2005–2013), does not speak English with an accent. Still, hiring a

Cuban American actor to play Cha-Cha was likely a conscious decision on the part of the show. According to veteran voice actor Ron Paulsen, from the 1990s on, there was a general movement among the voice acting community to find actors that match, rather than mimic, an actor's heritage or discourse community (Eakin, "Voice Actor Rob Paulsen"). Using a Latinx actor to play a Latinx character does not absolve *Bob's Burgers* from the kind of racism *The Simpsons* perpetrated in the form of Apu.[4] Addressing these problems in animation means confronting both the limits and the possibilities of this medium. In live action, viewers can conflate a character's race with that of their portrayer. The color palette of animated programs traditionally is very limited, so an exaggerated accent is used as a signifier. Thus, in case naming her after a Cuban dance wasn't enough, Nuñez gives Cha-Cha an exaggerated Cuban accent.

Not every non–White character gets the Cha-Cha treatment. Ken Jeong's Dr. Yap speaks General American English, despite the actor's demonstrated abilities, particularly in the *Hangover* series of movies, to speak with an exaggerated East Asian accent. The other most prominent characters of Asian descent come out of Bob and Louise's obsession with a fictional series of Japanese films featuring a father and daughter samurai theme, *Hawk & Chick*. In discussing the casting of Keisuke Hoashi, an American of Japanese descent, as Hawk, Rich Renaldi talked about the difficulty in filling a role outside of their usual repertory, but because Hawk/Shinji Kojima would have to speak both Japanese and English, they needed an actor who was either Japanese or of Japanese descent. Hoashi, an Asian American actor who was thrilled to be on the show, noted that a Japanese actor would not have been able to deliver the same performance as they would have been unlikely to get the jokes ("Behind *Bob's Burgers* Live Episode 11"). The role of daughter Yuki Kojima allowed for more flexibility, but the show was consistent and cast another actor of Japanese descent, Suzy Nakamura.

What is never said directly, but seems clear when looking at the way casting BIPOC works, is that using an actor of color lends credibility to what might otherwise be baldly offensive. Ken Jeong's accent in *The Hangover* would have sparked protests had it come from the mouth of a White actor. Even though Jeong, who was a practicing physician before becoming a performer, is so apolitical that he blithely sat next to brazen anti-vaxxer Jenny McCarthy as a fellow judge on *The Masked Singer*, he might not do a part like that now. In any case, when BIPOC are cast in animated roles, they are often used to legitimize racial stereotypes, like

9. *"You're so good at touching strangers"*

Oscar Nuñez' Cha-Cha. If this seems less offensive than, say, Mel Blanc's work as the voice of Speedy Gonzales, the reliance on ethnic stereotypes for laughs cheapens the show in which it appears, and of course, *Bob's Burgers* seems recent enough to know and do better.

Making an effort to create more diverse roles can make a difference, but the utility of actors of color is only recognized by non–White animated showrunners like Aaron McGruder. McGruder's show *The Boondocks* had a predominantly Black cast, including Black comedian Charlie Murphy as White drug dealer Ed Wuncler III. As a general rule, however, White actors can be cast because they are the funniest ones for the role, while non–White actors are sought and cast specifically to play non–White roles, and rarely cross-cast, leading to an animation landscape where voice talent like David Herman (Marshmallow on *Bob's Burgers*) and Hank Azaria (Apu on *The Simpsons*) regularly don black and brownface.

On June 24, 2020, Jenny Slate refused to maintain the charade that this was simply a matter of being the funniest voice. Jenny Slate portrayed Missy, a biracial adolescent girl on the Netflix animated sitcom *Big Mouth*, for four seasons. She explained why she would no longer do so on Instagram:

> At the start of the show, I reasoned with myself that it was permissible for me to play "Missy" because her mom is Jewish and white—as am I. But "Missy" is also Black, and Black characters on an animated show should be played by Black people. I acknowledge how my original reasoning was flawed, that it existed as an example of white privilege and unjust allowances made within a system of societal white supremacy, and that in me playing "Missy," I was engaging in an act of erasure of Black people. Ending my portrayal of "Missy" is one step in a life-long process of uncovering the racism in my actions.

Jenny Slate stops short in calling what she did blackface, but it seems like the world is coming around to seeing cross racial casting in that light.

Slate's announcement impacts *Bob's Burgers* on several levels. First, any regular viewer of *Bob's Burgers* recognizes Jenny Slate's talent as a voice actor; she has appeared as Tina's antagonist, Tammy, in over 40 episodes. Due to Slate's visibility and the momentum of the Black Lives Matter movement, just hours after Slate's post, Loren Bouchard, along with the other executive producers of his latest series, *Central Park*, released a statement regarding the casting of White actor Kristen Bell as Molly, a biracial girl:

> Kristen Bell is an extraordinarily talented actress who joined the cast of Central Park from nearly the first day of the show's development—before there

was even a character for her to play—and she has since delivered a funny, heartfelt, and beautiful performance.

But after reflection, Kristen, along with the entire creative team, recognizes that the casting of the character of Molly is an opportunity to get representation right—to cast a Black or mixed race actress and give Molly a voice that resonates with all of the nuance and experiences of the character as we've drawn her. Kristen will continue to be a part of the heart of the show in a new role but we will find a new actress to lend her voice to Molly.

We profoundly regret that we might have contributed to anyone's feeling of exclusion or erasure.

Black people and people of color have worked and will continue to work on Central Park but we can do better. We're committed to creating opportunities for people of color and Black people in all roles, on all our projects—behind the mic, in the writers room, in production, and in post-production. Animation will be stronger for having as many voices, experiences, and perspectives as we can possibly bring into the industry. Our shop and our show will be better for respecting the nuances and complexity around the issue of representation and trying to get it right.

On her own Instagram, Bell called playing Molly "an act of complicity" and "wrong." Unlike the executives, she makes no attempt to deflect from her culpability. Of course, Bell, also the voice of Anna in the incredibly popular *Frozen* films, has very little to lose by ceasing her association with a streaming television show, but the fact that it takes the actors, not the creators of the show, to confront these problems is disheartening, as it suggests that better, more thoughtful content will have to come from an entirely different set of voices.

If the problems with the diversity of representation on *Central Park*, or, more germane to this book, *Bob's Burgers*, could be attributed to a single person, it would be creator Loren Bouchard, who seems, by all accounts, to be a generous and thoughtful man. However, he is a man of his times. His vision of the world saw no problem using David Herman as the voice of Marshmallow. Bouchard consistently explains his casting decisions by leaning on the chemistry between actors and his own reluctance to work with new people. While discussing voice casting in a 2011 interview, Bouchard said, "I tend to think of all new voices as a potential for failure, and all the people I've worked with before as the greatest potential for success" (Keller "Loren Bouchard"). This explains why Herman, also the voice of Mr. Frond, would be used rather than attempting to find an actor who could relate to the experience of a Black transgender woman.[5] However, when asked several months before making the apology and pledging to recast Molly on *Central Park*, Bouchard made it sound like those decisions were so artistically driven as to be beyond his control. In January 2020, six months before the kerfuffle, Bouchard defended the choice to cast a White actress as a biracial girl by leaning on the particular talents of that White actress, saying, "Kristen needed to be Molly, like we couldn't not make her Molly. But then we couldn't make Molly white and we couldn't make Kristen mixed race, so we just had to go forward" (Murphy "Kristen Bell"). This seems like a shocking failure of imagination on Bouchard's part. Bell and Bouchard had not worked together before, but Bell's status as an actress, from the neo-noir series *Veronica Mars* (2004–19), to the comedy *The Good Place* (2016–20), along with her starring role in one of the most successful animated films of all time, *Frozen*, probably allayed some of Bouchard's anxiety about working with new people. That he could overcome his aversion to new people to cast Bell is not surprising, but that he never considered a Black or biracial actress to play the character is shameful. *Bob's Burgers* owes its warm, silly heart to Bouchard and the people he hires. Historically, it has included more women in the writers' room than comparable shows, and more women and girls' stories on screen, which goes a long way to explain its popularity. However, success in one kind of diversity can't excuse failures in another, and I think it's clear that *Bob's Burgers* has failed in its representation of BIPOC thus far.

Shortly after Bouchard shared the *Central Park* statement on his *Twitter* account, a fan commented, "now do the same for our girl, Marshmallow." Bouchard replied, "yes. On it." Committing to recast Marshmallow, a character who, despite her popularity, has, as of this writing, only appeared in 11 episodes, will not be arduous. As a fan, I'm glad Bouchard will do it, because Marshmallow could just as easily disappear from the show entirely, as Darryl did when Aziz Ansari became a divisive figure. Alison Foreman, writing in *Mashable*, criticizes the show for using Marshmallow as an empty symbol for *Bob's Burgers'* commitment to depicting diversity, noting that Marshmallow not only has almost no character development, but that she doesn't even appear in an episode with a plot devoted to Marshmallow's shoe. I explore Marshmallow's role in more detail in an earlier chapter, but it's worth noting here that Foreman's valid concerns will likely never be addressed.

The possibilities for *Bob's Burgers* are determined by the interests of its creator and writing staff. Unfortunately, as difficult as it might seem to get diversity in the voice cast, it's far more challenging to achieve in the writers' room, where the ranks are often filled by known quantities—friends, or, notoriously in the case of the *Simpsons*, people who worked on the *Harvard Lampoon*. Joey Soloway circumvented this in creating *Transparent* by simply hiring people they thought would be able to accurately represent the characters and then teaching them how to write for television. They solicited essays from queer and transgender artists, activists, and academics. Soloway spent a week with those they hired giving the writers new to the medium a crash course in television (Levy). Of course, the process of assembling a team for a prestige streaming program will differ from that of a network sitcom. *Transparent* never had more than ten episodes for each of its five seasons, while the writers for *Bob's Burgers* must churn out more than twice as many, with buttons every few minutes to send the audience into commercial with a chuckle—a rhythm that streaming television does not require. What reaches the screen is obviously dependent on what happens in the writers' room. Television, particularly animated television, is much more driven by its writers and producers—who are often promoted from the writing ranks—than film. *Bob's Burgers* has had a very stable core of writers over its run so far, with only 20 different writers credited over its ten seasons as of 2020.[6] Of those twenty writers, six are women, and one, Asian American writer and performer Kelvin Yu, is a person of color. If these demographics are woefully out of line with *Bob's Burgers'* audience, they are not unusual for an animated sitcom, or, honestly, most mainstream American entertainment. For comparison, *The Simpsons* has 150 different credited writers as of the close of the 2019–2020 season. Among them, only 17 are women. *Bob's Burgers* at least closes the gender gap significantly with women making up 30 percent of its credited writers. As relatively progressive as *Bob's Burgers* has been in areas like gender and sexuality, the current voice cast and writing staff does not auger a lot of hope for future with broader and better representation of BIPOC.

As I write I can only anticipate the way that this time in the United States will be understood by history, but given the civil unrest sparked by the murder of George Floyd and the popular uprising calling for justice in every aspect of society for BIPOC, it seems like this pandemic and this moment/movement of reckoning for white supremacy will be inextricable. The fact that *Bob's Burgers* depends so much on talent that came up through the improv and stand-up circles of the 1990s and early 2000s means that when Bouchard assembles his troupe, he starts with the people who were there: overwhelmingly, these worlds were populated by cis White men.

While teaching my course, "Bob's Burgers' Onion-Tended Consequences," I found that my students' enthusiasm for discussing the show's

portrayal of family dynamics, adolescent desire, gen
economic realities of the lower middle class vastly o
est in discussing race. I taught the course at the Unive
Davis, during the 2018–19 school year. At that time,
cent of the student population self-identified as White
number of students, though not a majority, identifying
Islander. The next largest group was students identify...g as Hispanic.
My class accurately reflected the overall demographics of UC Davis,
which is to say that most of the students were BIPOC. Thus, I was surprised, as a queer cis White woman, that they did not want to explore
issues of race. Looking back, having conducted my own exploration, I
see now that my students' instincts may have come from a desire to preserve their love for a *Bob's Burgers*. From the cultural margins, we are
trained to imagine ourselves into the narrative rather than call it out for
not having seen us and given us our space from the start.

A friend of mine, a Black woman, messaged me to let off some
steam about micro aggressions in her workplace. As a White woman, my
first response was empathy and commiseration: even I have to deal with
racism in the workplace, and I'm just writing about cartoons. Quickly
I realized this was the wrong approach, because, of course, my experience writing about racism bears very little resemblance to her experience as the direct object of racism. Instead, I wrote her something that
I would love to see in *Bob's Burgers*. I asked if she could imagine a time
when noting that something was cruel, thoughtless, and informed by
systemic oppression was met not with defensiveness, but with sincere
contrition followed by restorative action. What does that look like on
a cartoon built around what Bouchard admits is a cozy repertory company? It might mean new characters, but, as a true fan of *Bob's Burgers*, I think what it actually means is Bouchard should leverage his clout
as a producer and his experience in bringing wonders like *Bob's Burgers*
into our homes and make a concentrated effort to mentor a new troupe,
brought together by a vision that can bring more inclusive stories. Now
that it's been airing for over a decade, it seems like a *Bob's Burgers* without the four White men and one White woman who make up its core
cast wouldn't be *Bob's Burgers*. Maybe *Bob's Burgers* simply doesn't have
the voices America needs to hear from right now.

Chapter Notes

Introduction

1. I encourage readers looking for an overview of the technical history of animation to consult Nichola Dobson's introduction to *The A to Z of Animation and Cartoons* (Scarecrow, 2010).

1. From Womb to the Tomb

1. Leman uses sex and gender interchangeably throughout, suggesting that it is, for him, an objective and static category at least.

2. Lindsey Weber provided a delightful primer on the source and uses of the meme on *Vulture* in 2016. As this is not necessarily a "smart" book, I recommend that you take a moment and look up "A Very Brady Meme" on your personal device.

3. Fans quickly recognized this kinship—a Google image search for "Louise Scissorhands" produces screenshots, but more striking are the photos of *Bob's Burgers* fans in homemade versions of Louise's bunny ears, covered in duct tape, holding scissors in black-on-black outfits.

4. Of course, I draw this comparison between Gene and Queen Latifah as a public figure, not from any biographical knowledge. Queen Latifah could technically be termed a middle child, as she is the second of four siblings.

5. The issue of Gene's gender and sexuality is explored in more depth in the "Gene-der Trouble" chapter.

6. She would later come to wider fame as an actress and personality, including an Academy Award nomination for *Chicago*

in 2003 and two daytime talk shows, *The Queen Latifah Show* from 1999 until 2001 and *The Queen Latifah Show* from 2013 to 2015.

7. Louise, on Future Darryl's mustache: "Do they not have razors in the future?"

8. *The Terminator* was recently the subject of a piece in the romance-focused webzine, *The Silver Petticoat Review*, and *Cinemablend*'s "*The Terminator* and 4 Other Great Movies with Unexpected Love Stories." *Terminator 2* as a story of maternal devotion is a reading widely explored by critics, particularly "Just a Woman Among the Cyborgs: Sarah Connor in *Terminator 2: Judgment Day*," by Catherine Summerhayes, and James Clarke's *The Cinema of James Cameron: Bodies in Heroic Motion*.

9. Pilot Viruet notes the homage to *Jurassic Park* without mentioning the references to the *Terminator* films in their recap of the episode for *The AV Club*.

10. Somewhat ironically, for a piece celebrating *Bob's Burgers* as a wholesome family program, writer Ron Hogan characterizes Louise as "a budding sociopath. She lies constantly, she's manipulative, she's prone to violence, she constantly wears her pink bunny ears hat, and she's the Belcher most likely to get the other two in trouble alongside her." This is not far from Leman's description of lastborn traits, cited above.

11. I refer specifically to Jill and Jessa Duggar, who starred in the TLC reality series *17 Kids and Counting* (2008–2009), *18 Kids and Counting* (2009), *19 Kids and Counting* (2010–2015), and *Jill and Jessa: Counting On* (2015–present).

...elberger of the Day

1. Other Spielberg homages pop up throughout the series. For example, the most direct reference to Spielberg's follow-up to *Jaws*, 1977's *Close Encounters of the Third Kind*, comes in season ten episode "Wag the Song" as something of a throwaway. One of the burgers of the day is called "Cloves Encounters" (10.14). There's also an homage to the raptor chase from *Jurassic Park* in "The Frond Files" and likely sight gags that my weary eyes fail to catch (4.12).

2. Major characters from *The Goonies* include Brand, Chunk, Data, and Sloth.

3. Just try to say Brand and Andy once, not even three times fast, and you'll understand that this union is doomed.

4. I think it's far more likely that Andy would drop out and get her GED so that she would definitely never have to see Brand again than actually date him after making out with his little brother. Ewww.

5. The internet loves discussing *The Goonies*. Jennifer Arbues wrote a concise and convincing dissection of the film's various plot holes for *Looper* in 2019, but simply mentioning the film on Facebook as a member of Generation X will pull dozens of acquaintances out of the woodwork, each with Very Strong Feelings.

6. The whale in *Moby Dick* is in fact a sperm whale, which is a terrible name for a boat. I think the allusion to Melville holds even if Quinn has named his boat after a different variety of whale.

7. A case can be made tracing the influence of *Duel* well before "Christmas in the Car." Each episode of *Bob's Burgers* opens with two gags, one for the shop next door, and one for the pest control truck. *Duel* feels taut, with little room for whimsy. One of the few places it can be found is late in the film when Mann believes he sees a police vehicle. When he inspects it further, it turns out to be advertising Grebleips Pest Control—Spielberg spelled backwards.

8. In *Duel*, the gas station attendant suggests that Mann's radiator hose might need a replacement. When Mann says no, the attendant shrugs and says, "You're the boss." Mann responds, "Not in my house, I'm not!"

9. Bob is not only secure in his masculinity, he knows how to romance a lady!

3. "We're not not-going to a toy-pony convention"

1. Cosplay is portmanteau of "costume" and "play," which many fans engage in when attending fan conventions, also called cons or fanccons.

2. As someone who enjoys naming and talking to the items in my home and office, I do not appreciate pphemerson13 pathologizing what is super normal, healthy adult behavior.

3. Nonbinary would mean that Gene identifies as neither a boy or a girl, while genderfluid implies that Gene moves back and forth, sometimes taking on a masculine, feminine, or nonbinary identity.

4. Truly, Louigan starts with "Earsy Rider." A *Reddit* post simply commemorating the eighth anniversary of that episode earned dozens of comments and over a thousand up votes (Yahoo201027).

5. There are three major platforms for fan fiction, *Archive of Our Own*, *Wattpad*, and *Fanfiction.net*. *Wattpad* does not always date its posts, so its possible that some of its Louigan content is even earlier.

6. As of October 1, 2020, Tina/Zeke had 46 entries and Tina/Jimmy Jr. had 45.

7. As of this writing, Bowden currently works for Apple, suggesting that he might be pretty good at his day job.

8. I use here the terminology Dave Navarro employs on the tattoo competition program, *Ink Master* to refer to recipients of tattoos.

4. *Our Father Who Art in Apron*

1. Zaddy is a term that emerged in late 2016. It can be traced back to a Ty Dolla $ign song, "Zaddy." According to a contributor on *Genius*, the term is a kind of portmanteau of "sugar daddy," but it has come to mean a sexy, well-dressed older man who seems like he could take care of you. Clover Hope gives several useful

illustrations in her 2017 *Jezebel* piece, "A List of Zaddys," in which she includes the actors John Slattery, Idris Elba, Justin Theroux (in sweatpants) and *Bob's Burgers'* own Jon Hamm.

2. Denise DuVernay gives an excellent assessment of how *The Simpsons* centers community engagement in her essay, "This Town Is a Part of Them (and Us) All" in *The Simpsons' Beloved Springfield* (2019).

3. Any similarities between the unnamed town in *Bob's Burgers* and the original Monopoly are not entirely accidental, as the game is based on Atlantic City, New Jersey, model for many boardwalked burgs on the eastern seaboard.

4. The series first came to the United States in a much different form. The "good parts" of the six films in the *Lone Wolf and Cub* series were edited into *Shogun Assassin* (1980), which became a cult classic. Patrick Macias gives an excellent summary of the history and reception of *Lone Wolf and Cub* in his essay, "Samurai and Son" in honor of the Criterion Collection's DVD release of all six films.

5. Tomisaburo Wakayama, the actor who plays Ogami in all six of the *Lone Wolf and Cub* films, does not cut a particularly threatening figure. Unlike the character from the manga, Wakayama looked paunchy and middle-aged, but it actually benefits the films, as his grace and efficiency takes the viewer by surprise.

6. While both parties are forced into this encounter by the renegades who have taken over the village, apparently the encounter is so enchanting for the prostitute that she attempts to follow Itto and Daigoro, but Itto, truly a lone wolf, threatens to destroy the bridge rather than expand his little band of outcasts beyond himself and his cub.

7. The baby cart, which is in the title of four of the six films, turns out to be a little like the Batmobile, with new capabilities in every film.

5. Burger Boss

1. This scene is not only a crossover with *Bob's Burgers*, but an homage to the opening of David Cronenberg's 2005 film, *A History of Violence*.

2. See Michael V. Tueth, *Laughter in the Living Room*, 119.

3. As Bonnie Dow notes, when workplace sitcoms use the family sitcom as a template, their ability to truly innovate in their portraits of politics and gender are limited by the extent to which they simply reproduce old problems in a new setting.

4. The bar, the bed and breakfast, and the night shift at the municipal court, respectively.

5. Jeffrey Griffin does an extensive comparison of the British and American versions of *The Office*, but limits himself to the first two seasons of the American program.

6. In the fourth season finale, "Goodbye, Toby," Ryan, *The Office*'s Icarus, is fired.

6. "Boys are from Mars, girls are from Venus"

1. June Foray passed in 2017, and remained very active into her later years, returning as Rocket J. Squirrel to star in 2000's *The Adventures of Rocky and Bullwinkle* and bemoaning Rocky's lack of Oscar recognition in *Variety*.

2. For context, The Cartoon Network, which specializes in animated programming for both children and adults, did not have a single program created by a woman until Rebecca Sugar's *Steven Universe* debuted in 2013.

3. Kristen Schaal, who provides Louise's voice, might be the most recognizable, as she has costarred in two cult sitcoms, Fox's *Last Man on Earth* and HBO's *Flight of the Concords*. Still, she's only the second-most-famous Kristen with repeating vowels (I see you, Kristen Wiig). Many reoccurring characters, most notably Kevin Kline's Mr. Fischoeder, are voiced by actual famous people.

4. Briefly, gender refers to social roles and expectations that come with being understood as a man or a woman. Masculinity and femininity describe the extent to which an individual is fulfilling the

expectations of their culture. Sex refers to the biological markers used to differentiate male from female. Sex and gender work independently, as glands drive one and women's magazines and commercials for cologne drive the other. For example: Linda's breasts mark her biological sex as female. Depending on her culture, her love for Angel Babies marks her gender as woman.

5. The ghost of thirteen-year-old Jeff, trapped in a shoebox after an exorcism in the restaurant basement, becomes a contentious object of desire once Tina takes him to school and begins introducing him as her boyfriend in "Tina and the Real Ghost." The Jimmy Jr. storyline ebbs and flows throughout the season, but Tina's relationship with Jeff might best typify *Bob's Burgers'* insight into middle school romance: a love entirely dependent upon one party's willingness to imagine a personality for the another.

6. In fact, the shift from the Henley to the V-neck was likely due to occasional gaffes in which the buttons were on the wrong side of her placket, so her dress has become less fussy over time.

7. Gene-der Trouble

1. The specific episodes in which these occur are "Work Hard or Die Trying, Girl," "Full Bars," "The Kids Run the Restaurant," "I Get a Psy-chic Out of You," and "Bobby Driver."

2. Swayze's mother Patsy actually contributed to the eighties cult of manly dancing by choreographing Travolta in *Urban Cowboy* (1980).

3. The scene in the dance class owes a great deal to a clip from an instructional video by Dena Rizzo that went viral in 2010 commonly called "This Is Hip Hop" (Incrediblous).

4. As defined in a previous chapter, "headcanon" refers to any element in a media property that is not explicitly stated within the property itself (the "canon") but that fans intuit (theduedliest-firearm).

5. Genderfluid is a term used by individuals whose gender identity (how they feel) and expression (their external appearance) freely incorporates masculine and feminine elements to varying degrees, sometimes simultaneously (think a boxy suit with rouge and lipstick) or sequentially (one day dirty coveralls, the next day a flirty romper).

8. The Marshmallow Test

1. *South Park*'s crude animation style allows it to be produced on a *Saturday Night Live*–like schedule, as depicted in Arthur Bradford's documentary, *6 Days to Air*. As the title suggests, unlike *Family Guy*, which has a one-year lead time, *South Park* episodes are written and animated within a week. Thus, while both programs are irreverent, only *South Park* is designed to be topical. Of course, transgender individuals and their families had long been on television as guests on daytime talk shows, beginning with Nancy Hunt's appearance on *The Phil Donahue Show* in the late seventies (Phipps).

2. In the LGBTQ+ or Gay/Trans Panic defense, assailants claim diminished rational capacity due to the "surprise" that the victim was of a gender or sexual orientation that the perpetrator did not recognize at first. Because "gayness," masculinity, and femininity are all incredibly subjective traits, anyone's assault or murder could conceivably be excused on this basis. The LGBT Bar provides an interactive map tracking work against the "Gay Panic" defense across the United States at lgbtbar.org/programs/advocacy/gay-trans-panic-defense/gay-trans-panic-defense-legislation/.

3. Crenshaw, a legal scholar, originally used the term to discuss how impoverished the legal definition of discrimination is when someone who experiences multiple vectors of discrimination—in her example, a Black woman—must sue on the basis of either racial discrimination or gender discrimination, as if a Black woman would not be subjected to racism and misogyny at the same time.

9. *"You're so good at touching strangers"*

1. According to many anonymous sources, Tyler Perry might also be able to go back to work more quickly because of his willingness to use non-union labor.

2. The precedent for this kind of substitution can be found in Christian filmmaking. While doing publicity rounds for 2008's *Fireproof*, lead Kirk Cameron told Kathie Lee Gifford and Hoda Kotb on *Today* that he was unwilling to kiss the actress playing his wife, Erin Bethea. Instead, the scene where his character kisses his wife was lit so that the wife appears in silhouette and thus the role could be, for that moment, recast with Cameron's wife, the actress Chelsea Noble. Cameron retold the story throughout the junket, proud of to be "honoring marriage behind the scenes" (Celizic).

3. In terms of appearances by characters that are meant to be BIPOC, Mike has appeared in 20 episodes, Darryl in 17, Ms Jacobson in 14, and Marshmallow in 11. These are not all speaking appearances.

4. On *The Simpsons*, many characters of color are voiced by white actors, including Harry Shearer's Dr. Hibbert, Hank Azaria's Carl, and most notoriously Apu Nahasapeemapetilon, also performed by Hank Azaria. Hari Kondabolu, an American comedian of Indian descent, developed his tweets and bits about the way Apu had become a racist slur into the 2017 documentary feature, *The Problem with Apu*. Kondabolu integrates his own experience with being called "Apu" and dreading going to convenience stores with white friends with an exploration of how such a stereotyped portrayal had managed to stay on television for over 25 years.

5. David Herman has an even longer history with *Bob's Burgers* other, less public-facing, creator, Jim Dauterive, as they worked together on *King of the Hill* (1997–2010).

6. By contrast, a show like *American Dad*, which, as of the 2019–2020 television season, has aired about a third more episodes than *Bob's Burgers*, has credited more than three times as many writers. Even *King of the Hill*, creator Jim Dauterive's previous animated sitcom, went through more than twice as many writers as *Bob's Burgers* despite having aired 250 episodes compared with *Bob's Burgers'* 194.

Bibliography

Abel, Sam. "The Rabbit in Drag: Camp and Gender Construction in the American Animated Cartoon." *Journal of Popular Culture*, vol. 29, no. 3, 1995, pp. 183–202.

Adams, Erik. "*Bob's Burgers* Showrunner Loren Bouchard Breaks Down the Show's Third Season Part 1." *AVClub*, 26 August 2013, tv.avclub.com/bob-s-burgers-showrunner-loren-bouchard-breaks-down-the-1798240599.

_____. "*Bob's Burgers* Showrunner Loren Bouchard on Season Three's Most Musical Episodes (3 of 5)." *AVClub*, 28 August 2013, tv.avclub.com/bob-s-burgers-showrunner-loren-bouchard-on-season-three-1798240580.

_____. "*Bob's Burgers* Showrunner Loren Bouchard on the End of the Show's Third Season." *AVClub*, 30 August 2013, Tv.avclub.com/bob-s-burgers-showrunner-loren-bouchard-on-the-end-of-t-1798240586.

_____. "Showrunner Lorne Bouchard on Sympathetic Leg Hair and *Bob's Burgers'* Third Season (2 of 5)." *AVClub*, 27 August 2013, Tv.avclub.com/showrunner-loren-bouchard-on-sympathetic-leg-hair-and-b-1798240675.

_____. "Showrunner Loren Bouchard on Talking Toilets and Other Pieces of *Bob's Burgers'* Third Season (4 of 5)." *AVClub*, 29 August 2013, Tv.avclub.com/showrunner-loren-bouchard-on-talking-toilets-and-other-1798240654.

"*AfterBuzz TV's Bob's Burgers* Review and After Show." *AfterBuzzTV*, https://www.afterbuzztv.com/bobs-burgers-afterbuzz-tv-aftershow/.

airplanesoda. "The Belcher Sisters." *Tumblr*, airplanesoda.tumblr.com/post/176570174851/the-belcher-sisters.

alexh2458. "Start of My *Bob's Burgers* Half-sleeve Tattoo." *Reddit*, 6 September 2020, www.reddit.com/r/BobsBurgers/comments/innnj7/start_of_my_bobs_burgers_halfsleeve_tattoo/.

Allison, Tanine. "Blackface, *Happy Feet*: The Politics of Race in Motion Capture and Animation." *Special Effects: New Histories, Theories, Contexts*, edited by Dan North, Bob Rehak, and Michael Duffy, BFI/Palgrave, 2015, pp. 114–126.

allmilhouse. "Feelings Under the Fridge." *Archive of Our Own*, 8 March 2020, archiveofourown.org/works/23071066.

_____. "I Love You So Much (It's Hairy)." *Archive of Our Own*, 15 March 2018, archiveofourown.org/works/13828983.

Anderson, Tre'vell. "Visibility Matters: Transgender Characters on Film and Television Through the Years." *Los Angeles Times*, 18 December 2015, timelines.latimes.com/transgender-characters-film-tv-timeline/.

Andreeva, Nellie. "*Family Guy* and *Bob's Burgers* Get Two Season Renewals at Fox." *Deadline*, 23 September 2020, deadline.com/2020/09/family-guy-bobs-burgers-renewed-two-season-fox-seasons-19–20–12–13–1234582825/.

_____. "*One Day at a Time* to Do Animated Special Amid Coronavirus-Related Production Shutdown." *Deadline*, 28 April 2020, https://deadline.com/2020/04/one-day-at-a-time-animated-special-coronavirus-related-production-shutdown-1202919412/.

Bibliography

Andrews, Nellie. "*The Bold and the Beautiful* Returns to Production with Safety Protocols in Place." *Deadline*, 15 June 2020, deadline.com/2020/06/the-bold-and-the-beautiful-returns-production-covid-19-protocols-season-33-1202960103/.

"Animal Tools." *The Ultimate Flintstones Site*, 24 June 2002, i-flintstones.tripod.com/tools.htm.

Arbues, Jennifer. "Dumb Things Everyone Ignores in *The Goonies*." *Looper*, 8 October 2019, www.looper.com/169216/dumb-things-everyone-ignores-in-the-goonies/.

Arnett, Robert. "Eighties Noir: The Dissenting Voice in Reagan's America." *Journal of Popular Film & Television*, vol. 34, no. 3, Fall 2006, pp. 123–129. EBSCOhost, doi:10.3200/JPFT.34.3.123–129.

Astin, Sean, and Layden, Joseph. *There and Back Again : An Actor's Tale*. 1st ed., St. Martin's Press, 2004.

Aurthur, Kate, and Adam B. Vary. "Extras on $et: Inside Hollywood's Pricey Plan to Restart Production." 20 May 2020, *Variety*, variety.com/2020/biz/features/restarting-production-coronavirus-pandemic-hollywood-1234611125/.

Bahr, Sarah. "*Bold and the Beautiful* to Resume Production with On-Set Covid Rules." *New York Times*, 16 June 2020, www.nytimes.com/2020/06/16/arts/television/bold-beautiful-resumes-cbs-coronavirus.html.

Bailey, Marlon M. "Gender/Racial Realness: Theorizing the Gender System in Ballroom Culture." *Feminist Studies*, vol. 37, no. 2, 2011, pp. 365–386. *JSTOR*, JSTOR, www.jstor.org/stable/23069907.

Barsanti, Sam. "After *Central Park* Recasting, Loren Bouchard Discusses *Bob's Burgers'* Representation Issues." *AVClub*, 26 July 2020, news.avclub.com/after-central-park-recasting-lauren-bouchard-discusses-1844511449.

Beeden, Alexandra, and Joost de Bruin. "The Office: Articulations of National Identity in Television Format Adaptation." *Television & New Media*, vol. 11, no. 1, January 2010, pp. 3–19, DOI:10.1177/1527476409338197.

Behind *Bob's Burgers*. "Behind *Bob's Burgers* Live: Episode 11." Hosted by Jon Schroeder, guests Rich Rinaldi, Tyree Dillihay, and Shinji "Koji" Kojima, *YouTube*, 22 December 2015, www.youtube.com/watch?v=AxeG_7GXkQ8&list=PLpq9ud5PfXszjQOiQJcyo6z1ukyy9LsD-&index=5&t=0s.

Bell, Kristen. Green Slide with White Text. *Instagram*, 24 June 2020, https://www.instagram.com/p/CB1coy7JkDG/.

Benjamin, Walter. *The Work of Art in the Age of Its Technological Reproducibility and Other Writings on Media*, edited by Michael W. Jennings, Brigid Doherty, and Thomas Y. Levin, translated by Edmund Juphcott, Rodney Livingstone, Howard Eiland, and others, Belknap Press of Harvard UP, 2008.

Blank, Elana. "Transphobia in *Bob's Burgers'* 'Sheesh! Cab, Bob?'" *QIPC '14*, 26 March 2014, https://qipc2014.wordpress.com/2014/03/26/transphobia-in-bobs-burgers-sheesh-cab-bob/.

BleekLondon. "AMAZING Bob's Burgers Cosplay!" *Twitter*, 9 February 2015, 8:54 a.m., twitter.com/bleeklondon/status/564829718533640192.

BoboftheDay. "Gene's Biggest Oopsie." *Fanfiction.net*, www.fanfiction.net/s/13571166/2/Gene-s-Biggest-Oopsie.

Bob's Burgers. Created by Loren Bouchard and Jim Dauterive, voice performances by H. Jon Benjamin, Kristin Schaal, Eugene Mirman, Dan Mintz, and John Roberts, Fox, 2011–present.

"Bob's Burgers Crime." *Bob's Burgers Crime*, 28 May 2019, podcasts.apple.com/us/podcast/bobs-burgers-crime/id1466122542?ign-mpt=uo%3D4.

Bobsburgersstories. "The Origin of the Ears." *Fanfiction.net*, www.fanfiction.net/s/13551430/2/The-Origin-of-the-Ears.

Bode, Lisa. "In Another's Skin: Typecasting, Identity, and the Limits of Proteanism." *Making Believe: Screen Performance and Special Effects in Popular Cinema*, Rutgers University Press, 2017, pp. 70–98.

9. Bibliography

Bollinger, Alex. "Black Trans Woman Character in *Bob's Burgers* Is Played by a White Man. That Will Change." *LGBTQNation*, 1 July 2020, www.lgbtqnation.com/2020/07/black-trans-woman-character-bobs-burger-character-played-white-man-will-change/.

Bouchard, Loren, and the writers of *Bob's Burgers*. *The Bob's Burgers Burger Book*. Recipes by Cole Bowden. Universe Publishing, 2016.

Bowman, Sabienna. "*Bob's Burgers'* Gene Is Super Underrated." *Bustle*, 26 July 2015, www.bustle.com/articles/99867-9-quotes-that-prove-gene-from-bobs-burgers-is-the-most-underrated-belcher-of-them-all.

Boynton, Robert S. "The Birth of an Idea." *New Yorker*, 30 September 1996, 72. www.newyorker.com/magazine/1996/10/07/the-birth-of-an-idea.

Bradford, Arthur, dir. *Six Days to Air: The Making of South Park*. Comedy Central, 2011.

The Brady Bunch. Created by Sherwood Schwartz, Paramount, ABC, 1969–1974.

Brooks, Katherine. "About That *Bob's Burgers* Theory That Bob Is Dead." *Huffpost*, 7 March 2017, www.huffpost.com/entry/bobs-burgers-fan-theory-family-is-dead_n_58bec496e4b0d8c45f468b34.

_____. "Uhh This *Bob's Burgers* Fan Art Would Make Tina Proud." *Huffpost*, 19 March 2016, www.huffpost.com/entry/bobs-burgers-art-gallery-1988_n_573ce634e4b0ef86171d3877.

Bryan and Ryan. "Season 3 Episode 21: Boyz4Now." *Burgers and Fries*, 21 July 2018, https://www.burgersfriespodcast.com/episodes?offset=1544101200377.

Bult, Laura. "A Timeline of 1,944 Black Americans Killed by the Police." *Vox*, 30 June 2020, www.vox.com/2020/6/30/21306843/black-police-killings.

Burt, Stephanie. "The Promise and Potential of Fan Fiction." *New Yorker*, 23 August 2017, www.newyorker.com/books/page-turner/the-promise-and-potential-of-fan-fiction.

Butler, Judith. *Bodies That Matter: On the Discursive Limits of Sex*. Routledge, 1993.

_____. *Gender Trouble: Feminism and the Subversion of Identity*. 2nd ed., Routledge, 1999.

Cameron, James, dir. *The Terminator*. Orion Pictures, 1984.

_____. *Terminator 2: Judgment Day*. Tri-Star Pictures, 1991.

Cantwell, Elizabeth. "It's Only an Island If You Look at It from the Water." *Bright Wall/Dark Room*, issue 15 part 2, 1 April 2016, www.brightwalldarkroom.com/2016/04/01/its-only-an-island-if-you-look-at-it-from-the-water/.

Carnage678. "Is It Weird I Want to See Louise and Regular-Sized Rudy as a Couple?" *Reddit*, 23 November 2016, www.reddit.com/r/BobsBurgers/comments/5ehnsj/is_it_weird_i_want_to_see_louise_and_regularsized/?sort=qa.

cavemanda. "My Brother and I Have Always Wanted Matching Sibling Tattoos and Since Our Last Name Is Actually Belcher, We Could Think of No Better Option." *Reddit*, 30 May 2020, https://www.reddit.com/r/BobsBurgers/comments/gtpj4k/my_brother_and_i_have_always_wanted_matching/.

Celizic, Mike. "Kirk Cameron: I'll Only Kiss My Wife." *Today*, 23 September 2008, www.today.com/popculture/kirk-cameron-ill-only-kiss-my-wife-2D80555063.

Chappel, Caitlin. "The Bleakest *Bob's Burgers* Fan Theory Is Still the Most Popular." *CBR.com*, 14 August 2020, www.cbr.com/bleakest-bobs-burgers-fan-theory-most-popular/.

Chmielewski, Dawn. "*The Bold and the Beautiful* Is Back with a Plan to Keep Covid from Stealing the Sex." *Forbes*, 16 June 2020, www.forbes.com/sites/dawnchmielewski/2020/06/16/the-bold-and-the-beautiful-is-back-with-a-plan-to-keep-social-distancing-from-stealing-the-sex/?sh=684e956860e6.

"The Cissy." *South Park*, written and directed by Trey Parker, season 18, episode 3, Comedy Central, 8 Oct. 2014.

Close Encounters of the Third Kind. Directed by Steven Spielberg, performances by Richard Dreyfus, Teri Garr, Melinda Dillon, and François Truffault, Columbia, 1977.

Cooper, Gael Fashingbauer. "*Bob's Burgers* Cooking Up New Episodes, but Not About Coronavirus." *CNet*, 26 May 2020, www.cnet.com/news/bobs-burgers-making-new-episodes-during-pandemic-but-not-about-the-virus/.

Bibliography

Courneen, Trevor. "Cole Bowden of *The Bob's Burger Experiment* Talks Putting Puns Between Buns." *Paste*, 25 June 2015, www.pastemagazine.com/food/cole-bowden-of-the-bobs-burger-experiment-talks-pu/.

Crenshaw, Kimberlé. "Demarginalizing the Intersection of Race and Sex: A Black Feminist Critique of Antidiscrimination Doctrine, Feminist Theory and Antiracist Politics." *University of Chicago Legal Forum,*1989, chicagounbound.uchicago.edu/uclf/vol1989/iss1/8.

Cronin, Brian. "TV Legends Revealed: Does Marge Simpson Have Rabbit Ears Under Her Hair?" *CBR.com*, 27 April 2016, www.cbr.com/tv-legends-revealed-does-marge-simpson-have-rabbit-ears-under-her-hair/.

Davison, Candace Braun. "13 Things You Didn't Know About Sandra Lee." *Delish*, 25 July 2016, www.delish.com/restaurants/a48384/things-you-dont-know-about-sandra-lee/.

dawnheart. "All I Wanted." *Archive of Our Own*, 24 May 2020, archiveofourown.org/works/24362275.

Denison, Rayna. "Star-Spangled Ghibli: Star Voices in the American Versions of Hayao Miyazaki's Films." *Animation*, vol. 3, no. 2, 2008, pp. 129–146.

Detweiler, Eric. "'I Was Just Doing a Little Joke There': Irony and the Paradoxes of the Sitcom in *The Office.*" *Journal of Popular Culture*, vol. 45, no. 4, August 2012, pp. 727–748.

Dhaenens, Frederik, and Sofie Van Bauwel. "Queer Resistances in the Adult Animated Sitcom." *Television & New Media* 13.2 (2012): 124–138. Academic Search Complete. Web. 4 Jan. 2017.

Diagnosis Murder. Performances by Dick Van Dyke, Barry Van Dyke, and Victoria Rowell, CBS, 29 October 1993–11 May 2001.

diggitySC. "Zeke Has a Crush on Tina Evidence Compilation." *Reddit*, 23 July 2018, www.reddit.com/r/BobsBurgers/comments/91ekxh/zeke_has_a_crush_on_tina_evidence_compilation/.

DingoJingoJango. "Psyched." *Archive of Our Own*, 5 January 2020, archiveofourown.org/works/18922075/chapters/44920543.

Dirty Dancing. Directed by Emile Ardolino, performances by Jennifer Grey, Patrick Swayze, Jerry Orbach, and Cynthia Rhodes, Great American Films, 1987.

Djinnkj. "Bob Is the Only Sober Person in This Show." *Reddit*, 22 December 2016, www.reddit.com/r/FanTheories/comments/5jtuys/bobs_burgers_bob_is_the_only_sober_person_in_this/.

Dobson, Nichola. *The A to Z of Animation and Cartoons*. Scarecrow Press, 2010. *ProQuest Ebook Central*, https://ebookcentral.proquest.com/lib/washington/detail.action?docID=1037548.

Dow, Bonnie J. *Prime-Time Feminism: Television, Media Culture, and the Women's Movement Since 1970*. U of Pennsylvania P, 1996.

the-duedliest-firearm. "Headcanon." *Urban Dictionary*, 12 July 2012, https://www.urbandictionary.com/define.php?term=headcanon.

Duel. Directed by Steven Spielberg, performance by Dennis Weaver, Universal, 1971.

Du Vernay, Denise. "This Town Is Part of Them (and Us) All." *The Simpsons' Beloved Springfield*, edited by Karma Waltonen and Denise Du Vernay, McFarland, 2019, pp. 15–21.

Eakin, Marah. "Voice Actor Rob Paulsen Says He Won't Play a Character of Color Again." *AvClub*, 30 June 2020, tv.avclub.com/voice-actor-rob-paulsen-says-he-won-t-play-a-character-1844183726.

Edge, John T. *Hamburgers and Fries: An American Story*. Putnam, 2005.

"Eek, a Penis!" *South Park*, written and directed by Trey Stone, season 12, episode 5, Comedy Central, 9 April 2008.

EloiseBelcher. "Boyz5Now." *Fanfiction.net*, www.fanfiction.net/s/11149705/1/Boyz-5-Now.

9. Bibliography

E.T.: The Extra-Terrestrial. Directed by Steven Spielberg, performances by Henry Thomas, Dee Wallace and Peter Coyote, Universal, 1982.

Fame. Created by Christopher Gore, performances by Debbie Allen, Olivia Barash, Jesse Borrego and Lee Curreri. NBC, 1982–1983, syndication 1983–1987.

_____. Directed by Alan Parker, performances by Eddie Barth, Irene Cara, and Lee Curreri, United Artists, 1980.

The Fan Girl. "*Bob's Burgers* Fan Theory: Gene Belcher Is an Autism Role Model." *You-Tube*, 12 July 2017, www.youtube.com/watch?v=DdUy58qNH50.

Fatdude6. "Regarding Louise's Bunny Ears." *Reddit*, 9 April 2014, www.reddit.com/r/FanTheories/comments/22lp76/bobs_burgers_regarding_louises_bunny_ears/cgoar5x/.

Faughnder, Ryan. "California Says Film and TV Shoots Can Start June 12, but Big Changes Are Coming." *Los Angeles Times*, 5 June 2020, www.latimes.com/entertainment-arts/business/story/2020–06–05/gavin-newsom-hollywood-production.

Ferguson, Christopher J., and Moritz Heene. "A Vast Graveyard of Undead Theories: Publication Bias and Psychological Science's Aversion to the Null." *Perspectives on Psychological Science*, vol. 7 iss. 6, 2012, pp. 555–561.

"Finale." *The Office*, directed by Ken Kwapis and written by Greg Daniels, NBC, 16 May 2013.

Fiske, John, and John Hartley. *Reading Television*. Routledge, 2004.

Fleming, D.M., et al. "Gender Difference in the Incidence of Shingles." *Epidemiology and Infection*, vol. 132, no. 1, 2004, pp. 1–5.

Footloose. Directed by Herbert Ross, performances by Kevin Bacon, Lori Singer, Dianne Wiest, and Jon Lithgow, Paramount, 1984.

Foray, June. "Scrapbook of the Century: Mickey, Bugs, Rocky: Didn't Even Get a Dinner." *Variety*, 6 December 1999, 377.

Foreman, Alison. "It's Time for *Bob's Burgers* to Do Right by Marshmallow." *Mashable*, 27 June 2020, mashable.com/article/bobs-burgers-marshmallow-black-trans-character/.

Førland, Tor Egil, Trine Rogg Korsvik, and Knut-Andreas Christophersen. "Brought Up to Rebel in the Sixties: Birth Order Irrelevant, Parental Worldview Decisive." *Political Psychology*, vol. 33 no. 6, 2012, pp. 825–838.

fowlerni. "Is Jimmy Jr Gay?" *Reddit*, 7 September 2016, www.reddit.com/r/BobsBurgers/comments/51p1je/is_jimmy_jr_gay/.

"Fugues and Riffs." *Archer*, F/X, 17 January 2013.

Gabbard, Krin. *Black Magic : White Hollywood and African American Culture*. Rutgers UP, 2004.

Gabreyes, Rachel. "H. Jon Benjamin Says This *Bob's Burgers* Character Could Be Gay." *Huffington Post*, 23 Sept. 2015, www.huffingtonpost.com/entry/h-jon-benjamin-bobs-burgers-gene-belcher-gay_us_5602e410e4b00310edf9a246.

Geargirl. "Bob's Burgers Is About Bob Coping with the Death of His Family." *Reddit*, 29 July 2014. www.reddit.com/r/FanTheories/comments/2c29cw/bobs_burgers_is_about_bob_coping_with_the_death/.

Girls Just Want to Have Fun. Directed by Alan Metter, performances by Sarah Jessica Parker, Lee Montgomery, Morgan Woodward, Jonathan Silverman, and Helen Hunt, New World, 1985.

The Goonies. Directed by Richard Donner, story by Steven Spielberg, performances by Sean Astin, Josh Brolin, Jeff Cohen, Corey Feldman, Kerri Green, Martha Plimpton, Ke Huy Quan, Amblin Entertainment, 1985.

Goscilo, Margaret. "Deconstructing the Terminator." *Film Criticism* vol. 12, no. 2, 1987, pp. 37–52.

Green, Willow. "Edgar Wright Interviews Steven Spielberg About *Duel*." *Empire*, 27 March 2018. www.empireonline.com/movies/features/edgar-wright-interviews-steven-spielberg-about-duel/.

Bibliography

Griffin, Jeffrey. "The Americanization of *The Office*: A Comparison of the Offbeat NBC Sitcom and Its British Predecessor." *Journal of Popular Film and Television*, vol. 35, no. 4, August 2008, pp. 154–163.

Griffin, Mackensie. "Trendsetters: The Strange, Creative, and Occasionally Tacky History of Table Settings." *Slate*, 5 May 2015, slate.com/human-interest/2015/05/history-of-table-setting-from-service-a-la-russe-to-sandra-lees-tablescapes.html.

Gross, Terry. "From *Hill* Kid to *Californication*." Interview with Pamela Adlon, *Fresh Air*, 4 January 2012, www.npr.org/templates/transcript/transcript.php?storyId=1443 19352.

Gwynne, Joel. "'Might as Well Be Dead': Domesticity, Irony and Feminist Politics in Contemporary Animation Comedy." *Critical Studies in Television: The International Journal of Television Studies*, vol. 10, no. 2, 2015, pp. 55–70.

Haraway, Donna J. "A Cyborg Manifesto: Science, Technology, and Socialist-Feminism in the Late Twentieth Century." *Simians, Cyborgs, and Women: The Reinvention of Nature*. Routledge, 1991, pp.149–181.

Harrison, Skylar, and Max Miller. *Bob's Credits*. bobscredits.com.

Hartinger, Brent. "Is *Family Guy*'s Seth MacFarlane a Complete Idiot?" *NEWNOWNEXT*, 10 May 2010, www.newnownext.com/is-family-guys-seth-macfarlane-a-complete-idiot/05/2010/.

Haskell, Molly. *Steven Spielberg*. Yale University Press, 2017.

Heer, Jeet. "My Epiphany About the Problem with Apu." *New Republic*, 14 April 2018, newrepublic.com/article/147980/epiphany-problem-apu-simpsons.

"He's All Yours." *The Mary Tyler Moore Show*, directed by Jay Sandrich, written by Bob Rodgers, ABC 12 December 1970.

HeWasAZombie. "Regarding Louise's Bunny Ears." *Reddit*, 9 April 2014, www.reddit.com/r/FanTheories/comments/22lp76/bobs_burgers_regarding_louises_bunny_ears/cgoar5x/.

Hibberd, James. "Fox's Midseason Schedule Revealed!" *Entertainment Weekly*, 1 December 2011, ew.com/article/2011/12/01/fox-midseason-schedule/.

Hicks, Heather J. "Hoodoo Economics: White Men's Work and Black Men's Magic in Contemporary American Film." *Camera Obscura* 1 September 2003; 18 (2 [53]): 27–55.

Hill, Alexandra Merley. "Motherhood as Performance: (Re)Negotiations of Motherhood in Contemporary German Literature." *Studies in 20th & 21st Century Literature*, 2011, vol. 35, iss. 1, Article 6.

Hill, Evan, Ainara Tiefenthäler, Christiaan Triebert, Drew Jordan, Haley Willis and Robin Stein. "How George Floyd Was Killed in Police Custody." *New York Times*, 32 May 2020, www.nytimes.com/2020/05/31/us/george-floyd-investigation.html.

Hilton-Morrow, Wendy, and David McMahan. "*The Flintstones* to *Futrama*: Networks and Prime Time Animation." *Prime Time Animation : Television Animation and American Culture*, edited by Carole Stabile and Mark Harrison, Taylor & Francis, 2003, pp. 74–88.

Hirji, Faiza. "Goodbye Apu—Here's What You Meant to Us." *The Conversation*, 4 November 2018, https://theconversation.com/goodbye-apu-heres-what-you-meant-to-us-105948.

Hirsch, Marianne. *The Mother/Daughter Plot*. Indiana UP, 1989.

A History of Violence. Directed by David Cronenberg, performances by Viggo Mortensen and Maria Bello, New Line, 2005.

Hogan, Ron. "How Bob's Burgers Teaches the True Meaning of Family Love." *Den of Geek*, 14 September 2015, https://www.denofgeek.com/tv/how-bobs-burgers-teaches-the-true-meaning-of-family-love/.

homersqueack. "What Ethnicity Is DRL?" *Reddit*, 21 March 2017, www.reddit.com/r/BobsBurgers/comments/60szsq/what_ethnicity_is_drl/.

9. Bibliography

Hope, Clover. "A List of Zaddys." *Jezebel*, 17 June 2017, jezebel.com/a-list-of-zaddys-1796062207.

Hugar, John. "How *King of the Hill* Led Directly to *Bob's Burgers*." *Vulture*, 14 March 2017, www.vulture.com/2017/03/how-king-of-the-hill-led-directly-to-bobs-burgers.html.

Hughes, John, director. *Sixteen Candles*. Channel Productions, 1984.

Human Rights Campaign. "Fatal Violence Against the Trans and Gender Non-Conforming Community in 2020." *HRC*, www.hrc.org/resources/violence-against-the-trans-and-gender-non-conforming-community-in-2020?utm_source=GS&utm_medium=AD&utm_campaign=BPI-HRC-Grant&utm_content=454864016094&utm_term=violence%20against%20trans%20people&gclid=Cj0KCQiAqo3-BRDoARIsAE5vnaKEw5u0HpSwTp9GSLksmsBkgh0J3Vd48ZkrzQed67-SsvemjQ1vlrkaAhyTEALw_wcB.

HumanDictionary. "Sympesto for the Devil: The Story of James Poplopovich." *Fanfiction. net*, www.fanfiction.net/s/13677282/1/Sympesto-for-the-Devil-The-story-of-James-Poplopovich.

Incrediblous. "This Is Hip Hop!" *YouTube*, 5 July 2010, www.youtube.com/watch?v=IS2KQ46Kf84.

Isaacson, Cliff, and Kris Radish. *The Birth Order Effect: How to Better Understand Yourself and Others*. Adams Media, 2002.

Itzkoff, Dave. "*Simpsons* Creator Matt Groening Says Debate Around Apu Character Is 'Tainted.'" *New York Times*, 18 July 2018, www.nytimes.com/2018/07/18/arts/television/simpsons-matt-groening-apu.html.

Jackson, Lauren Michelle. "The Messy Politics of Black Voices—and 'Black Voice'— In American Animation." *New Yorker*, 30 June 2020, www.newyorker.com/culture/cultural-comment/the-messy-politics-of-black-voices-and-black-voice-in-american-animation?fbclid=IwAR3JuaEWNulT_i3uy5wIxAzvSLg8zRM2Gy3zb91MHQtNMXwuQo0997_wBuY.

Jaffe, Jenny. "Bob's Burgers Is Better Than Game of Thrones and Every Other Sunday Show, Trust Me." *Bustle*, 24 April 2014, www.bustle.com/articles/22589-bobs-burgers-is-better-than-game-of-thrones-mad-men-every-other-sunday-show-trust.

Jaws. Directed by Steven Spielberg, performances by Roy Scheider, Robert Shaw, and Richard Dreyfus, Universal, 1975.

Jen and Briddany. *Pod's Burgers*. Podsburgers.com.

Johnson, Kjerstin. "*Family Guy*: Reaching New Transmyginic Lows." *Bitchmedia*, 11 May 10, www.bitchmedia.org/post/family-guy-reaching-new-transmysogyny-lows.

Jones, Blake. "*Bob's Burger* X Gallery 1988." *The Ranting Robot Blog*, 3 May 2016, www.blakebot5000.com/rantingrobot/2016/5/3/bobs-burgers-x-gallery-1988.

Jurassic Park. Directed by Steven Spielberg, performances by Sam Neil, Laura Dern, and Jeff Goldblum, Universal, 1993.

Kaiser, Rowan. "*Bob's Burgers*: Broadcast Wagstaff School News." *AVClub*, 28 January 2013, tv.avclub.com/bob-s-burgers-broadcast-wagstaff-school-news-1798175622.

_____. "*Bob's Burgers*: 'The Belchies.'" *AVClub*, 11 March 2012, tv.avclub.com/bob-s-burgers-the-belchies-1798171907.

Kandell, Steve. "Pleased to Meat Me: *Bob's Burgers* Creators on the Finale and Season Two's High Points." *Spin*, 23 May 2012, www.spin.com/2012/05/pleased-meat-me-bobs-burgers-creators-finale-and-season-twos-high-points/.

Keller, Joel. "Loren Bouchard." *AVClub*, 19 May 2011, tv.avclub.com/loren-bouchard-1798225766.

_____. "Stream It or Skip It: *One Day at a Time* Animated Special on Pop TV, a Remotely-Produced Episode That's One of the Series' Funniest." *Decider*, 16 June 2020, decider.com/2020/06/16/one-day-at-a-time-animated-special-pop-tv-stream-it-or-skip-it/.

Kenzie. "Drew Some Gene Beans in Fashionable Outfits." *Tumblr*, 1 November 2015, cactul.tumblr.com/post/132326336540/drew-some-gene-beans-in-fashionable.

Bibliography

Keyes, Cheryl L. "Empowering Self, Making Choices, Creating Spaces: Black Female Identity Via Rap Music Performance." *The Journal of American Folklore*, vol. 113, no. 449, 2000, pp. 255–269.

kieraplease (Kiera Please). "?" *Instagram*, 4 October 2018, https://www.instagram.com/p/BohnFAyl6kx/.

King of the Hill. Created by Mike Judge and Greg Daniels. Fox, 12 January 1997–6 May 2010.

Lane, Laura. "What's a Writers' Room Without Junk Food?" *New Yorker*, 25 May 2020, https://www.newyorker.com/magazine/2020/06/01/whats-a-writers-room-without-junk-food.

Leeds, Sarene. "*One Day at a Time*'s Animated 'Politics Episode' Can't Avoid Feeling Dated." *Vulture*, 16 June 2020, www.vulture.com/article/one-day-at-a-time-animated-episode-recap-review-season-4-episode-7.html.

Leman, Kevin. *The Birth Order Book: Why You Are the Way You Are.* Third Edition. Grand Rapids, Revell, 2009.

Levy, Ariel. "Dolls and Feelings: Jill Soloway's Post-patriarchal Television." *New Yorker*, 7 December 2015, www.newyorker.com/magazine/2015/12/14/dolls-and-feelings.

The LGBT Bar. "The LGBTQ+ Panic Defense." *The LGBT Bar*, https://lgbtbar.org/programs/advocacy/gay-trans-panic-defense/.

Lime_and_Coconut. "S5E17 of Bob's Burgers, Gene Is Kicked Out of a Band, One Reason Being That He Can Only Play 3 Chords, but in S3E16 He Creates an Orchestrated Work That the School Band Plays and Mr. Fischoeder and Gayle Sing." *Reddit*, 1February 2017, www.reddit.com/r/PlotDivots/comments/5rib80/in_s5e17_of_bobs_burgers_gene_is_kicked_out_of_a/.

Lindsay, Benjamin. "What It's Like Being a Voice Actor on *Bob's Burgers*." *Backstage*, 22 September 2016. www.backstage.com/magazine/article/like-voice-actor-bobs-burgers-6584/.

Lone Wolf and Cub: Sword of Vengeance. Directed by Kenji Misumi, written by Kazuo Koike, performances by Tomisaburō Wakayama and Akihiro Tomikawa, Katsu, 1972.

lorenbouchard (Loren Bouchard). "movie." *Twitter*, 22 February 2018, 9:14 a.m., twitter.com/lorenbouchard/status/1098994372895330304?ref_src=twsrc%5Etfw%7Ctwcamp%5Etweetembed%7Ctwterm%5E1098994372895330304%7Ctwgr%5Eshare_3&ref_url=https%3A%2F%2Fwww.cnet.com%2Fnews%2Fbobs-burgers-the-movie-everything-we-know-about-the-belchers-film%2F.

_____. "This Is Really Sweet and Sad but Also Hopeful. to Clarify: We Have Episodes Coming That We Made DURING Corona. but None About It. Hoping to Avoid That." *Twitter*, 26 May 2020, twitter.com/lorenbouchard/status/1265190589517033472.

Lyle, Timothy. "'Check with Yo' Man First; Check with Yo' Man': Tyler Perry Appropriates Drag as a Tool to Re-Circulate Patriarchal Ideology." *Callaloo*, vol. 34 no. 3, 2011, pp. 943–958.

Lyons, Margaret. "Best TV Parents of the Year: Bob and Linda Belcher from *Bob's Burgers*." *Vulture*, 10 June 2013, www.vulture.com/2013/06/best-tv-parents-of-the-year-the-belchers.html.

Macias, Patrick. "Samurai and Son: The Lone Wolf and Cub Collection." *Criterion*, 8 November 2016, https://www.criterion.com/current/posts/4287-samurai-and-son-the-lone-wolf-and-cub-saga.

Marie, Jane. "They Had a Tablescape Competition at the Fair." *The Hairpin*, 6 September 2012, www.thehairpin.com/2012/09/they-had-a-tablescape-competition-at-the-fair/.

Martin, Brett. *Difficult Men: Behind the Scenes of a Creative Revolution.* Penguin, 2013.

Martinelli, Marissa. "How One Dedicated Blogger Became the Chef Behind the Official *Bob's Burgers* Cookbook." *Slate*, 7 October 2015, slate.com/culture/2015/10/bobs-burgers-cookbook-contributor-cole-bowden-talks-about-his-blog-and-recipes.html.

McCall, Alexander. "Feminism in a Run-down Taffy Factory: The Women of *Bob's*

9. Bibliography

Burgers." *Pop Culture Happy Hour, NPR,* 23 August 2014, www.npr.org/2014/08/23/342397137/feminism-in-a-run-down-taffy-factory-the-women-of-bobs-burgers.

McLaughlin, Colin. "The Sadness of Louise Belcher." *Stand in the Fire,* 8 July 2016, stands inthefire.com/2016/07/08/the-sadness-of-louise-belcher/.

MDef255. "Regarding Louise's Bunny Ears." *Reddit,* 9 April 2014, www.reddit.com/r/Fan Theories/comments/22lp76/bobs_burgers_regarding_louises_bunny_ears/cgoar5x/.

Michelle and G. "Sheesh! Cab, Bob?" *Two for T/JJ,* open.spotify.com/episode/6jwQGa C2IRG7Hm7KicJ8On.

"Middle Child Syndrome." *TV Tropes.* http://tvtropes.org/pmwiki/pmwiki.php/Main/MiddleChildSyndrome.

Milloy, Cristin. "*South Park*'s 'Cissy' Episode Was Great on Trans Issues." *Slate,* 9 October 2014, www.slate.com/blogs/outward/2014/10/09/south_park_s_cissy_episode_was_great_on_trans_issues.html.

Mills, Brett. *The Sitcom.* Edinburgh UP, 2009.

Mills, Rebecca. "*Bob's Burgers*: Would the Restaurant Survive a Pandemic?" *Fansided,* 26 May 2020, hiddenremote.com/2020/05/24/bobs-burgers-restaurant-survive-pandemic/.

"Mr. Garrison's Fancy New Vagina." *South Park,* written and directed by Trey Parker, season 9, episode 1, Comedy Central, 9 March 2005.

Morgan, Joan. *When the Chickenheads Come Home to Roost: My Life as a Hip-hop Feminist.* Simon & Schuster, 1999.

Morris, Nigel. *The Cinema of Steven Spielberg: Empire of Light.* Columbia UP, 2007. *JSTOR,* www.jstor.org/stable/10.7312/morr476489. Accessed 13 Aug. 2020.

Moss, Gabrielle. "Tina Belcher's Sexual Revolution." *Bitchmedia,* 6 May 2014, bitchmagazine.org/post/tina-belcher-sexual-revolutionary-how-bobs-burgers-is-changing-the-way-tv-depicts-teen-sexualit.

Mtrembrulee557. *Reddit,* 22 May 2017, www.reddit.com/r/BobsBurgers/comments/6cptxx/help_me_diagnose_louise/.

muddywaffles86. "My Wife and I Got Matching Tattoos for Our Anniversary." *Reddit,* 26 August 2019, www.reddit.com/r/BobsBurgers/comments/cvvpth/my_wife_and_i_got_matching_tattoos_for_our/.

Murphy, Chris. "Kristen Bell Will Also No Longer Voice an Animated Black Character on *Central Park.*" *Vulture,* 24 June 2020, www.vulture.com/2020/06/kristen-bell-no-longer-voicing-black-character-central-park.html.

Nahar, Jasmin. "22 Times Gene Belcher Was the Best Character on *Bob's Burgers.*" *BuzzFeed,* 5 June 2016, www.buzzfeed.com/jasminnahar/times-gene-belcher-was-the-true-star-of-bobs-burgers?utm_term=.ur7VapWJy#.tvMMEXbrz.

Nguyen, Hanh. "*Bob's Burgers*: The Secret Ingredient for Its Girl-Powered Emmy Episode Are Two Hilarious Sisters." *IndieWire,* 7 August 2018, www.indiewire.com/2018/08/bobs-burgers-season-8-episode-8-v-for-valentine-detta-kristen-schaal-emmy-1201991871/.

Nicholson, Amy, and Paul Scheer. "113: *Jaws.*" *Unspooled,* Earwolf, 1 July 2020, earwolf.com/episode/jaws-2/.

nitsirklea. "Got Bob's Tattoo from the Equestranauts. My First (but Not Last) BB Tattoo!" *Reddit,* 12 October 2017, www.reddit.com/r/BobsBurgers/comments/761t1u/got_bobs_tattoo_from_the_equestranauts_my_first/.

notawalnut. "The Long P-arm of the Law (comes with Parmesan Cheese)." *Archive of Our Own,* 19 September 2020, archiveofourown.org/works/26518303/chapters/64633627.

O'Donnell, Carey. "Chatting Early YouTube, Music, and Moms with Comedian and *Bob's Burgers* Star John Roberts." *Paper,* 24 May 2016, www.papermag.com/chatting-with-john-roberts-bobs-burgers-1817453764.html.

Olmstead, Kathleen. *Archer and Bob's Burgers: The Untold History of Television.* Kindle edition, HarperCollins, 2015.

Bibliography

Opam, Kwame. "*Bob's Burgers* Is Using Fan Art to Make Its Eight Season Premiere."
3 March 2017, *The Verge*, www.theverge.com/2017/3/3/14807322/bobs-burgers-fanart-season-eight-premiere.

_____. "*Steven Universe* Creator Rebecca Sugar on Animation and the Power of Empathy." *The Verge*, 1 June 2017, www.theverge.com/2017/6/1/15657682/steven-universe-rebecca-sugar-cartoon-network-animation-interview.

Otterson, Joe. "How Loren Bouchard Built a *Bob's Burgers* Retail Empire." *Variety*, 11 November 2020, variety.com/2020/tv/features/bobs-burgers-merchandise-album-volume-2-1234823351/.

Ozersky, Josh. *The Hamburger: A History*. Yale UP, 2009.

Peeples, Jase. "Transgender Actress Shakina Nayfak Joins Cast of *Difficult People*." *The Advocate*, 25 February 2016, www.advocate.com/television/2016/2/25/transgender-actress-shakina-nayfack-joins-cast-difficult-people.

Perea, Katia. "Gender and Cartoons from Theaters to Television: Feminist Critique on the Early Years of Cartoons." *Animation*, vol. 13, no. 1, Mar. 2018, pp. 20–34, doi:10.1177/1746847718755591.

Petski, Denise. "*The Simpsons* Showrunner Gets Back at George H.W. Bush." *Deadline*, 27 October 2017. deadline.com/2017/10/the-simpsons-showrunner-al-jean-george-h-w-bush-1202196474/.

Phipps, Keith. "Hollywood's Cringey Transgender Evolution." *Daily Beast*, 14 April 2017, www.thedailybeast.com/hollywoods-cringey-transgender-evolution.

Poniewozik. James. "You Can Stream, but You Can't Hide." *New York Times*, 18 March 2020, www.nytimes.com/2020/03/18/arts/television/coronavirus-binge-watching.html.

"Popular Baby Names." US Department of Social Security, www.ssa.gov/cgi-bin/babyname.cgi.

Pphemerson. "*Bob's Burgers* Fan Theory. Bob's Conversations with Inanimate Objects." *Reddit*, 9 December 2018, www.reddit.com/r/FanTheories/comments/a4qzux/bobs_burgers_fan_theory_bobs_conversations_with/.

Putterman, Barry. *On Television and Comedy: Essays on Style, Theme, Performer and Writer*. McFarland, 2013.

"Quagmire's Dad." *Family Guy*, written by Tom Devanney, season 8 episode 18, Fox, 9 May 2010.

Queen Latifah. "U.N.I.T.Y." *Black Reign*, Motown, 1993.

Reset-363. "Gene Is Genderfluid?" *Reddit*, 2 December 2018, www.reddit.com/r/BobsBurgers/comments/a2h48l/gene_is_genderfluid/.

Rhodes, Joe. "Her Life as a Mom, an Actress, and a Boy." *New York Times*, 21 November 2008, www.nytimes.com/2008/11/23/arts/television/23rhod.html.

Ridlehoover, John. "*Bob's Burgers* Will Recast Show's Black Transgender Character, Marshmallow." *CBR.com*, 30 June 2020, www.cbr.com/bobs-burgers-recast-black-transgender-character-marshmallow/.

Roush, Matt. "Roush Review: A Super Busy TV Sunday." *TV Guide*, 7 January 2011, www.tvguide.com/news/roush-review-super-1027438/.

Rutsch, Poncie. "Watch *Bob's Burgers*? Now You Can Eat Them, Too." *NPR*, 27 January 2015, www.npr.org/sections/thesalt/2015/01/27/381880392/watch-bobs-burgers-now-you-can-eat-them-too.

sanibels. "The Porch." *Fanfiction.net*, www.fanfiction.net/s/13219790/1/The-Porch.

Saraiya, Sonia. "Bob's Burgers' Tina Makes the Series a Must-watch and 2013's Third-best Show." *AVClub*, 18 December 2013, www.avclub.com/article/bobs-burgers-tina-makes-the-series-a-must-watch-an-200663.

Sayre, Dana. "*Bob's Burgers* and Genderfluid Gene." *All the World's a Stage*, 10 July 2014, www.danasayre.com/bobs-burgers-and-genderfluid-gene/.

Schenkel, Katie. "Sexual Agency and Zombie Butts: Why *Bob's Burgers*' Tina Belcher

Mattiers." *The Mary Sue*, 19 May 2014, https://www.themarysue.com/bobs-burgers-tina-belcher-butts/.

"Secrets of Shark Island." Directed by William Hanna and Joseph Barbera, performances by Cher and Sonny Bono. *The New Scooby-Doo Movies*, CBS, 28 October 1972.

Semi-Homemade Cooking with Sandra Lee. Performance by Sandra Lee, Food Network, 2003–2011.

Sepinwall, Alan. *The Revolution Was Televised*. Alan Sepinwall, 2012.

Shane, Charlotte. "*Bob's Burgers* Is the Most Sex Positive Show on TV." *Salon*, 20 August 2013, www.salon.com/2013/08/19/bobs-burgers-is-the-most-sex-positive-show-on-tv.

Silvio, Teri. "Animation: The New Performance?" *Journal of Linguistic Anthropology*, vol. 20, no. 2, 2010, pp. 422–438.

Sinha-Roy, Piya. "*Bob's Burgers* Creator Promises to Improve Gender Balance in Show's Voice Cast." *Entertainment Weekly*, 20 July 2018, ew.com/tv/2018/07/20/bobs-burgers-gender-balance-voice-cast/.

Slafer Eugene. "A Conversation with Bill Hanna." *The American Animated Cartoon: A Critical Anthology*, edited by Gerald Peary and Danny Peary, Dutton, 1980, pp. 255–260.

Slate, Jenny. Text Slide. *Instagram*, 24 June 2020, www.instagram.com/p/CB1JISqFXT8/?igshid=xv3bw2tqldk4.

Spielberg, Steven. *Jurassic Park*. Universal, 1993.

Squires, Bethy. "Breaking Down the Role of Each Belcher on *Bob's Burgers*." *Vulture*, 13 June 2017, www.vulture.com/2017/06/breaking-down-the-role-of-each-belcher-on-bobs-burgers.html.

Stabile, Carol, and Mark Harrison. *Prime Time Animation: Television Animation and American Culture*. Taylor & Francis, 2003. *ProQuest Ebook Central*, https://ebook central.proquest.com/lib/washington/detail.action?docID=1397153.

Stanhope, Kate. "*Bob's Burgers* Originally Featured a Family of Cannibals and Other Secrets Revealed in *THR*'s Oral History." *The Hollywood Reporter*, 19 May 2016, www.hollywoodreporter.com/features/bobs-burgers-oral-history-894588.

Stevens, Ashlie D. "The Business of *Bob's Burgers*: From Labor Issues to the Cost of Meat, the Offbeat Family Cartoon Rings True." *Salon*, 23 January 2017, www.salon.com/2017/01/22/the-business-of-bobs-burgers-from-labor-issues-to-the-cost-of-meat-the-offbeat-family-cartoon-rings-true/.

Stewart, Alan E. "Issues in Birth Order Research Methodology: Perspectives from Individual Psychology." *Journal of Individual Psychology*, vol. 68, no. 1, 2012, pp. 75–106.

StirfryedShana. "All *Tumblr* Talks About Is Tina but What About Gene Belcher?" *Tumblr*, stirfryedshana.tumblr.com/post/108489739445/all-tumblr-talks-about-is-tina-belcher-but-what.

Stuever, Hank. "*Bob's Burgers*: Another Gross Cartoon Where Jokes Are Burnt to a Crisp." *Washington Post*, 7 January 2011, www.washingtonpost.com/lifestyle/style/tv-review-bobs-burgers-another-gross-cartoon-where-the-laughs-are-burnt-to-a-crisp/2011/01/03/ABbm6jD_story.html.

Sulloway, Frank J. "Birth Order and Sibling Competition." *The Oxford Handbook of Evolutionary Psychology*, edited by R.I. M. Dunbar and Louise Barrret, Oxford UP, 2007, pp. 297–311.

_____. *Born to Rebel: Birth Order, Family Dynamics, and Creative Lives*. Pantheon Books, 1996.

T-lasagna. "Regarding Louise's Bunny Ears." *Reddit*, 9 April 2014, www.reddit.com/r/FanTheories/comments/22lp76/bobs_burgers_regarding_louises_bunny_ears/cgoar5x/.

"Tablescaping Rules." Los Angeles County Fair, 2018, www.lacountyfair.com/docs/default-source/2018/competitions/tablescaping-combined.pdf?sfvrsn=eaed795a_2.

Bibliography

Talmadge, Stephanie. "*Bob's Burgers* Star H. Jon Benjamin Is Always There for You." *GQ*, 15 October 2019, www.gq.com/story/h-jon-benjamin-profile.

thatCutesyPie2. "Millie's Infatuation." *Wattpad*, 21 July 2019, www.wattpad.com/story/183867872-mille%27s-infatuation-yandere-millie-frock-x-louise.

Thornton, Max. "The Uniquely Lovable Tina Belcher." *Bitch Flicks*, December 2013, www.btchflcks.com/2013/12/bobs-burgers-the-uniquely-lovable-tina-belcher.html#.

Tomothy37. "S5E17 of Bob's Burgers, Gene Is Kicked Out of a Band, One Reason Being That He Can Only Play 3 Chords, but in S3E16 He Creates an Orchestrated Work That the School Band Plays and Mr. Fischoeder and Gayle Sing." *Reddit*, 1 February 2017, www.reddit.com/r/PlotDivots/comments/5rib80/in_s5e17_of_bobs_burgers_gene_is_kicked_out_of_a/.

Tueth, Michael V. "Back to the Drawing Board: The Family in Animated Television Comedy." *Prime Time Animation : Television Animation and American Culture*, edited by Carole Stabile and Mark Harrison, Taylor & Francis, 2003, pp. 133–146.

_____. *Laughter in the Living Room*. Peter Lang, 2005.

Twisp, Steve. "Brainstorm: A *Bob's Burgers* Fan Comic." *Tumblr*, 4 August 2018, https://stevetwisp.tumblr.com/post/176612262219/brainstorm-a-bobs-burgers-fancomic-thanks-for-10k.

_____. "Headcanons for Characters on *Bob's Burgers*." *Tumblr*, 16 October 2018, stevetwisp.tumblr.com/post/179115267489/what-are-ur-headcanons-for-everyones-sexualities.

u/homersqueak. "What Ethnicity Is DRL," *Reddit*, 2016, https://www.reddit.com/r/BobsBurgers/comments/60szsq/what_ethnicity_is_drl/.

UC Davis Profile. https://www.ucdavis.edu/sites/default/files/upload/files/uc-davis-student-profile.pdf.

Urban Cowboy. Directed by James Bridges, performances by John Travolta, Debra Winger, and Scott Glenn, Paramount, 1980.

VanArendonk, Kathryn. "Fixing Your Color-Blind Casting Problem Is Actually Very Easy." *Vulture*, 25 June 2020, https://www.vulture.com/2020/06/big-mouth-central-park-colorblind-casting.html.

Vary, Adam B. "Coronavirus Spike Puts Hollywood's Back-to-Work Plans in Serious Jeopardy." *Variety*, 1 July 2020, variety.com/2020/film/news/coronavirus-spike-hollywood-back-to-work-plans-1234695168/.

Viruet, Pilot. "*Bob's Burgers*: Linda-Pendant Woman." *AVClub*, 17 February 2013, tv.av-club.com/bob-s-burgers-lindapendant-woman-1798175843.

_____. "The Creator of *BoJack Horseman* Doesn't Want to Ignore Animation's Diversity Problem Anymore." *Uproxx*, 30 January 2018, uproxx.com/tv/bojack-horseman-diversity-diane-interview-raphael-bob-waksberg-alison-brie/.

Waggoner, Nate. "Meet Lizzie and Wendy: 'Bob's Burgers' Hilarious Sister Writing Duo." *KQED*, 3 December 2013.

Wallace, Benjamin. "The Ravenous and Resourceful Sandra Lee." *New York*, 25 March 2011, nymag.com/news/features/sandra-lee-2011–4/index5.html.

Weber, Lindsey. "20 Years After Its Release, a Brady Bunch Movie Meme Emerges." *Vulture*, 16 January 2015, www.vulture.com/2015/01/20-years-after-its-release-a-very-brady-meme.html.

Weiss, Norman. "Watching TV Under the Coronavirus Quarantine Is Challenging When You See So Much Face-touching." *Primetimer*, 19 March 2020, www.primetimer.com/item/Watching-TV-under-the-coronavirus-quarantine-is-challenging-when-you-see-so-much-face-touching-ElS16X.

Wellen, Brianna. "The Belchers Fall Victim to a Fad in a Middling *Bob's Burgers*." *AVClub*, 11 March 2018, www.avclub.com/the-belchers-fall-victim-to-a-fad-in-a-middling-bobs-bu-1823688938.

_____. "*Bob's Burgers* Returns with a Little Help from Its Fans." *AVClub*, 1 October 2017, www.avclub.com/bobs-burgers-returns-with-a-little-help-from-its-fans-1819045168.

9. Bibliography

_____. "10 Episodes of Belcher Family Values from *Bob's Burgers*." *AVClub*, 21 November 2016, tv.avclub.com/10-episodes-of-belcher-family-values-from-bob-s-burgers-1798254659.

White, Abby. "11 Wonderful Gene Belcher Quotes to Live By." *Paste*, 21 April 2016, www.pastemagazine.com/articles/2016/04/11-quotes-from-bobs-burgers-gene-belcher.html.

Wilkins, Alasdair. "*Bob's Burgers*: Best Burger." *AVClub*, 30 November 2014, tv.avclub.com/bob-s-burgers-best-burger-1798182082.

_____. "*Bob's Burgers* Pulls Off the Impossible: A Gene Belcher Love Story." *AVClub*, 14 February 2016, tv.avclub.com/bob-s-burgers-pulls-off-the-impossible-a-gene-belcher-1798186872.

_____. "*Bob's Burgers*: 'The Dawn of the Peck.'" *AVClub*, 23 November 2014. tv.avclub.com/bob-s-burgers-dawn-of-the-peck-1798182033.

_____. "*Bob's Burgers*: Work Hard or Die Trying, Girl." *AVClub*, 5 October 2014, tv.avclub.com/bob-s-burgers-work-hard-or-die-trying-girl-1798181493.

_____. "Linda Remains the Trickiest *Bob's Burgers* Character." *AVClub*, 20 March 2017, https://tv.avclub.com/linda-remains-the-trickiest-bob-s-burgers-character-1798190817.

Wolfe, Alan. "Up from Scientism: Review of *Born to Rebel: Birth Order, Family Dynamics, and Creative Lives*, by Frank Sulloway." *The New Republic*, 23 December 1996, pp. 29–35.

Wright, Andy. "The Fiercely Precise World of Competitive Table-Setting." *Atlas Obscura*, 26 July 2017, www.atlasobscura.com/articles/tablescaping.

Wright, Megh. "Jenny Slate Says She Will No Longer Voice an Animated Black Character." *Vulture*, 24 June 2020, https://www.vulture.com/2020/06/jenny-slate-missy-big-mouth-recast.html.

Yahoo201027. "On This Day in 2012: When Louise Gets Her Prized Bunny Ears Stolen by a High School Bully, She Won't Stop Until She Gets Her Hat Back, While Bob and Linda Had to Deal with a Biker Gang While Attending Their Leader's Funeral in the First Episode of Season 3, "Ear-sy Rider." *Reddit*, 30 September 2020, www.reddit.com/r/BobsBurgers/comments/j2o423/on_this_day_in_2012_when_louise_gets_her_prized/.

"'Zaddy' Ty Dolla Sign." *Genius*, genius.com/Ty-dolla-sign-zaddy-lyrics.

Index

183

Index

Index

185

Index

Index

Index

Index

Index

Index

Index